TANOREEN

A NEW AND EXPANDED EDITION OF *OLIVES, LEMONS AND ZA'ATAR*

TANOREEN

PALESTINIAN HOME COOKING IN DIASPORA

RAWIA BISHARA

PHOTOGRAPHY BY PETER CASSIDY

Interlink Books
An imprint of Interlink Publishing Group, Inc.
Northampton, Massachusetts

DEDICATION

To my mother and father, Monira and Anton, for sharing a love of food, family and the value of togetherness around our dinner table.

First published in 2025
by Interlink Books,
an imprint of Interlink Publishing Group, Inc.
46 Crosby Street
Northampton, MA 01060
www.interlinkbooks.com

All rights reserved. No part of this publication may be reproduced, stored in a retrieval system or transmitted, in any form or by any means, without the prior written permission of the publisher.

Text copyright © Rawia Bishara and Jumana Bishara, 2014, 2025
Photography copyright © Peter Cassidy, 2014, 2025, except the photographs on page 249, courtesy of Rawia Bishara; and on page 246 courtesy of Nick Dabas

Library of Congress Cataloging-in-Publication Data available
ISBN 978-1-62371-630-1

Project editors Anja Schmidt and Vicki Murrell
Updated edition editor Leyla Moushabeck and John Fiscella
Photographer Peter Cassidy
Food styling Linda Tubby
Prop styling Iris Bromet
Copy editors Sarah Scheffel and Jennifer McKenna
Designer Paul Palmer-Edwards and Louise Evans at Grade Design
Book design, 2014 edition Kyle Cathie Ltd
Book design updates, 2024 edition Pam Fontes-May
Cover design Harrison Williams

Printed and bound in China

10 9 8 7 6 5 4 3 2 1

CONTENTS

Introduction ...6
The Pantry ...10

1. Breakfast ...12

2. Mezze ...30

3. Salads ...70

4. Soups & Stews ...88

5. Main Courses ...120
Vegetarian ...124
Fish & Shellfish ...135
Chicken ...152
Lamb & Beef ...164

6. Sides ...190

7. Pickles, Sauces & Seasonings ...206

8. Desserts ...226

Index ...250
Acknowledgments ...256

Introduction

A HOMESTYLE CULINARY JOURNEY

When I opened Tanoreen in 1998, I never imagined the journey it would take me on. Over the years, I've witnessed a remarkable shift in how people perceive and appreciate Palestinian cuisine. What was once familiar only to those from our region has now captured the hearts and appetites of food lovers across the globe. I see it in the diversity of our diners and guests at the restaurant on a nightly basis. It brings me joy to see dishes from my childhood gaining recognition alongside other celebrated cuisines.

My daughter Jumana, co-owner of Tanoreen, has been instrumental in this journey, bringing fresh perspectives while honoring our culinary heritage. Together, we've strived to share not only our food but the stories, traditions, and love woven into every dish we serve.

Rawia, in Arabic, means storyteller. But rather than share stories about my family, life, and culture through words alone, I opened my restaurant, Tanoreen, to express them through cooking. In my mind, how ingredients are procured, dishes are served, and meals are celebrated speak volumes.

CREATING TANOREEN

It all began with my mother, Monira Hanna. I opened Tanoreen as a tribute to her and to reinterpret her delicious Middle Eastern cooking. The name comes from the Arabic word for traditional clay ovens, *tannour*.

My mother was a passionate and inventive cook who crafted meals for our family of seven—and often numerous guests—on a modest budget. While inspired by the cooking traditions of her native Galilee, she wasn't afraid to go off the beaten path. She understood the value of bending culinary rules, a practice we celebrated at our dinner table. She would introduce handfuls of fresh herbs, unexpected spices, or even wine into classic savory dishes and cakes, creating spectacular results where these ingredients seemingly didn't belong. I adored this about her and strive every day to infuse my food with the same creative spirit that defined my mother's cooking.

> "In southern Galilee, I was surrounded by a rich culinary heritage. My grandmother's ceramic urns filled with fruity olive oil, my mother's homemade vinegar and goat cheese and the sun-dried herbs and fruits that adorned rooftops—these were the ABCs of my culinary education."

ROOTS IN GALILEE

Born into a food-loving Palestinian-Arab family in Nazareth, a beautiful town in southern Galilee, I was surrounded by a rich culinary heritage. My grandmother's ceramic urns filled with fruity olive oil, my mother's homemade vinegar and goat cheese, and the sun-dried herbs and fruits that adorned rooftops—these were the ABCs of my culinary education.

Summers spent in the villages of Ramah and Tarshiha in Galilee left an indelible mark on me. The drive there was a feast for the senses, with rooftops laden with drying vegetables, herbs, and fruits—a colorful mosaic stretching to the horizon.

FROM NAZARETH TO NEW YORK

Marriage brought me to Bay Ridge, Brooklyn, where I found myself immersed in a culinary landscape of different cultures. My passion for food led me to explore many cuisines, dramatically influencing my cooking style. Family trips, both to Europe and back to the Middle East, further expanded my culinary repertoire and ensured my children connected with their heritage through food.

EMBRACING CHANGE AND MIXING IT UP

My cooking celebrates tradition while embracing change and community. I recreate time-honored dishes and experiment with contemporary twists, adding unexpected spices or offering modern shortcuts. Popular creations like Brussels sprouts with panko and tahini, or eggplant Napoleon with baba ghanouj, exemplify this approach.

A PERSONAL CULINARY JOURNEY

The recipes in this cookbook reflect my commitment to ingredients, respect for my Palestinian heritage, and passion for cooking. They offer a unique take on Middle Eastern cuisine, distinguished by subtlety, variety and accessibility.

I encourage you to experiment. Use spices liberally, embrace the tang of lemon and, most importantly, cook with love. Season to your liking and enjoy the process of preparing food for those you care about.

My hope is that these recipes help create an atmosphere of welcome and trust that celebrates both heritage and hospitality—the true essences of cooking.

The significance of preserving and sharing our cultural heritage has never been more profound than now. Our cuisine, with its rich flavors and time-honored traditions, serves as a powerful connection to our roots and identity, as an act of cultural preservation. At the same time, gathering around the table with others is an invitation to nourish both body and soul, and to find comfort in the simple yet profound act of breaking bread together in ever widening circles of community.

The Pantry

Allspice: This is a ground, dried berry (not a mixture of spices as its name suggests), used frequently in the Levant. It features notes of cinnamon, nutmeg and cloves.

Tip: Use this on lamb, especially, as it eliminates the "gamey" flavor.

Basmati rice: This long-grain rice has a soft texture and nutty flavor. In Arabic, Basmati means "my smile."

Black pepper: This ubiquitous ground spice is used in all my dishes to add a base flavor element.

Tip: Grind peppercorns as you need them for the freshest taste.

Bulgur: This high-fiber whole grain is used throughout the Middle East for soups, salads and main dishes. It comes in various sizes from whole to fine. For example, the bulgur we use in tabouleh is a smaller grain than for kibbeh.

Tip: It's a great substitute for rice in vegetarian grape leaves, page 53.

Cardamom: This spice pod is something we grind into our own Tanoreen spice blend. We use cardamom in savory dishes, desserts and even grind a few pods in with our Arabic coffee.

Tip: Open a pod and chew on the seeds to instantly freshen your breath.

Cinnamon: This spice is derived from a particular tree bark and was imported to Egypt as early as 2000 BC. It's uniquely "sweet" in aroma, but can be added to many Middle Eastern dishes as a savory seasoning as well.

Tip: Sprinkle sparingly over a plain rice pilaf for an instant flavor boost.

Citric acid: Found in most citrus fruits, this "sour salt" adds a concentrated, lemony flavor, without adding the additional juice. It's also used in cheese and wine production.

Tip: Since it looks exactly like salt, but with a slightly larger crystal structure, take care not to mix these up!

Coriander: This antioxidant rich, intensely flavored seed of the cilantro plant is ground into a powder and used in many of our dishes.

Tip: Throw a few coriander berries in with your pickling brine to give great flavor.

Cumin: This seed is famous for its distinctive smoky/nutty flavor. It's used in cuisines around the world, stretching from Mexico to Italy to India and beyond. Surprisingly, it's a member of the parsley family. In the old days it was used to alleviate stomach upset, which is why it is traditionally used in grain dishes.

Tip: Cumin boiled with ginger makes a great digestive tea.

Freekeh: Freekeh is smoked green wheat berries. It has a smoky aroma and a nutty, toasted flavor. The green wheat hull is placed over an open flame during which the straw is burned off, leaving behind a unique flavor.

Tip: Freekeh can be used instead of rice to stuff chicken or in soups and stews.

Ghee: Ghee is clarified, evaporated butter. After butter is melted and simmered long enough to evaporate, the moisture becomes richer in flavor than oil and has a higher smoking point than butter.

Tip: Ghee keeps at room temperature for several weeks and for months in the refrigerator. You can make your our own or buy it in most ethnic grocery stores or online.

Grape leaves: These are the leaves of the grape vine. Green and slightly sour, most varieties are sold in a brine that you should rinse off the leaves before use.

Tip: If you can find fresh grape leaves, use them to scoop up tabouleh, page 81, for a fantastic bite.

Lentils: This legume has been cultivated since antiquity. After soy beans, they have the highest protein content of any vegetable and are also fiber packed.

Tip: I usually use red lentils for soups, as I find them tender.

Maftool: A pasta traditionally made by hand-rolling flour around wheat berries to make pearl-sized grains that are then steamed in chicken broth. Today packaged maftool is available in most Middle Eastern markets.

Mahlab: A spice made from the seeds of the St. Lucy's cherry, mahlab gives a subtle floral taste to desserts.

Mastic: A plant resin with a somewhat piney flavor, liquid mastic is dried into small hardened chunks that are crushed into a powder before being added to a recipe. Mastic gives *sahlab* (page 230) its unique flavor.

Nutmeg: A strong, slightly sweet spice from the nutmeg tree, this is best freshly grated.

Olive oil: For fresh salads, drizzling or quick sautéing, we recommend using only the extra-virgin variety. You can use a lighter variety for cooking.

Tip: Experiment with different kinds of olive oil, as Spanish olive oil is different in flavor and color from Italian or California varieties. Some are sweeter and some more peppery.

Orange blossom water: Orange blossom water is the distilled essence of the orange blossom flower. It's intensely floral and excellent in desserts.

Tip: Boil water and add a few drops of orange blossom to make a great digestive "white tea" or add some to fresh mint lemonade.

Pomegranate molasses: Made from the seeds of the pomegranate fruit, this thick, sweet syrup imparts a perfect sweet-sour note into many Middle Eastern dishes.

Tip: Drizzle this into salad dressings, make it into a sorbet or pour some into a cocktail.

Red pepper paste (harissa): Harissa is a combination of chile, garlic, coriander (and/or cumin) and some olive oil. You can substitute your own chile paste with the above ingredients if it's not readily available.

Tip: Spread some on a sandwich or spoon it in soup to kick up the flavor factor.

Rose water: Distilled from rose petals, this aromatic ingredient adds a unique flavor to many Middle Eastern desserts.

Tip: As it has a very strong flavor and aroma, start with a small amount and add more to taste.

Sesame seeds: I suggest purchasing them raw and dry-roasting them until golden brown so you get the full flavor punch. They quickly turn rancid so store them in your freezer.

Tip: High in calcium, iron and anti-oxidants, sprinkle some on your salad, or try *halva*, a delicious confection of sesame seed paste and honey.

Sumac: Sumac is a spice made from the dried, powdered berries of a shrub that is common in the Middle East. Tangy in flavor, deep purple in color, sumac grows in dense clusters. It is often sprinkled in salads like fattoush or used as a garnish.

Tip: Toss some sumac into your kebab mix or marinades for a tangy twist.

Tahini: Essentially sesame paste, tahini is made by grinding raw or toasted sesame seeds.

Tip: Tahini will separate from the natural sesame oil; stir to recombine and store upside down.

Za'atar: Dry oregano or thyme is often mixed with sumac, toasted sesame seeds and salt and served with olive oil and Arabic bread as a traditional breakfast in the Middle East.

Tip: You can use za'atar to garnish hummus (page 38) or labneh (strained yogurt spread) or toss it into salad dressing.

BREAKFAST

Breakfast Traditions

Some of my fondest memories of returning to Nazareth as an adult with my own family are of sitting around my parents' formidable breakfast table, recalling our morning traditions to my own children.

Each day began the same way: My mother roused her five stubborn children out of bed before she dashed off to her job as a schoolteacher. She didn't leave until she was positive we were *out of bed and standing up*. Though she didn't eat breakfast with us, she was as much a part of it as any of us. To this day, I marvel at the effortlessness with which she laid out an elaborate breakfast spread during busy weekdays. We were routinely treated to a dizzying array of jams and preserves, olives, honey, warm Arabic bread, olive oil, garden tomatoes, za'atar and labneh.

I can still taste the sunny flavor of my mother's homemade apricot jam, slathered on a chunk of toasted bread spread with a thin layer of sweet, creamy butter. The apricots came straight from the fruit trees in our backyard, as did the grapes and raspberries she used to boil with sugar and pectin to make the most delicious spreads. She prepared enough jams and fruit spreads to last until the trees bore fruit again the following year. My dad broke open the apricot pits, removed the seeds and roasted them so they could be boiled with the jam, giving it an intense apricot flavor and a wonderful crunch.

Labneh, the tangy goat milk yogurt cheese that can be found in every Middle Eastern pantry, was another staple on the breakfast table. My mother made several batches at a time, enough to last for a few months. She poured the goat milk into a huge cheesecloth-lined sieve, sea salted it, then let the whey drain overnight, or until it reached a consistency similar to farmer's cheese. She rolled the cheese into golf ball–size orbs, dropped them in big jars and then filled them to the lip with the extra-virgin olive oil her family harvested from their grove in the nearby village of El Rameh. In just a few days, the cheese was ready to eat.

And then there was za'atar. *Ahhhh*, za'atar. I so love this vibrant mix of wild thyme and oregano, lemony sumac, and toasted sesame seeds that I ate it by the spoonful when I was pregnant with my children. On my family's breakfast table there always was—and still is and probably always will be—a dish of za'atar next to one of olive oil and a plate piled high with warm Arabic bread. There is perhaps no more delicious a way to start the day than tearing a piece of bread from the loaf, dunking it first in fruity olive oil, and then dipping it in za'atar mix. The exception being when my mother treated us to her

"We were routinely treated to a dizzying array of jams and preserves, olives, honey, warm Arabic bread, olive oil, garden tomatoes, za'atar and labneh."

homemade *manakeesh*, a flatbread topped with a mix of olive oil and za'atar and then baked.

Along with all of that, my mother always provided tomatoes cut in wedges and thinly sliced cucumbers—both picked from our garden, a big bowl of honey from my uncle's bee farm, chile-oil-cured green olives and slices of halloumi (a semi-hard brined cheese made from either goat, sheep or cow milk) topped with fresh picked mint. The breakfast table fairly heaved with food! And although it may sound extravagant, the truth is, such a feast is long on assembly, but short on preparation, requiring little, if any, actual cooking come breakfast time. Most of what we ate was either prepared months in advance or came straight from the garden. When it was time to go off to school, we simply covered the platters in plastic wrap and put them in the pantry or refrigerator until the next morning.

WEEKEND BREAKFASTS

Come the weekend, breakfasts were a bit more involved as they always included an egg dish or classic *foul* (a dip made from fava beans) in addition to the usual weekday repertoire. Since my mother worked on Saturdays, my father was the rare man, back in those days, who stepped into the kitchen to prepare his specialty egg dishes: Eggs and Potatoes, page 17, and Meat and Eggs, page 19. Such an arrangement was quite unusual back then—Middle Eastern men generally did not cook and women did not hold jobs on the weekend. These days, my husband, Wafa, has developed quite a reputation with our houseguests for his Eggs with Za'atar, page 16. I make my own version of *foul*, page 24, which is inspired by the classic, page 21, that my mother so lovingly prepared on Sunday, her only day off.

Eggs with Za'atar

BAYID BI ZA'ATAR

Most households in the Levant place small dishes of olive oil and za'atar on the kitchen counter for snacking throughout the day. This recipe features eggs seasoned with those ingredients to create an excellent brunch dish. Whenever we have guests staying at our home in New York, which seems to be quite frequently (my son dubbed it the Hotel Bishara), my husband makes this fragrant meal, often cracking nearly a dozen eggs because one batch is never enough! To temper the assertive flavor of the za'atar and sumac, serve this with sliced tomatoes, cucumbers and some olives and a piece of feta, if desired.

In a small bowl, stir together the za'atar, sumac, salt and pepper; set aside.

Scoop out a quarter-size hole in the center of each slice of bread.

Heat ¼ cup oil in a large skillet over medium heat until hot. Arrange half of the bread slices in the skillet and brown about 1 minute on each side. Reduce the heat to low and crack one egg into the hole in each slice of bread. Sprinkle the za'atar mixture evenly over each egg, cover, and cook until the eggs have reached your desired doneness, 2 to 3 minutes. If you like your yolk cooked really well, scoop up some oil from the bottom of the skillet and drizzle on top of each egg. Using a spatula, transfer the toasts to a platter or serving plates and keep warm. Repeat with the remaining ¼ cup of oil and bread slices.

Serve warm with the tomatoes, cucumbers and feta cheese.

SERVES 6

3 tablespoons za'atar
1 tablespoon sumac
Pinch sea salt
½ teaspoon freshly ground black pepper
1 Italian country-style loaf, cut into 2-inch-thick slices (about 6 slices)
½ cup extra-virgin olive oil
6 large eggs
Sliced tomatoes, cucumbers and feta cheese for serving

Eggs and Potatoes

BAYID WA BATATA

This dish brings back very fond memories of Saturday mornings at home with my father, who prepared this while my mother was at work. The funny thing is, he always closed the kitchen door for privacy while he cooked, but we were treated to quite a performance when my father ate. He did so quite ceremoniously, with lots of physicality, forming each bite with the exact same ratio of bread to egg every time, then popping an olive and a slice of tomato into his mouth afterward. You can add chopped fresh tomatoes and a minced bell pepper to the mix if you like. Add them after sauteing the onions. Serve this egg dish straight from the skillet with Arabic flatbread, sliced tomatoes and lemon wedges alongside.

> **INGREDIENT NOTE** When cooking with chile peppers, I use long hots because they are milder than jalapeños, but if you like a bit more heat by all means use jalapeños. For an even milder pepper, use poblanos instead of long hots.

Heat the oil in a medium skillet until hot, 2 to 3 minutes. Add the onion and saute, stirring frequently, until golden brown, about 2 minutes. Stir in the chile pepper, if using, and saute until soft and fragrant, about 2 minutes. Toss in the potatoes and saute until they are browned and softened, 5 to 7 minutes.

Meanwhile, in a large bowl, crack the eggs and whisk them together, then whisk in the pepper, allspice and nutmeg.

Pour the egg mixture into the potato mixture and cook, stirring constantly, until the eggs have reached your desired consistency, 2 to 3 minutes for the that of scrambled eggs. Transfer to a serving platter and garnish with the lemon wedges.

SERVES 4 TO 6

8 tablespoons extra-virgin olive oil
1 small yellow onion, finely chopped
1 long hot chile pepper, finely chopped (optional)
3 to 4 small russet potatoes, peeled and cut into ½-inch pieces
12 large eggs
1½ teaspoons freshly ground black pepper
2 teaspoons ground allspice
⅓ teaspoon ground nutmeg (optional)
Lemon wedges for serving

Meat and Eggs

BAYID WA LAHMEH

My husband loves this breakfast of fluffy eggs and lamb seasoned with earthy spices, a classic my dad made on Saturday mornings. It makes a wonderful lunch or light dinner, too. Serve with a platter of olives, pickles, chile peppers, spring onions and radishes, all of which are refreshing to eat in between bites of the creamy eggs. If you don't want to spend time chopping the lamb by hand, ask the butcher to pass it through the meat grinder once—you don't want the pieces to be too small.

Heat the oil in a large skillet over medium-high heat. Stir in the shallot and saute until soft and lightly browned, 3 minutes. Add the chile pepper and saute until soft, about 2 minutes. Stir in the allspice, salt, black pepper, nutmeg, cinnamon and cardamom, if using, and cook until fragrant, 30 seconds. Toss in the lamb and cook until it loses its pink color, 4 to 5 minutes.

In a large bowl, whisk together the eggs. Pour the eggs over the lamb mixture in the skillet and let set for 1 minute, then cook, stirring occasionally, until the eggs reach desired consistency. Serve with Arabic bread for scooping.

SERVES 4 TO 6

¼ cup extra-virgin olive oil or corn oil
1 shallot, cut into ¼-inch pieces
1 chile pepper, preferably jalapeño, seeded, if desired, and finely chopped
½ teaspoon ground allspice
½ teaspoon sea salt
¼ teaspoon freshly ground black pepper
Pinch ground nutmeg
Pinch ground cinnamon
Pinch ground cardamom (optional)
1 pound lamb meat from the leg, chopped into ½-inch pieces
10 large eggs
Warm Arabic Bread (page 61) for serving

Scrambled Eggs with Halloumi

BAYID WA HALLOUMI

Halloumi is a firm, salty, cheese made from a mix of goat and sheep milk. It's excellent for grilling or frying, as it holds together beautifully. Here it is cut into cubes and browned before the eggs are scrambled into it. The more frequently you make this dish, the more confident you will become at tinkering with the seasonings—or adding some new ones, like fresh cilantro or basil.

Heat the oil in a large skillet over high heat until hot. (Don't choose a nonstick skillet for this job.) Add the halloumi and brown on all sides until golden, about 2 minutes total. Stir in the tomatoes, salt, pepper and nutmeg and cook until the tomatoes have just softened, but are not falling apart.

Crack the eggs directly into the skillet. Cook for 1 minute after cracking the last egg, then, using a fork, scramble the eggs, 2 to 3 minutes or longer, depending on the texture you desire.

Transfer the eggs to a large platter. Serve warm with the Arabic bread and olives.

SERVES 6

½ cup extra-virgin olive oil
8 to 10 ounces halloumi, cut into 1-inch cubes
2 plum tomatoes, peeled and diced
1 teaspoon sea salt
½ teaspoon freshly ground black pepper
¼ teaspoon ground nutmeg
10 to 12 large eggs
Arabic Bread (page 61) and black or green olives for serving

Simple Omelet

IJII ARABIA

All of the ingredients for an Arab omelet are whisked together and cooked at once, unlike in its French brethren, which rolls a filling into the center of the cooked omelet. And while *ijii* literally translated means "omelet," this egg dish more closely resembles a frittata: It is open-faced and the fillings are cooked right into the eggs. This is my mother's recipe, but there are endless variations.

SERVES 4 TO 6

12 large eggs
3 tablespoons chopped red or white onion
1 chile pepper, finely chopped (optional)
3 tablespoons chopped fresh parsley
1 tablespoon chopped fresh mint
Pinch sea salt or to taste
Pinch ground nutmeg (optional)
¼ cup extra-virgin olive oil

In a large bowl, combine the eggs, onion, and, if desired, the chile pepper with the parsley, mint, salt and nutmeg, if using. Whisk until the eggs are pale yellow.

Heat the oil in a medium skillet over medium-high heat until hot, about 2 minutes. Pour the egg mixture into the skillet and let cook, untouched, for 3 minutes. Using an offset spatula, lift up an edge of the omelet to check the color of the bottom. When it is golden brown, run the spatula along the edge of the skillet and flip the omelet over. Cook for 2 minutes more. Slide the omelet onto a platter, cut into wedges and serve warm.

VARIATION *For a fancier version, my mother made six very thin individual omelets. She whisked finely chopped plum tomatoes and a jalapeño into the egg mixture, then arranged cheese (depending on what she had on hand—Arabic, Cheddar, keshkaval, a yellow sheep milk cheese that tastes somewhat like Cheddar, or goat cheese) down the middle after she flipped it. To finish she folded the egg in thirds. Cook 1 minute per side.*

BREAKFAST ON THE GO

My favorite weekday breakfast growing up was a sliced egg tucked inside warm bread, spread with labneh, topped with tomato slices and seasoned with a generous sprinkle of za'atar and pepper. *Kaak*, a delicious, chewy flatbread that's coated in sesame seeds and resembles an oversized bagel, was a close second. While it used to be baked at home, *kaak* is now widely available from the food carts that dot the streets of major Middle Eastern cities. Like the egg and cheese sandwich beloved in the States, it is the favored breakfast for those on the go. If you can't find *kaak*, use Arabic flatbread.

To prepare the sandwich, tear open the *kaak* or Arabic flatbread, drizzle with a little olive oil and za'atar, then stuff with a sliced hard-boiled egg. I like to add a little chopped tomato and cucumber, too. The bread is available at Middle Eastern stores and some gourmet food stores. If you can't find *kaak*, use thin Arabic bread to make this nourishing portable breakfast.

Fava Bean Breakfast

FOUL MUDAMMAS

Though this ancient dish is enjoyed all over the Middle East—particularly in the Levant—its roots lay in Egypt. *Foul* is a breakfast staple, but when I was growing up, it was a dish reserved for weekend eating, especially brunch. We would travel five hours to Jerusalem to walk the old market and eat *foul* at a diminutive place with just four tables—and a long line outside. It was *the* place to eat *foul* because the beans were prepared the traditional way—in clay pots set over a low fire and cooked for twelve hours. The table was also spread with boiled eggs, radishes, spring onions, long hot peppers, pickled vegetables and, of course, hummus. It was set for lingering—and that's what we did, eating the best *foul* in the world while sipping coffee or tea. At Tanoreen, *foul* is a mainstay on our Sunday brunch menu—a big draw for those looking for a traditional Middle Eastern breakfast.

SERVES 4 TO 6

2 cups dried fava beans, soaked and boiled (see right), or 2 (14-ounce) cans, drained and rinsed
½ cup extra-virgin olive oil, plus more for drizzling
½ cup fresh lemon juice
4 cloves garlic, finely chopped
1 teaspoon sea salt
½ teaspoon ground cumin (optional)
2 tablespoons chopped fresh parsley

If using canned beans, drain off all but a third of the water from the cans. Combine the beans and ¼ cup oil in a large skillet and bring to a boil over medium heat. Turn the heat off and add the lemon juice, garlic, salt and cumin, if using, to the skillet. Smash the bean mixture with a potato masher until the beans are just split or to the desired texture.

Spoon the *foul* into a serving bowl, smoothing the top with the back of a spoon. Use the back of the spoon to make a well in the *foul*. Drizzle the remaining ¼ cup olive oil into the well. Garnish with the parsley and serve. The *foul* will keep, covered, in the refrigerator up to one week.

> **COOKING TIP** My version of *foul* is slightly chunkier than most—I like to mash the beans only just until they split, but you can mash them smoother or to whatever consistency you desire. Serve it with *Tetbileh*, page 145, or Homemade Hot Sauce, page 220, or Siracha (an Asian chile sauce that's readily available in the States), along with the traditional accompaniments mentioned above.

A GOOD SOAK

I always presoak dried beans at the restaurant, but I understand that it is not necessarily the most convenient technique for making bean dishes at home. That said, if you make extra-large batches of beans and freeze some for later use, it's worth the effort as most of the cooking time isn't active. Here's my method.

Soak your desired amount of beans in a heavy-bottomed pot for 12 hours in enough water to cover by 4 inches. Drain and return to the pot. Add enough water to cover by 4 inches and add 1 tablespoon of salt for every 4 cups (2 pounds) of beans. Cover, place over high heat and bring to a boil. (If boiling dried chickpeas, add ½ teaspoon of baking soda to speed the cooking time.) Boil until you can crush a bean between your thumb and forefinger, 1 to 2 hours, depending on the beans.

For a more intensely "beany" flavor, simply bring the unsoaked beans, water and salt to a boil over high heat, reduce the heat to low and cook for 4 to 5 hours. Drain, reserving the cooking water if boiling fava or chickpeas. To freeze, place the beans in 2-cup portions in resealable freezer bags and do the same with the fava or chickpea cooking water.

Chickpea and Fava Bean Breakfast

MAKHLOOTA

Makhloota, literally translated, means "mixture," which is precisely what this is. There are dozens of variations—some feature various kinds of beans, rice and bulgur—but my favorite is a traditional Palestinian version: chickpeas and favas seasoned with cumin, garlic and lemon juice. Serve this with Homemade Hot Sauce, page 220, or *Tetbileh*, page 145, and Arabic bread for scooping.

SERVES 4 TO 6

1½ cups dried fava beans, soaked and boiled (see page 21), 1 cup cooking liquid reserved, or 2 (14-ounce) cans fava beans, liquid from 1 can reserved
1 cup dried chickpeas, soaked and boiled (see page 21) or 1 (15-ounce) can chickpeas, drained
¾ cup extra-virgin olive oil
¾ cup fresh lemon juice
6 cloves garlic, finely chopped
1 tablespoon ground cumin or to taste
1 teaspoon sea salt or to taste
½ teaspoon freshly ground black pepper
3 tablespoons chopped parsley for garnish
1 jalapeño chile, with seeds, cut into small cubes for garnish
Arabic Bread (page 61) for serving

In a large skillet, combine the favas and chickpeas with the reserved cooking liquid or the liquid reserved from 1 can. Set over medium heat and bring to a boil. Reduce the heat to low and cook for 15 minutes, or until the liquid has almost completely evaporated. If the mixture goes dry before the beans are cooked, add a little water.

Pour in ¼ cup olive oil, reduce the heat, and bring to a simmer. Cover and cook for 5 minutes. Add the lemon juice, garlic, cumin and salt, cover, turn off the heat and let sit for 2 minutes. Transfer to a serving bowl, drizzle with the remaining ½ cup olive oil and garnish with the parsley and jalapeño. Serve with Arabic bread.

Tanoreen's Specialty Fava Beans

FOUL ALLA TANOREEN

The impulse to tinker with classics came to full bloom when I created this version of *foul* for Tanoreen. I integrated items typically served alongside traditional *foul into* the dish. The recipe calls for twice as many fava beans as you need. I did this as a favor to you; freeze them for next time.

SERVES 4 TO 6

½ cup extra-virgin olive oil, plus more for drizzling
4 cups dried fava beans, soaked and boiled (see page 21), or 3 (12-ounce) cans, drained and rinsed
3 shallots or 1 yellow onion, diced
5 cloves garlic, finely chopped
1 chile pepper, preferably poblano, cored, seeded and finely chopped
1 cup chopped fresh cilantro
3 plum tomatoes, diced
½ cup fresh lemon juice
1 teaspoon ground cumin
1 teaspoon sea salt
1 teaspoon freshly ground black pepper (optional)
Chopped fresh parsley for garnish
Arabic Bread (page 61) for serving

In a large skillet, combine ¼ cup oil with the beans and bring to a boil over high heat. Meanwhile, in another large skillet, heat the remaining ¼ cup oil over medium until hot. Toss in the shallots and saute until golden brown and fragrant, about 3 minutes. Add the garlic and cook until softened and fragrant, about 2 minutes. Add the chile pepper and saute, stirring, until softened, about 2 minutes. Sprinkle in the cilantro and cook, stirring, until darkened and wilted, about 2 minutes. Toss in the tomatoes and cook until they soften and release their juices, about 3 minutes more.

Add 4 cups of the fava beans to the tomato mixture, along with the lemon juice, cumin, salt and pepper, if using. Using a potato masher, mash until smooth. Transfer to a serving bowl and, using the back of a spoon, make a moat in the *foul* and drizzle some olive oil into it. Garnish with the parsley and serve with warm Arabic bread.

Yogurt Tahini with Chickpeas

TISKAI

My Syrian friends shared this traditional breakfast with me when I first arrived in New York. It's been on the menu at Tanoreen since we opened our doors and is a favorite among my vegetarian customers. It's not a weekday breakfast dish, but rather a hearty brunch offering when paired with pickles, scallions and radishes. I use low-fat yogurt because it's tangier than the full-fat version. You can toast the pine nuts in olive oil if you like, but they are traditionally toasted in ghee or butter for this dish.

In a large pot over high heat, combine the chickpeas with the lemon juice, oil, garlic, cumin, salt and pepper. Bring to a boil, then immediately remove the pot from the heat; the chickpeas should be falling apart.

Heat a dash of oil or ghee in a small skillet over medium heat. Add the pine nuts and cook, stirring, until golden brown, about 2 minutes. Using a slotted spoon, transfer the nuts to paper towels to drain.

In a medium bowl, combine the yogurt and tahini sauce. Using a wooden spoon or a hand mixer, beat until smooth. Transfer the mixture to a small skillet and heat over medium-low heat until just heated through—do not bring to a boil. Season to taste with lemon juice and salt if you need it.

To serve, arrange the toasted Arabic bread pieces in the bottom of a rimmed serving dish. Spoon the chickpeas into the center of the dish, nudging the pieces of bread to the edge of the dish. Spoon the warm yogurt mixture over the chickpeas. Garnish with the fried pine nuts and parsley. Serve with the chile paste on the side, if desired.

SERVES 6 TO 8

- 2 cups dried chickpeas, soaked and boiled (see page 21), or 3 (15-ounce) cans, drained and rinsed
- ½ cup fresh lemon juice, plus more for seasoning
- ¼ cup extra-virgin olive oil or ghee or butter, plus more for frying the nuts
- 5 cloves garlic, finely chopped, or to taste
- 1½ teaspoons ground cumin
- 1 tablespoon sea salt, plus more for seasoning
- ¼ teaspoon freshly ground black pepper
- 1 cup pine nuts
- 1 cup plain low-fat yogurt
- ½ cup Thick Tahini Sauce (page 221; omit the parsley)
- 2 pieces Arabic Bread (page 61), cut into 1-inch squares, fried or toasted
- 3 tablespoons chopped fresh parsley
- 1 tablespoon seedless Middle Eastern or Turkish chile paste (optional)

Hummus with Meat

HUMMUS BIL LAHMEH

A heartier version of hummus, this features tender lamb seasoned with allspice and nutmeg that is then topped with toasted pine nuts and almonds. It's a wonderful brunch dish, but is just as appropriate for lunch or as a mezze. Be sure to use a tender cut of meat, since it is so quickly cooked. I always use more olive oil than butter but you can swap the proportions if you like. Serve this with a small platter of Arabic bread, scallions, onions, long hot peppers, olives, Pickled Turnips and Beets, page 210, and radishes.

Spread the hummus onto a shallow platter and make a well in the middle. Set aside.

Heat the oil and ghee in a small skillet over medium heat. Add the almonds and cook, stirring, for 1 minute. Toss in the pine nuts and cook, stirring, for 2 minutes more until golden brown. Remove the nuts with a slotted spoon and transfer to paper towels.

Add the lamb or sirloin, the allspice, pepper, salt and nutmeg to the skillet and saute, stirring occasionally, until medium to well done, 3 to 5 minutes. Return the nuts to the skillet, stir to combine and cook for 30 seconds. Remove from the heat. Spoon the meat into the well on the plate and serve with fresh or toasted Arabic bread.

SERVES 4 TO 6

2 cups Hummus (page 38)
3 tablespoons extra-virgin olive oil
1 tablespoon ghee or butter
2 tablespoons slivered almonds
2 tablespoons pine nuts
½ pound lamb from the leg or filet mignon, cut into ½-inch pieces
½ teaspoon ground allspice
¼ teaspoon freshly ground black pepper
Pinch sea salt
Pinch ground nutmeg
Arabic Bread (page 61) for serving

MEZZE

Eat, Talk and Drink

The Italians have antipasto, the Spanish tapas, the Americans appetizers, the Chinese dim sum. In the Middle East, there is mezze, small plates of food served all at once before the main course, to provide a bounty of tastes and textures. That said, one or two plates can comprise a snack, while a few more can add up to a whole meal. Mezze is invariably served with arak, an anise-flavored spirit, to sip in between swipes of creamy dip on Arabic bread, forkfuls of fried or raw kibbeh and bites of spicy meat pies.

The simplest mezzes are made up of whatever is on hand in the garden and the pantry. When I was growing up, this meant *makdous*, labneh, olives, hummus, Arabic bread, cucumbers and tomatoes.

At its core, though, mezze is a mood. In Arabic, the verb for mezze is, *mezmiz*, which loosely translated means "eat, talk and drink"—all at once. Imagine friends and family sitting around a table, passing heaping plates of hummus, baba ganouj, falafel and za'atar bread, and laughing, talking—and of course debating heatedly—amid the clang of glasses and plates. Mezze is a ritual about sharing—not just bites of delicious food, but stories, experiences, laughter and opinions.

There are no real rules when it comes to serving mezze; several small plates and good company are the keys! When I visit one of my friends to play cards, she offers Hummus, page 38, romaine lettuce cups for scooping Tabouleh, page 81, and a bowl of roasted nuts served with chilled glasses of arak or cold beer. When my children entertain guests, they serve *Mhammara*, page 46, with toasted Arabic Bread, page 61, and some cheese with honey and crisp crackers. It can be that simple.

Admittedly, I tend toward the extravagant with my own mezze spreads, both at home and at Tanoreen. It is part of my culture to offer food in abundance, and it begins with these small treasures. There are plenty of inspiring options to choose from in this chapter as well as in the salad chapter that follows. From among all of these recipes, you can create an array of dishes that beautifully capture the flavors and spirit of the Middle Eastern mezze table. The trick is not to overindulge if a main course follows; in fact, I often advise customers against ordering too much for fear they will be sated before the main course arrives!

The mezze dishes in this chapter easily cross over to other mealtimes—hummus is a favorite breakfast for many and an essential part of a wedding or cocktail party spread. Falafel, page 56, is a mezze staple, of course, but also makes an excellent lunch, tucked into Arabic bread and dressed with Thick Tahini Sauce, page 221.

But, always remember, to *"mezmiz"* is not so much dependent on the selection of dishes you provide at the table, as it is about the atmosphere you create around it. So, eat, talk, drink—and enjoy!

"Admittedly, I tend toward the extravagant with my own mezze spreads, both at home and at Tanoreen. It is part of my culture to offer food in abundance, and it begins with these small treasures."

Hossi for Kibbeh

KIBBEH BIL HOSSI

I will never forget my mother making kibbeh this way. She would shape the meat mixture into small cones and then make the impression of a cross on them with the side of her hand. Along with a bottle of arak (it isn't proper to bring just a glass—the bottle is always on the table so that guests can have as much as they like) that always accompanied kibbeh, she put a bowl of *hossi*, chile paste fragrant of marjoram and cumin, in the center of the table, then served one cone per plate. We flattened the kibbeh with the back sides of our forks, then spooned the *hossi* over it. There was always *saj*, a paper-thin bread, and a bowl of bright green olive oil. We dipped the bread in the olive oil, then used it to scoop up the kibbeh and *hossi*.

Heat ½ cup of oil in a skillet over medium-high heat. Add the onions and cook for about 15 seconds without stirring to prevent them from releasing their liquid. Continue cooking for 8 to 10 minutes, stirring only every 15 seconds or so, until the onions begin to caramelize. Using a slotted spoon, transfer the onions to a bowl.

To the same skillet, add the allspice, salt, cumin, pepper, marjoram, and nutmeg and saute, stirring, until the spices are fragrant, about 10 seconds. Add the meat and sear on all sides, about 2 minutes total. Reduce the heat to medium and cook 3 minutes more, stirring occasionally. Return the onions to the skillet and cook the onion and meat mixture to desired doneness, 3 to 5 minutes more. Turn off the heat and stir in the chile paste, if using. Stir in the almonds, pine nuts and walnuts, if using, until evenly incorporated. Transfer to small bowls, one for each plate of kibbeh, and drizzle the remaining ½ cup olive oil equally over each.

Remove the kibbeh from the refrigerator. Using your hands, shape about ½ pound of the kibbeh mixture into a 5- by 2-inch log. Using the side of your hand, make an impression of a cross in the top of each log. Repeat with remaining kibbeh to create 4 to 6 logs total. Serve 1 log per plate and invite diners to spoon the *hossi* over the kibbeh.

SERVES 4 TO 6

For the *Hossi*

1 cup extra-virgin olive oil, plus more for dipping
2 to 3 large yellow onions, diced (about 3 cups)
1 tablespoon ground allspice
1 teaspoon sea salt
⅔ teaspoon ground cumin
½ teaspoon black pepper
¼ teaspoon dried marjoram
¼ teaspoon ground nutmeg
2 pounds lamb meat from the leg or lean beef, chopped
1 to 2 tablespoons seedless Middle Eastern or Turkish chile paste (optional)
1 cup slivered almonds, toasted
½ cup pine nuts, toasted
½ cup walnuts, toasted (optional)

Kibbeh (page 37), chilled

Kibbeh: The Sound of One Village Pounding

An ominous title, but quite accurate. Galilean food traditions are many, but perhaps none is more significant than the preparation of kibbeh, a paste made from the freshest, leanest part of the goat or lamb mixed with fine bulgur and regional spices. Traditionally, its presence on the table meant only one thing: There was something major to celebrate. It was otherwise too labor intensive, not to mention costly, to prepare for everyday eating. The only large gatherings that took place without kibbeh, in fact, were those veiled in sadness, such as the passing of a loved one.

Kibbeh is always made on the morning of the celebration. In the old days, every home had a huge stone mortar and pestle, typically stored out on the veranda, reserved for making this very special dish. The fresh meat was pounded with a pestle twice the width of a baseball bat that turned the ground meat into a paste-like dough. It's a tradition that continues to this day. I can still hear the booming of those pestles hitting the meat; the sound filled the air of my village, from house to house and street to street, welcome background music that left everyone in anticipation for a taste of this beloved dish.

I love all versions of kibbeh, but scooping it—raw—onto Arabic bread, then topping it with *hossi* (page 34), a seasoned chile paste, is a Proustian experience for me. It takes me straight back to those weekend mornings in the pretty village, Tarshiha, where I spent so much of my childhood. Today, kibbeh remains one of the most popular dishes in the Middle East. My father used to tell us there were over one hundred versions of kibbeh prepared in Aleppo, Syria, alone. When I moved to the States, where I made many Syrian friends, they confirmed this astonishing fact.

The basic and most traditional version of kibbeh is a dough made from the freshest ground goat meat kneaded together with bulgur wheat and spices. At my restaurant, I replace the goat with lamb and the consistency remains the same. Whichever meat you use, just remember: It must be extremely fresh so purchase it only from a butcher you trust. There is nothing quite like raw kibbeh spread thinly on a plate, drizzled with fruity olive oil and chile paste and topped with fresh mint and onion. It is the Middle Eastern version of steak tartare. The day after it is eaten raw, the kibbeh dough is traditionally layered in a tray with *hossi* then baked, or the kibbeh dough can be shaped into a cone filled with the *hossi* then deep-fried.

Cooked versions of kibbeh can be prepared from a dough made with ground fish (snapper, tilapia or tuna) accompanied by a *hossi* made from the same fish that's been chopped together with roasted pine nuts. I even make a vegan version of kibbeh at Tanoreen using ground pumpkin (mixed with spiced bulgur) instead of meat. It's filled with a stuffing of fresh spinach and roasted walnuts bound together by pomegranate molasses.

Raw Kibbeh

No matter the preparation—raw or cooked, hot or cold, shaped into balls or patties, spread onto a tray, baked, broiled, boiled, grilled or frozen—only the freshest, top-quality meat is acceptable for making kibbeh. In Nazareth, raw kibbeh was typically prepared on Saturday because that was always the day when meat was slaughtered and sold. The most tender, lean cuts of lamb or goat make the best kibbeh, but these days many people make it with beef because it's less expensive. As opposed to a good steak for grilling, the perfect meat for kibbeh has no fat and shows no marbling. In fact, I remember my mother drawing a fork through the meat after chopping it to remove any fatty strands or tendons. Here, kibbeh is served the Lebanese way, with mint and onions.

> **COOKING TIPS** As with almost all Middle Eastern dishes, there are as many ways to spice kibbeh as there are cooks. In general, Palestinians like an assertively spiced kibbeh and serve it with hot sauce, while the Lebanese season it with a light hand.
>
> When making raw kibbeh, make sure everything it touches—your hands, the bowls, the tray—is ice cold. Soak the bulgur well; if you don't, it will take on excess water as you knead the dough.

Fill a small bowl with ice water. In a large bowl, combine the allspice, cumin, pepper, marjoram and nutmeg and stir in half the bulgur. Dip your hands in the ice water and allow them to drip into the bulgur mixture. Using both hands, press handfuls of the mixture between your palms to incorporate the spices, pressing and pushing it away from you as if kneading bread. Continue dipping your hands in the ice water and allowing the water to drip into the bowl until you can squeeze a handful of the bulgur mixture in your hand and it stays together.

Add the remaining half of the bulgur, the salt, chile paste, yellow onion and ground meat and knead to incorporate as described above, until it forms a dough. (You will use about ½ cup water in total to moisten the bulgur and meat.)

If you plan to serve immediately, prepare an ice-water bath in an extra-large bowl; set the bowl of kibbeh in the ice water. If not serving right away, cover the kibbeh tightly with plastic wrap and refrigerate up to 1 hour while you prepare accompaniments, such as *hossi* (page 34). If there are leftovers, freeze in resealable plastic bags to bake or fry for up to 2 months. Press it into a tray or shape into balls before freezing. Frozen kibbeh is never served raw again.

To serve, spread ½ cup raw kibbeh on a small oval plate. Garnish with the mint leaves and onion slices. Drizzle with the olive oil.

SERVES 4 TO 6

1 teaspoon ground allspice

½ teaspoon ground cumin or to taste

½ teaspoon black pepper

¼ teaspoon dried marjoram

¼ teaspoon ground nutmeg

1 cup fine bulgur (#1), soaked in cold water for 30 minutes

1 teaspoon sea salt

1 tablespoon seedless Middle Eastern or Turkish chile paste

½ yellow onion, grated or finely chopped in a food processor and drained on a paper towel

1 pound very lean, red lamb or goat meat from the leg, ground to a paste

Fresh mint leaves and sliced white onion for garnish

Good-quality olive oil for drizzling

Hummus

Hummus is perhaps the single most recognizable Middle Eastern dish in America. It is essential on the mezze table, but it also serves as the base for Hummus with Meat, page 29, and the chickpea half of Chickpeas and Fava Bean Breakfast, page 24. I serve hummus more than any other dish at Tanoreen; it is one of the items on our menu that has distinguished us from other Middle Eastern restaurants in the city.

How, you might wonder, can a combination of chickpeas, tahini, lemon juice and garlic vary so much from one kitchen to the next? The secret—apart from being fearless with the lemon juice and garlic—is in the cooking of the chickpeas. You must boil dried chickpeas until they not only lose their skins but are easily crushed between your thumb and forefinger. The boiling time can vary greatly depending on the quality of the chickpeas. I always boil far more chickpeas than I need; drain the excess and freeze them in resealable plastic bags for up to six months.

In a small bowl, set ¼ cup of chickpeas aside for your garnish.

In the bowl of a food processor, combine the remaining chickpeas, tahini, lemon juice, reserved liquid, garlic and salt. Process until smooth and creamy, adding more water or lemon juice to reach the desired consistency. (If you plan to refrigerate the hummus before serving, make it a little looser; it thickens up when chilled.) Taste and adjust the lemon juice and salt.

Transfer to a serving dish and, using the back of a spoon, make a well around the circumference of the dip, about ½ inch from the edge. Drizzle the olive oil in the well and garnish with the reserved chickpeas and the parsley. Serve with Arabic bread.

SERVES 6 to 8

1 pound dried chickpeas, soaked and boiled (see page 21), 1 cup cooking liquid reserved, or 2 (15-ounce) cans, liquid from 1 can reserved

1¼ cups tahini (sesame paste)

1½ cups fresh lemon juice or to taste

5 cloves garlic or to taste, finely chopped

1 teaspoon sea salt

¼ cup extra-virgin olive oil

2 tablespoons chopped fresh parsley for garnish

Arabic Bread (page 61) for serving

My Mother's Hummus

HUMMUS BELZEIT

Whenever a dish called for tahini, my mother tried leaving it out because she felt omitting it instantly lightened the dish. One of her most successful alterations was this version of hummus—prepared without tahini and with extra lemon juice—resulting in a much tarter spread. She also mashed the chickpeas by hand and left the mixture somewhat chunky. It is especially wonderful served warm with *Tetbileh*, page 149, drizzled over it. Serve this not only on the mezze table but also for breakfast with warm Arabic bread, smeared on sandwiches for lunch and as a spread with grilled meats for dinner.

In a large pot, combine the cooked chickpeas with the reserved cooking liquid or the reserved liquid from 1 can. Place over low heat and bring to a gentle boil. Using a potato masher, crush the chickpeas until they are coarsely mashed. Turn the heat off.

Add ¼ cup of oil, the lemon juice, garlic, chile paste, if using, cumin and salt; stir with a wooden spoon. Using the potato masher, mash again to incorporate all the ingredients. If the hummus is too stiff, gradually add a bit of bottled water (never tap) until it reaches the desired consistency. Taste and adjust the lemon juice, chile paste and salt.

To serve, spread the hummus in a shallow rimmed bowl, drizzle with the remaining ¼ cup oil and garnish with the parsley.

SERVES 8 TO 10

1 pound dried chickpeas, soaked and boiled (see page 21), 1 cup liquid reserved, or 2 (15-ounce) cans, liquid from 1 can reserved

½ cup olive oil

¾ to 1 cup freshly squeezed lemon juice

6 cloves garlic or to taste, finely chopped

1 teaspoon seedless Middle Eastern or Turkish chile paste (optional)

1 teaspoon ground cumin, plus more to taste

1 teaspoon sea salt or to taste

2 tablespoons chopped fresh parsley for garnish

Tahini with Parsley Sauce

BAKDONSIYYEY

This versatile sauce, known perhaps more widely by its Lebanese name, *taratour*, is both a dip and a sauce on the mezze table. Swab it onto a small folded piece of Arabic bread in between sips of arak, or drizzle it over falafel to give the chickpea patties a lemony kick. *Bakdonsiyyey* is always served alongside Whole Fried Fish, page 145, and is sometimes converted into a salad to accompany the fish by adding chopped fresh tomatoes and cucumbers.

In a small bowl, stir together the tahini sauce, parsley and lemon zest. If you prefer a thinner sauce, add the lemon juice or 2 tablespoons water. Stir in the jalapeño for a spicy kick, if desired. The sauce will keep, tightly covered in the refrigerator, for a few days if the parsley is incorporated, up to 1 week if the parsley is added as you serve it.

MAKES 1½ CUPS

1 cup Thick Tahini Sauce (page 221)
1 cup chopped fresh parsley
Zest of half a lemon
Juice of half a lemon, or 2 tablespoons water (optional)
½ jalapeño chile, grated (optional)

Eggplant Pâte

I came up with this recipe when I discovered the very large, deep purple eggplants in American markets. The idea that I could slice an eggplant into 8-inch-wide rounds was revelatory! So, rather than char them and scoop out the flesh, I decided to slice and fry (or roast) these jumbo eggplants, then use them as a base for a salad. This recipe calls for a lot of lemon juice, but keep in mind that the eggplant soaks up sauce like a sponge. For this dish, I prefer to peel tomatoes, but it is not absolutely necessary. In addition to making a creative mezze, these salad-topped rounds make a great vegan sandwich: Just tuck one into pocket bread or serve alongside falafel in Arabic bread.

Arrange the eggplant slices on a sheet pan, sprinkle with salt and set aside for 30 minutes or until eggplants begin to sweat. Pat dry.

Add ¼ inch corn oil to a large skillet and heat over high until hot. Working in batches, use a spatula to slide the eggplant slices into the skillet and fry, turning once, until they are medium brown on both sides, about 4 minutes total. Repeat with remaining eggplant, adding more corn oil to the skillet if necessary. Alternatively, brush the eggplant slices with olive oil on both sides and roast in a 500°F oven until golden, turning once, about 15 minutes. Set aside to cool.

Meanwhile, finely dice 2 chile peppers, removing seeds if desired. Finely slice the other 2 chile peppers. In a medium bowl, combine the tomatoes, chopped chiles, garlic, ⅓ cup of the olive oil, lemon juice, salt and pepper, stirring to incorporate. Gradually add as much of the remaining olive oil to achieve your desired consistency. Spoon enough of the tomato mixture onto each eggplant slice to leave a narrow border around the rim. Garnish with the sliced chiles and serve.

SERVES 8

3 medium eggplants (2½ to 3 pounds total), cut into ½-inch rounds

Sea salt for sprinkling

Corn oil for frying

4 long hot or jalapeño chile peppers

8 plum tomatoes or 3 beefsteak tomatoes, peeled and diced

6 garlic cloves, minced

⅓ to ½ cup extra-virgin olive oil for tomato topping, plus more for roasting

Juice of 2 lemons

Baba Ghanouj

Every country in the Levantine region claims this earthy, robust spread as its own. And, in truth, it might simply be because there are many ways to season *"baba."* On the West Bank and in Gaza, most cooks use red tahini made from sesame seeds that are roasted for a longer time than the white seeds. Many cooks use pomegranate molasses instead of lemon juice. Some garnish with parsley, others with pistachios, and still others with pomegranate seeds. And it goes on and on.

My version is rather straightforward, intensely smoky and a touch more tart than most. In Nazareth, we call this spread *mutabal* (I had never heard it called baba ghanouj until I came to New York), a name used in other parts of the Middle East for an entirely different eggplant spread made without tahini (for that recipe, see opposite page).

> **COOKING TIP** My dad used to say that the key to making excellent *baba* is to begin with grilled eggplant made by setting the vegetable directly over hot coals or the flame of a gas stove, imparting a lovely smoky flavor. But if you want a milder flavor, roast the eggplants in the oven; directions are provided for both methods below. You can use any kind of eggplant you like, but ideally choose a variety with few seeds and avoid especially large eggplants, as they taste bitter. I prefer the black Italian eggplant; I find it has the least amount of seeds.

SERVES 6 TO 8

3 medium eggplants (2½ to 3 pounds total)

1½ cups Thick Tahini Sauce (page 221)

2 cloves garlic, minced

Fresh lemon juice or pomegranate molasses to taste

¼ cup extra-virgin olive oil

2 tablespoons chopped fresh parsley for garnish

Arabic Bread (page 61) for serving

Prepare a charcoal or gas grill for grilling over high heat, or turn a gas burner to high. Place the eggplants directly onto the coals or one at a time on the flame and grill, using tongs to turn the vegetables as the skin chars, until blackened all over. Set aside to cool.

Alternatively, to roast the eggplants, preheat the oven to 500°F and line a baking sheet with aluminum foil. Pierce the eggplants in a few places with a sharp knife, place them on the prepared baking sheet and roast, turning every 5 minutes or so, until the skin is blistered and begins to crack all over. Set aside to cool.

Slice the eggplants in half lengthwise and scoop out the flesh, transferring it directly to a strainer to allow the liquid to release.

Transfer the strained eggplant to a medium bowl. Add the tahini sauce to the eggplant and mash them together with a fork, breaking up the larger pieces of eggplant with a knife, if necessary. Stir in the garlic along with lemon juice to taste. Spoon the eggplant into a rimmed serving dish and, using the back of a spoon, make a well around the circumference of the dip, about ½ inch from the edge. Drizzle the oil into the well and garnish with the parsley. Serve with Arabic bread.

Mutabal

In most Middle Eastern countries (apart from Nazareth, where baba ghanouj is called *mutabal*)**, the ingredients in this dish are as simple as eggplant, garlic and lemon juice—a lightened up, tahini-free version of baba ghanouj. But when I arrived in America, I experimented with various ingredients and found myself adding tomatoes, chile pepper and a hint of cumin to my** *mutabal*. **I serve it with grilled meat and chicken. My children love this preparation, which is also great spread on toasted or fresh Arabic bread, crusty flatbread or crackers.**

Prepare a charcoal or gas grill for grilling over high heat, or turn 3 gas burners to high. Place the eggplants directly onto the coals or flame and grill, using tongs to turn them as the skin chars, until blackened all over. Set aside to cool.

Alternatively, roast the eggplants in the oven. Preheat the oven to 400°F and line a baking sheet with aluminum foil. Pierce the eggplants in a few places with a sharp knife, place them on the prepared baking sheet and roast, turning every 5 minutes or so, until the skin is blistered and begins to crack all over. Set aside to cool.

Slice the eggplants in half lengthwise and scoop out the flesh, transferring it directly to a strainer to allow the liquid to release.

Meanwhile, in a medium bowl, combine the tomatoes with the chile peppers, if using, garlic, shallot, ½ cup parsley, 3 tablespoons oil, lemon juice, cumin, pepper and a pinch of salt. Add the drained eggplant and mix together with a fork. Transfer the eggplant mixture to a serving bowl and drizzle with the remaining 3 tablespoons oil. Garnish with the remaining parsley and surround with the cucumber slices.

SERVES 6 TO 8

3 medium eggplants, 2½ to 3 pounds total
4 plum tomatoes, or 2 Jersey tomatoes, finely chopped
2 chile peppers, seeded and finely chopped (optional)
4 to 5 cloves garlic, minced
1 shallot, minced
1 cup chopped fresh parsley
6 tablespoons extra-virgin olive oil or to taste
Juice of 2 lemons, plus more for finishing
½ teaspoon ground cumin or to taste
½ teaspoon freshly ground black pepper
Sea salt to taste
Sliced cucumbers for garnish

Red Pepper and Walnut Spread

MHAMMARA

This very popular walnut and red bell pepper spread, similar to Spain's *romesco*, is both piquant and sweet. Some trace the dish's origins to Aleppo, Syria, while the Turks claim it as their own. I learned to make this version from Syrian friends I met in my early days in New York. *Of course,* I couldn't help fiddling with the recipe—mine is full of walnuts and homemade breadcrumbs to replace the traditional cracked wheat. I also strain it of most of its moisture. *Mhammara* is traditionally served with toasted pita chips, but it also makes an excellent addition to a crudité platter. Because the richness and texture of the walnuts lends a meatiness to this dish, I often suggest it as a vegetarian substitute for raw Kibbeh, page 37.

Combine the peppers and onion in the bowl of a food processor and puree until smooth. Line a strainer with a paper towel and transfer the mixture to the strainer; allow it to drain for at least 30 minutes. Transfer the pepper mixture to a medium bowl and set aside.

Place the walnuts in the bowl of the food processor and pulse just until coarsely chopped; do not process to a paste. Alternatively, chop with a knife. Set aside 2 tablespoons for garnish.

Add the rest of the walnuts, the breadcrumbs, 2 tablespoons pomegranate molasses, oil, cumin, allspice, nutmeg, chile paste, if using, salt and pepper to the pepper mixture and stir until thoroughly combined. Cover and refrigerate for 30 minutes or until cool.

Transfer the mixture to a serving dish, drizzle with the remaining pomegranate molasses and garnish with the reserved chopped and whole walnuts. Serve at room temperature.

SERVES 6 TO 8

4 large or 6 small red bell peppers, 1½ to 2 pounds total, seeded and chopped
1 small yellow onion, chopped
2 cups chopped walnuts plus a few whole walnuts for garnish
⅔ to 1 cup plain breadcrumbs
⅓ cup pomegranate molasses
6 tablespoons extra-virgin olive oil
1½ teaspoons ground cumin seeds
½ teaspoon ground allspice
¼ teaspoon freshly grated nutmeg
2 tablespoons seedless Middle Eastern or Turkish chile paste or to taste (optional)
Sea salt and freshly ground black pepper

Brussels Sprouts with Panko

Brussels sprouts were not part of the Palestinian kitchen when I was growing up. I discovered them here in the States and very eagerly tried to push them on my children. To that end, I did what any good mother would do—I pumped up their flavor by adding a little tahini sauce and sweet pomegranate molasses. It worked! In fact these Brussels sprouts were so delicious that they made it onto the original Tanoreen menu and I've never taken them off.

Pour ¼ to ½ inch corn oil in a large skillet and place over a high heat until hot. To test the temperature, slip half a Brussels sprout into the pan; if it makes a popping sound, the oil is hot enough. Working in batches, fry the Brussels sprouts, turning occasionally, until they are browned all over, 2 to 3 minutes. Using a slotted spoon, transfer the sprouts to a paper towel–lined plate to drain.

Meanwhile, whisk together the Thick Tahini Sauce, yogurt and pomegranate molasses in a medium bowl. Set aside.

In a small skillet, heat the olive oil over medium-high until hot. Add the garlic and saute until fragrant, about 1 minute. Add the panko and stir constantly until the crumbs are golden brown, about 2 minutes. Stir in the salt and remove the breadcrumbs from the heat. Transfer to a paper towel–lined plate to cool.

Place the Brussels sprouts in a serving dish, drizzle with the sauce and top with the panko crumbs. Serve immediately.

SERVES 6 TO 8

Corn oil for frying
4 pounds Brussels sprouts, outer leaves removed, cut in half
1 cup Thick Tahini Sauce (page 221)
1 cup low-fat plain yogurt
2 tablespoons pomegranate molasses
2 tablespoons extra-virgin olive oil
½ teaspoon finely chopped garlic
1 cup panko (Japanese-style breadcrumbs)
Pinch sea salt

Turkish Salad

SALATA TURKIYYA

This dish causes some confusion among my customers who expect a tomato salad, which is what most New York restaurants consider a Turkish salad. In Nazareth, the vegetables are chopped very finely and tossed with hot sauce thickened with tomato paste. Typically one of a trio of spreads on the mezze table, along with Hummus, page 38, and Baba Ghanouj, page 44, this is also great on Falafel sandwiches, page 56, or with Chicken Kebabs, page 162.

> **COOKING TIP** If making ahead, add the cucumber just before serving; without it, this salad, topped with a little olive oil, keeps in the fridge for up to ten days.

In a large bowl, combine the cucumbers and onions with the hot sauce, tomato paste, garlic, cumin, allspice, pepper, lemon juice and oil. Using a rubber spatula, gently stir until evenly distributed. Transfer to a serving dish, drizzle with olive oil and serve.

SERVES 8 TO 10

2 Persian seedless cucumbers, peel on, finely diced
2 small red or yellow onions, finely diced
1 cup Homemade Hot Sauce (page 220), or 6 ounces harissa paste
¼ cup tomato paste
3 to 4 cloves garlic, finely chopped
1 teaspoon ground cumin or to taste
1 teaspoon ground allspice
1 teaspoon freshly ground black pepper
Juice of 2 lemons
½ cup extra-virgin olive oil, plus more for drizzling

Pickled Stuffed Eggplants

MAKDOUS

Pickles of all sorts are a staple at every Middle Eastern meal. This particular pickle is generally served as part of an extensive mezze platter (although it makes a great hors d'oeuvres, too). It has a complex character and is more elaborate than most to prepare. I love the heat that the chile paste contributes to the stuffing, but you can use a milder chile or none at all. If sealed properly, *makdous* can last for months.

> **INGREDIENT NOTE** Primarily a preservative, lemon salt speeds the process of pickling so that you can eat the eggplant right away and I use it to avoid lemon juice, which, when mixed with the oil, will drain out of the eggplant.

Bring a large pot of salted water to a boil. Meanwhile, using a sharp kitchen knife, make two incisions anywhere on each eggplant to prevent them from floating in the water, taking care not to cut all the way through. Slide the eggplants into the boiling water and cook until tender, about 20 minutes; transfer to a large colander to drain. Lay a piece of waxed paper directly onto the eggplants, and place heavy cans on top to compress them. Let sit at least 4 hours or overnight to drain thoroughly.

In a medium bowl, combine the walnuts, garlic, oil, chile paste, if using, lemon salt and sea salt. Using a sharp kitchen knife, slit each eggplant lengthwise from stem to root end, cutting through the slits made in the previous step. Divide the walnut mixture evenly among the eggplant halves. Layer the eggplants, stuffing side up, in a sterilized glass container. Pour enough oil over them to cover completely. Place a piece of waxed paper on top, so that it is touching the eggplants. Seal tightly and refrigerate for 5 to 7 days. To serve, place the *makdous* on a platter and drizzle with olive oil. Serve with warm Arabic bread.

MAKES 10 TO 12

10 to 12 small Italian eggplants
3 cups chopped walnuts
10 cloves garlic, minced
¼ cup extra-virgin olive oil, plus more for jarring and serving
2 heaping tablespoons seedless Middle Eastern or Turkish chile paste (optional)
1 tablespoon lemon salt
2 tablespoons sea salt, plus more to taste
Arabic Bread (page 61) for serving

Vegetarian Grape Leaves

WARAK ANAB BIL ZAIT

Stuffed grape leaves should be about the length and width of a woman's pinkie finger—far more slender than most of the versions I see in the States. The size of the grape leaves themselves can vary; if they are larger than 4 inches across, cut them in half along the vein, beginning at the tip of the leaf. The stuffed leaves can be frozen in an airtight container for up to four months. To thaw, set them out on the counter or in the refrigerator overnight.

In a large bowl, combine the tomatoes and rice with the parsley, onions, oil, lemon juice, tomato paste, mint, allspice, 1 teaspoon salt, dried mint, pepper, nutmeg and cumin. Using a wooden spoon, stir the stuffing until thoroughly mixed together.

Working with 1 grape leaf at a time, snip the stem off with kitchen shears. Lay the grape leaf on a clean work surface, shiny side down with the stem end facing you. If the indentations in the leaf are deep, close them up by cutting them in half and overlapping the two segments or by patching the indentations with a piece of another leaf. Trim the rest of the leaves then stack them.

Arrange the carrot, potato or tomato slices on the bottom of a 4-quart pot (this prevents the grape leaves on the bottom layer from burning) and set aside.

Spoon 1 tablespoon of the stuffing at the base of a leaf, just above the stem. Bring the bottom of the leaf up over the filling, then fold the sides of the leaf into the filling. Roll the leaf away from you, wrapping it as tightly as possible around the filling to keep it all in. Repeat with the remaining filling and leaves. As each leaf is rolled, place it in the prepared pot, arranging the stuffed grape leaves in concentric rings, beginning from the outside and working your way to the center. Pack the rolls snugly side by side. When the bottom of the pot is covered, layer the remaining rolls on top.

Combine 2 cups water with the remaining ½ teaspoon salt and add to the pot. Invert a small, heatproof plate directly on top of the grape leaves, then place the lid on the pot. Bring to a boil over high heat, then reduce the heat to low and cook for 40 minutes to 1 hour, until the rice is tender and the grape leaves are easily pierced with a fork.

To serve, remove the plate from the grape leaves, and using a fork, gently transfer the grape leaves to a platter and garnish with the vegetables. Alternatively, using a kitchen towel, press the small plate against the rolls and tip the pot to drain off the liquid. Remove the plate. Invert a serving platter over the pot and flip the pot over to transfer the grape leaves and vegetables to the platter. Gently remove the pot. Serve with the lemon wedges.

MAKES 50 TO 60 GRAPE LEAVES (SERVES 8 TO 10)

6 plum tomatoes, or 5 beefsteak tomatoes, chopped
1½ cups Egyptian rice
1½ cups chopped fresh parsley
2 medium yellow onions, chopped
½ cup extra-virgin olive oil
Juice of 2 lemons or to taste
1 tablespoon tomato paste
1 tablespoon chopped fresh mint
1 tablespoon ground allspice
1½ teaspoons sea salt or more to taste
1 teaspoon dried mint
1 teaspoon freshly ground black pepper
½ teaspoon ground nutmeg
½ teaspoon ground cumin
1 (16-ounce) jar grape leaves, rinsed
Carrots, potatoes or tomatoes, cut into ¼-inch-thick slices (enough to line the bottom of a 4-quart pot)
Lemon wedges for garnish

Picture opposite, clockwise from top right: za'atar bread, pickled stuffed eggplant, vegetarian grape leaves, labneh, marinated olives, baba ghanouj, tabouleh, pickled chile peppers, and pickled cauliflower and carrots.

Of Marriage and Mezze

Galileans love a celebration, but there is perhaps none more ebullient than a wedding. And there was perhaps no better example from my youth than the marriage of my uncle Elia and aunt Marie. I was just seven years old and it was unlike any other gathering I had been to—it has become a defining memory of my childhood. I can still recall every whiff of aromatic spice and the gloriously vibrant platters of food as if I were there mere minutes ago.

A festive feeling filled the air long before the day of the actual wedding ceremony. Traditionally, the groom's parents host nightly get-togethers for his family and friends throughout the week leading up to the wedding day. Mezze is served every night.

During the day, the women in the family gathered and prepared vast amounts of food for the guests—fresh baked spinach pies, grassy chopped parsley, tomatoes and cucumbers picked fresh from their own gardens and chopped finely for tabouleh. Each night just before the feasts, the women made raw kibbeh so it was supremely fresh. It was an enormous amount of work, but Palestinians take pride in making every dish from scratch. Such a convivial spirit is as much a part of mezze as the spread of dishes itself.

A few days before the wedding, Uncle Elia drove from Tarshiha to collect my family in Nazareth. My brothers and sisters and I piled into the back of his covered pickup truck, while he and my parents sat three across, up front. Off we went, on a windswept, hour-long ride through the Galilean countryside. There were groves of banana and avocado trees, field after field of cucumbers, every fig varietal imaginable and trees bursting with olives. We sang ourselves hoarse with repeated renditions of our English ABCs, a tune my teacher mother insisted we sing until we knew it backward and forward!

As we approached Tarshiha, a hillside village of five thousand where my father was born and we spent our summers, the singing slowed and our eyes grew increasingly wide. The lush village, about eight miles south of the Lebanese border, was overrun with emerald green grape vines and citrus trees. The rooftops were quilted in trays of colorful fruits and vegetables set out to dry in the sun. Crimson tomatoes, earthy wheat berries, green okra, red peppers dried for mixing into kibbeh, *mhlookia* leaves, black figs, tobacco leaves and purple eggplant strung along rope with garlic were all part of the bountiful harvest, preserved for the winter months.

After the ceremony my uncle and new aunt walked arm in arm behind a *sahje*, a greeting line of men that stretched and moved from the village church to their new home. This ancient tradition isn't as closely observed these days as it once was, but back then, the ritual lasted for nearly an hour.

Later in the evening, the *real* celebration began—in a friend's backyard that was converted into a reception space. There were rows of banquet tables draped in crisp white linens, each one set with several bottles of arak, the anise-flavored aperitif that is the regional drink of the Levant, and most importantly . . . mezze.

Every table was covered from end to end with dishes of velvety hummus, smoky *mutabal*, the fluffiest tabouleh, crispy fried and raw kibbeh, labneh, mile-high piles of Arabic bread, and spinach and meat pies. (In the Middle Eastern culinary tradition, less is never more!) But as overwhelmed as I was by the abundance and joy of the occasion, it was the way my mother took charge of the cooking on this and so many other occasions that left the biggest and most lasting impression on me. She managed to create a feeling of togetherness and a sense of family that is hard to replicate. From my uncle's wedding day on, I dreamed of being able to cook like my mother. And I still do.

> "Every table was covered from end to end with dishes of velvety hummus, smoky *mutabal*, the fluffiest tabouleh, crispy fried and raw kibbeh, labneh, mile-high piles of Arabic bread, and spinach and meat pies."

Falafel

It is to Arabs what a hamburger is to Americans: Falafel is Middle Eastern fast food. In Nazareth, falafel stands are on what seems like every street corner. You order, add your own salads and pickles, and eat quickly. But as ubiquitous as it is, falafel can vary wildly in proportion of seasonings from vendor to vendor and from country to country.

Unlike at home, where falafel is typically served with tahini sauce or hot sauce (see my homemade versions on pages 221 and 220), street falafel offers a smorgasbord of toppings and sauces that turns the humble patties into something extraordinary. I love mine stuffed into Arabic bread and topped with fried eggplant, pickles, *Tetbileh*, page 145, fresh lemon juice, pickled purple eggplant, red cabbage salad, fresh chopped tomatoes as well as various sauces.

> **COOKING TIP** The beauty of the falafel mix is that you can refrigerate or freeze it. Of course, it always tastes best fresh, but if you have leftover mixture, place it in a resealable plastic bag, press all the air out and seal it. It will keep in the refrigerator up to 6 days and in the freezer for 2 months.

Place the onion in the bowl of a food processor and process until minced. With the motor running, add the garlic through the feed tube and mince, followed by the parsley, cilantro and chile pepper. Stop the motor, add the chickpeas and process until you can squeeze a portion of the mixture in your palm and it comes together easily but isn't pasty.

Transfer the falafel mixture to a mixing bowl. Add the coriander, cumin, sea salt and baking soda. Using your hands or a rubber spatula, gently incorporate the spices while tossing the mixture in the same way you would a salad. Set aside until ready to fry.

Fill a large, deep pot with 2 inches of the oil. Place over high heat until hot (365°F to 375°F) or when a tiny piece of the mix, dropped into the hot oil, creates bubbles and floats to the surface. Have two large trays ready, one lined with paper towels.

Meanwhile, shape the falafel. Using a falafel molder, known as an *aleb*, or, with dampened hands, scoop up a walnut-size portion of the dough and roll it into a ball. Press the ball between your palms to make a 1½- to 2-inch-wide patty, taking care not to compress the dough or squeeze the moisture out of it. Place the patty on the unlined tray and continue shaping half the dough.

Once the oil is hot, begin frying. Using a slotted spoon or your hands, carefully slip the patties into the pot, working in batches. Do not crowd the pot. When the patties float to the surface, flip them over with the slotted spoon and cook until mahogany brown, about 5 minutes. Transfer to the paper towel–lined tray to drain.

While the patties are frying and draining, shape the remaining dough into patties and fry as above. Serve hot with Arabic bread, tahini sauce and a selection of pickles.

SERVES 8

1 large yellow onion, quartered
6 cloves garlic, peeled
1 cup coarsely chopped fresh parsley
½ cup coarsely chopped fresh cilantro
1 chile pepper, preferably jalapeño, seeded if desired and coarsely chopped
2 pounds dried chickpeas, soaked
3 tablespoons ground coriander
2 tablespoons ground cumin
1 tablespoon sea salt
⅓ teaspoon baking soda
Corn oil for frying
Arabic Bread (page 61), pickles and Thick Tahini Sauce (page 221) for serving

SAVORY FLATBREADS & PIES

Meat Pies

SFEEHA

Sfeeha is a very traditional Levantine snack and one of my mother's favorite things to make when I was growing up. She would spend hours making the buttery dough, which turned out more like puff pastry than my version here. Though often served slightly larger, I have sized these as appetizers—plate a few next to a salad or soup if you want a proper meal. Traditional *sfeeha* fillings are mainly variations on cheese, spinach or meat. But, by all means, mix and match any manner of seasoned vegetables, cheeses or meat toppings as you like.

Make the dough: Combine the yeast and sugar in a small bowl. Stir in ¼ cup of the warm water; let stand until the yeast dissolves entirely and the mixture becomes a thin paste.

Meanwhile, sift the flour into a large bowl. Sprinkle the flour with the mahlab and mastic, if using. Make a well in the center of the bowl and sprinkle the salt into the well. Pour the yeast mixture into the well, then add the remaining 1¾ cups water. Add the yogurt and oil to the well and, using your hands, begin incorporating the flour into the liquid from the outside edge to the inside edge until it all comes together. Alternatively, combine the ingredients in the bowl of a stand mixer fitted with the dough hook and mix on medium speed until the dough comes together.

Turn the dough out onto a clean work surface and knead until it is smooth and pliable, 3 to 5 minutes. Divide the dough into 5 equal pieces. Shape into balls and set on a sheet pan. Cover with a kitchen towel and set in a warm, draft-free place for 30 minutes.

Shape the dough: Dust a clean work surface and a rolling pin with flour. Working with 1 ball at a time, roll out the dough into a 16-inch round. Using a 3-inch biscuit cutter, cut out the dough and transfer to a sheet pan, leaving 1 inch between each one. Cover with a kitchen towel and let the dough rest in a warm, draft-free place for about 40 minutes. Using your fingertips, tap the rounds all over, leaving indentations in them.

To make the pies: Preheat the oven to 350°F. Grease a baking sheet with the oil. Spoon 2 tablespoons filling into the center of the dough round. For the spinach pies, bring the edges of the dough together in three flaps to form a triangle. Using the back of a spoon, press the filling into the creases of the pie. For the meat pies and cheese pies, leave open-faced or pinch the dough together on opposite sides of the disc to form a boat, pushing the meat into the creases with the back of a spoon. Bake until the dough is golden and the filling is warmed through, 12 to 15 minutes.

MAKES ENOUGH FOR 8 (8-INCH) PIES OR 60 (3-INCH) PIES

1 tablespoon fast-acting dry yeast

1 tablespoon sugar

2 cups warm water, plus more if needed

4 cups all-purpose flour; 2 cups each whole-wheat flour and all-purpose flour; or 4 cups potato flour (for a gluten-free option)

1 teaspoon mahlab (optional)

Pinch mastic (optional)

1½ teaspoons sea salt or to taste

½ cup plain full-fat yogurt

¼ extra-virgin olive or corn oil

Meat, Spinach or Cheese Fillings (pages 59 to 60)

> **INGREDIENT NOTE** Although not essential, I like to use mahlab, a fragrant spice made from the ground kernels inside St. Lucie cherry pits in this dough. It is generally used for sweet doughs, but I love the subtle hint of floral, nutty, vanilla-like flavor that it lends to this savory dough. Mastic, the resin of the Greek *Pistacia lentiscus* tree, is another exotic flavoring that tinges the dough with a barely-there licorice flavor.

Meat Pie Filling
SFEEHA BIL LAHMEH

MAKES ENOUGH FOR 8 (8-INCH) PIES OR 60 (3-INCH) PIES

½ cup extra-virgin olive oil
2 cups finely diced yellow onion
1 tablespoon ground allspice
½ teaspoon ground nutmeg
⅓ teaspoon ground cinnamon
½ teaspoon ground cumin
½ teaspoon sea salt or to taste
½ teaspoon freshly ground black pepper
Pinch ground cardamom (optional)
3 pounds lamb meat from the leg, chopped
1½ cups low-fat plain yogurt
½ cup Thick Tahini Sauce (page 221)
1 tablespoon pomegranate molasses (optional)
Juice of 1 lemon
½ cup pine nuts, toasted
1 cup slivered almonds, toasted

Heat the oil in a medium skillet over medium-high heat. Add the onion and saute until soft and fragrant, about 5 minutes. Stir in the allspice, nutmeg, cinnamon, cumin, salt, pepper, cardamom, if using, and lamb. Cook, stirring, just until the meat is thoroughly coated with the spices. Do not overcook. Remove from the heat and stir in the yogurt, tahini sauce, pomegranate molasses, if using, lemon juice, pine nuts and almonds; mix to incorporate.

MASTIC MEMORIES

Whenever I open my jar of fragrant mastic, it takes me straight back to the church in Nazareth where my family and I attended Sunday services. Communion was not paper-thin wafers, but rather delicious chunks of bread baked with this aromatic sap of the mastic tree by the women from surrounding villages. They not only baked enough thick, tender loaves to serve in pieces, but provided every family with a loaf to take home. I suppose it is essentially nostalgia that inspires me to use mastic in my *sfeeha* dough—it's expensive and not really necessary—but I wouldn't want to miss out on that taste memory every time I take a bite of the savory little pies.

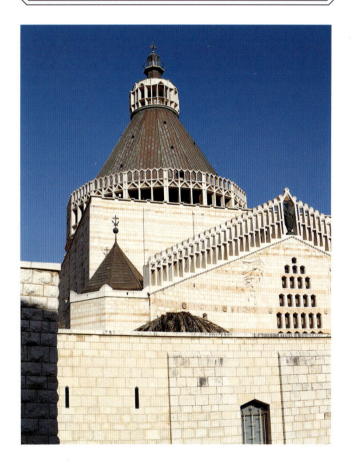

Spinach Pie Filling
FATAYER BIL SABANIKH

If you like your filling very lemony, use the optional lemon sea salt because most of the lemon juice is squeezed from the spinach when it is drained. This filling can be made a day in advance; cover tightly and refrigerate.

MAKES ENOUGH FOR 8 (8-INCH) PIES OR 60 (3-INCH) PIES

2 red onions, diced
½ teaspoon sea salt, plus more to taste
3 pounds fresh or frozen spinach, thawed, if necessary, and chopped
2 tablespoons sumac
½ teaspoon freshly ground black pepper
½ teaspoon lemon salt (optional)
Pinch crushed red pepper flakes (optional)
1 cup whole walnuts (optional)
½ cup extra-virgin olive oil
Juice of 2 lemons

Combine the onions and the sea salt in a bowl and, using your hands, rub the onions until they get soft and begin to release their water. Squeeze the onions of all their liquid, then transfer the onions to a large bowl and add the spinach. Rub the onions and spinach in your hands until the spinach softens and wilts. Squeeze as much liquid from the spinach as possible.

Add the sumac, pepper, lemon salt, red pepper flakes, walnuts (if using) and the olive oil and lemon juice to the spinach and onions in the large bowl; mix together with your hands until the seasonings are thoroughly incorporated. Transfer to a strainer to drain off the liquid (the dough will not adhere if there is excess liquid) and taste and adjust the sea salt.

Cheese Pie Filling
FATAYER BIL JIBIN

MAKES ENOUGH FOR 8 (8-INCH) PIES OR 60 (3-INCH) PIES

1½ pounds feta cheese, diced
4 plum tomatoes or 2 beefsteak tomatoes, diced (about 2 cups)
1 medium yellow onion, diced
1½ cups chopped fresh green za'atar, or 3 tablespoons dried
½ cup extra-virgin olive oil, plus more to taste
Juice of 1 lemon

In a large bowl, combine the cheese and tomatoes with the onion, za'atar, oil and lemon juice. Mix together with your hands until thoroughly incorporated.

BIG-BATCH BAKING

I generally make double batches of *sfeeha* and put some in the freezer, where they will keep for up to 3 months. If you are planning to freeze, bake the pies for 15 to 20 minutes, then let them cool on a wire rack. Pack them in airtight containers with waxed paper separating the layers. To serve, thaw the pies at room temperature for 2 to 3 hours, then bake in a preheated oven at 400°F until heated through, about 10 minutes.

Arabic Bread

KMAJ

When I was growing up, my mother made 40 to 50 loaves of this bread at one time. She would spread a huge piece of fabric in the bedroom and set the shaped discs of dough to rest on it—far from the constant activity in other parts of the house. When I was very young, everyone brought their bread to the village oven to be baked, but eventually, private homes had their own ovens—along with those intoxicating aromas. Fresh baked bread is a special treat; if you don't have the time to prepare it, buy good-quality packaged bread in Middle Eastern or specialty markets.

> **COOKING TIP** The dough can be made ahead and frozen for up to 3 months. Wrap it in waxed paper and place it in a resealable plastic bag. Thaw at room temperature before shaping into discs. If you are making this for the Chicken "Pizza" on page 158, be sure to place a drop of olive oil on each piece and tap all over with your fingertips. This will prevent the bread from splitting open.

In a small bowl, combine ½ cup warm water with the yeast and sugar, stirring every few minutes, until the yeast dissolves and begins to foam, about 5 minutes.

Into a large bowl, sift together the flour, powdered milk, if using, and salt. Make a well in the center of the flour mixture. Pour the yeast mixture into the well, then add the remaining 2 cups warm water, the olive oil and the yogurt (if you're not using powdered milk). Using a fork, mix the flour mixture into the yeast mixture, working from the outside in until thoroughly incorporated. Alternatively, put all of the ingredients in the bowl of a stand mixer fitted with the dough hook. Mix on medium speed for 10 to 12 minutes, or until the dough pulls away from the sides of the bowl and is hanging entirely on the hook.

Knead the dough in the bowl until it's soft yet slightly sticky, about 5 minutes. Add a drop of olive oil on top of the dough and turn it over in the bowl. Cover with a kitchen towel and place in the warmest part of the kitchen until it doubles in size, 30 minutes to 1 hour.

Line a sheet pan with waxed paper and rub with a thin coat of olive oil. Punch down the dough, then pull off pieces the size of oranges. Working with one piece at a time, fold the dough onto itself, then gather it up so that it looks like a moneybag. Grab the dough above the cinched portion and roll the dough ball around until the underside is completely smooth and is the size and shape of a hamburger bun. Place the ball, smooth-side-up, onto the waxed paper and continue with the remaining dough. Let rest for 20 minutes; the dough will expand slightly.

Preheat the oven to 450°F and grease 2 baking sheets with oil. Dust a clean work surface with flour. Roll out each piece of dough into a 9-inch round. Working in batches, transfer to the prepared baking sheets and let rest for a few minutes. Bake until the bottom is golden brown, 5 to 7 minutes. Serve warm.

MAKES 12

2½ cups warm water

4½ teaspoons active dry yeast

1 tablespoon sugar

6 cups all-purpose flour or whole-wheat flour, or 3 cups of each, plus more for dusting

½ cup powdered milk, or 1 cup plain yogurt

1 tablespoon sea salt

1 cup extra-virgin olive oil, plus more for greasing

Za'atar Bread

MANAKEESH

There's nothing quite like eating this aromatic flatbread warm, straight from the oven. Growing up, it was always on the weekday breakfast table. *Manakeesh* is found all over the Middle East, sold out of street carts. The vendor spoons mint and tomatoes onto the *manooshi*, rolls it all up into a cone, wraps it in a piece of waxed paper and, if you are lucky, presents it with a big smile. Normally, I like to make both the za'atar and red pepper and onion topping (see page 65) so I have an equal amount of each type of flatbread.

> **COOKING TIP** The dough can be made ahead and frozen for up to 3 months. Wrap it in waxed paper and place it in a resealable plastic bag. Alternatively, wrap the baked and cooled *manakeesh* in two layers of plastic wrap and freeze up to 4 months. To reheat, remove the plastic, wrap in aluminum foil and bake at 350°F until heated through.

MAKES 12 FLATBREADS

Arabic Bread dough (page 61)
1 cup za'atar with sesame seeds
1 cup extra-virgin olive oil

Prepare the Arabic Bread up to the point where it is resting on the baking sheets. Using your fingertips, make indentations in the dough. Alternatively, make a raised rim by pinching the perimeter of the dough as if crimping the crust of a pie.

In a medium bowl, combine the za'atar and olive oil and stir until thoroughly combined.

Spread each disc with ¼ cup za'atar topping to coat and bake on greased baking sheets until the bottom is golden brown, 5 to 7 minutes. Serve warm.

Me and My Za'atar

If somebody asks me, "Do you like za'atar?" I look at them dumbfounded and wonder, "Are you serious?" I savor it mixed with olive oil every morning—a testament to its addictive flavor and our age-old traditions.

Za'atar, which has been used in the Middle East for thousands of years, is more than just a spice blend. It's a staple of Palestinian food culture. Every household has it, we carry it with us when we travel, and we send it to our sons and daughters abroad, making sure they always have a taste of home.

As children, my siblings, cousins, and I would have friendly competitions to see who could forage the most wild za'atar—the herb in the thyme family that lends its name to the popular mixture—while our parents, aunts, and uncles harvested our olive groves. These childhood memories are deeply ingrained in our family history.

Za'atar is inextricably linked to our culinary traditions. Preparing traditional za'atar is a family affair, involving several steps: drying the herbs, hand-chopping (my mother insisted on chopping the dried za'atar leaves by hand because she believed they tasted better—and I wholeheartedly agree), and carefully blending with sesame seeds and sumac. While the preparation back in those days was time-consuming, it created memories that I find myself constantly recalling all these years later.

On the same day we mixed and jarred the spice blend, my mother would bake fresh bread for *Manakeesh* (Za'atar bread, see opposite page) for lunch. It's impossible to adequately describe the heavenly aroma that filled our home—a combination of warm bread, herbaceous za'atar, toasted sesame and the almost peppery scent of olive oil.

It brings a smile to my face that za'atar has now become a popular ingredient for home cooks and that it features prominently in upscale restaurants. However, this popularity is bittersweet. Unfortunately, the Israeli government's restrictions on harvesting wild za'atar have altered its traditional taste and significantly increased its cost. This has had a profound impact on a food that was once freely available to Palestinians and considered by many to be a birthright.

At Tanoreen, we honor this tradition by making our za'atar in-house. I encourage you to try making your own blend as well—it's a rewarding experience that connects you to centuries of culinary history!

Red Pepper and Onion Flatbread

KHUBZ BIL FILFIL

Wafa's sister Ikbal is known within the family for making the very best *khubz bil filfil*. She makes it the traditional way—in an outdoor clay oven known as a *taboun*, which gives the dough the perfect char. To this day, she bakes it dressed in a traditional housecoat and head scarf trimmed in crocheted flowers known as a *mandeel*. She has worn the same one ever since I can remember, and whenever she ties her *mandeel* on, we all know warm bread is in the offing.

> **COOKING TIP** If you're a purist, use lemon juice, but I have found that substituting lemon salt insures that the dough will not be overly moist and sticky.

Prepare the Arabic Bread up to the point where it is resting on the baking sheets. Using your fingertips, make indentations in the dough. Alternatively, make a raised rim by pinching the perimeter of the dough as if crimping the crust of a pie.

In a medium bowl, combine the chile paste, onion and tomatoes with the oil, lemon juice or lemon salt, sesame seeds, cumin and salt. Stir to thoroughly incorporate.

Spread each disc with ¼ cup of the onion mixture and bake on greased baking sheets until the bottom is golden brown, 5 to 7 minutes. Serve warm.

MAKES 12 FLATBREADS

Arabic Bread dough (page 61)
1 cup seedless Middle Eastern or Turkish chile paste
1 medium yellow onion, diced
2 plum tomatoes, peeled and grated, juices reserved
½ cup extra-virgin olive oil
Juice of 1 lemon or ⅓ teaspoon lemon salt
½ cup unhulled sesame seeds (shells on)
½ teaspoon ground cumin
½ teaspoon sea salt or to taste

Savory Pies

SAMBOSEK

A staple on every mezze spread, these little half moons are made with unleavened dough that results in a wonderfully crispy texture when fried. A forgiving and versatile dough, it can be flavored with onion or garlic powder, any dried herb, caraway or black nigella seeds. The fillings below are those on the Tanoreen menu, but you can just as easily make simple cheese pies using crumbled feta and za'atar, grated halloumi, goat or even pepper Jack cheese. Serve the pies on a platter alongside my homemade Thick Tahini Sauce and Hot Sauce (pages 221 and 220). Or try them with my Basil Pesto (page 215).

In a large bowl, combine the flour, water, oil, sugar and salt. Using a wooden spoon, stir until the mixture comes together. Turn out onto a clean work surface dusted with flour. Knead until the dough is tender. Alternatively, combine the ingredients in the bowl of a stand mixer fitted with the dough hook and beat on medium speed until the dough is tender. Shape into a ball, cover with a kitchen towel and let rest for 10 minutes.

Pull off a piece of dough about the size of an orange. Lightly dust a rolling pin with flour and roll out the dough as thinly as possible. Using a 2-inch biscuit cutter, cut out circles in the dough.

Spoon 1 tablespoon of the meat or vegetable filling onto one side of the circle, leaving a ¼-inch rim exposed around the perimeter. Fold the circle in half to make a half moon. Using a fork, crimp the edges to seal them. Repeat with the remaining dough. At this point, the pies can be sealed tightly in an airtight container and frozen up to 2 months.

Fill a skillet with ½ inch of oil and heat over high heat until hot. Working in batches without crowding the pan, fry the *sambosek*, turning once, until both sides are golden, about 4 minutes total. Using a slotted spoon, transfer the pies to a paper towel–lined tray to drain.

MAKES 24 PIES

4 cups all-purpose flour, plus more for dusting
2 cups water
¼ cup extra-virgin olive oil
1 teaspoon sugar
1 teaspoon sea salt
Meat or Vegetable Filling (recipes follow)
Corn oil for frying

Meat Filling

**MAKES 1½ CUPS
(ENOUGH FOR 24 PIES)**

¼ cup extra-virgin olive oil
1 small red onion, chopped (about 1 cup)
6 cloves garlic, finely chopped
1 chile pepper, seeded and diced (optional)
1 teaspoon ground coriander
1 teaspoon ground allspice
1 teaspoon ground cumin
½ teaspoon black pepper
2 pounds chopped lamb meat from the leg or lean beef such as sirloin or filet mignon
2 tablespoons pomegranate molasses
Juice of 1 lemon
2 teaspoons sea salt
½ cup slivered almonds, toasted
½ cup pine nuts, toasted

Heat the oil in a medium skillet over medium-high heat. Toss in the onion and saute until soft and translucent, about 3 minutes. Add the garlic and saute until fragrant and golden, 1 minute. Sprinkle in the chile pepper, if using, and saute until softened. Stir in the coriander, allspice, cumin and black pepper and count to five. Raise the heat to high, add the lamb and saute until the meat is cooked through, 7 to 10 minutes.

Stir in the pomegranate molasses, lemon juice and salt. Add the almonds and pine nuts and stir until well incorporated. Remove from heat and set aside.

Vegetable Filling

**MAKES 2 CUPS
(ENOUGH FOR 24 PIES)**

6 tablespoons extra-virgin olive oil
3 shallots, diced
3 cloves garlic, finely chopped
3 medium baking potatoes, diced (about 3 cups)
1 tablespoon ground coriander
1 teaspoon ground cumin
1 teaspoon freshly ground black pepper
½ cup chopped fresh cilantro
1 green chile pepper, seeded and cut into small dice (optional)
3 cups frozen baby peas
Juice of 1 lemon or to taste
2 tablespoons pomegranate molasses
1 teaspoon ground turmeric
1 teaspoon sea salt
Pinch saffron (optional)

Heat the oil in a large skillet over medium-high until hot. Toss in the shallots and saute until soft and fragrant, 3 to 4 minutes. Add the garlic and saute for 1 minute more. Tip in the potatoes and saute until they begin to take on color, about 5 minutes. Stir in the coriander, cumin, and pepper and count to five, then stir in the cilantro and chile pepper, if using, and cook until the cilantro changes color, about 1 minute. Toss in the peas and cook, stirring, for 3 to 5 minutes. Add the lemon juice, pomegranate molasses, turmeric, salt and saffron, if using; cook, stirring, 1 minute more. Taste and adjust the seasonings and lemon juice, as desired.

SALADS

Essential Side Notes

Salads in the Middle Eastern tradition are invariably served alongside every meal, essential keynotes that, unlike in Europe and the U.S., rarely make it to the center of the plate. No matter the composition or ingredients, salads are always on the table as an accompaniment, part of a mezze spread or a side dish.

What's more, the definition of a Middle Eastern salad is quite loose—it can be composed of leafy greens and vegetables as in Fattoush, page 78; a preponderance of herbs tossed with a few grains as in Tabouleh, page 81; or a mix of very finely chopped vegetables in a thick spicy sauce, somewhat like a chutney, as in Turkish Salad, page 49. This condiment-like salad is perfect for slathering on grilled Chicken Kebabs, page 162, and is a suitable counterpoint for hummus on a mezze spread. I often suggest that my customers order the Cauliflower Salad, page 85, tossed in a pomegranate-tahini sauce, as part of a mezze platter rather than as a side dish; it is as hearty and earthy as a main course, making it a lovely addition to an assortment of small dishes. Other salads are served as the *yin* to a main course's *yang*. One of my favorites is the easy-to-make Tomato Salad, page 77, which is as ubiquitous on the Middle Eastern table as the green salad is in the U.S.

It's tossed in a lemony vinaigrette and typically served as a cooling counterpoint to rich dishes such as Spiced Lamb Shank, page 184, and earthy *Mujadara*, page 198.

However you choose to enjoy the salads that follow, do as I do and season them to suit yourself. All of the spices, herbs, oils, vinegars and other flavorings can be adjusted according to your taste. I am an avowed lover of the brightening power of lemon juice, so I tend to use it quite liberally. If you love the earthy flavor nutmeg lends a dish, grind a pinch more. Add chile paste gradually to a vinaigrette, tasting as you go until you reach the heat level you're after. As with every other course on the Middle Eastern table, salads are prepared with care, respect and attention because they are an integral part of each and every meal.

> "No matter the composition or ingredients, salads are always on the table as an accompaniment, part of a mezze spread or a side dish."

Eggplant Salad

SALATET BAITENJAN

One of the first things I make myself when I go home to Nazareth is the eggplant sandwich we often ate on Friday afternoons when I was growing up. I always dressed mine with tomato slices and a simple sauce of garlic, lemon juice and olive oil. Perfection. This salad, a staple on the Tanoreen menu, is inspired by that beloved sandwich. It is excellent with *Mujadara*, page 198, or Falafel, page 56, tucked into a sandwich.

Preheat the oven to 500°F. Divide the eggplant pieces between two rimmed baking sheets and brush them all over with olive oil. Sprinkle with the salt and bake until the eggplants are lightly browned and softened, 20 to 30 minutes. Set aside to cool.

In a large mixing bowl, combine the tomatoes, green and red peppers, parsley, olives, shallots, garlic, lemon juice, 6 tablespoons oil and crushed red pepper, if using. Mix well with a wooden spoon, then taste and adjust the lemon juice and salt.

Gently fold in the cooled eggplant, distributing it evenly and taking care not to crush it. Transfer to a platter and serve.

SERVES 4 TO 6

3 medium to large eggplants (3 to 4 pounds total), peel on, cut into large cubes

6 tablespoons extra-virgin olive oil, plus more for brushing

1 teaspoon sea salt or to taste

8 plum tomatoes, cut into small cubes, or 3 beefsteak tomatoes, cut into large cubes (about 5 cups)

1 medium green pepper, seeded and diced

1 medium red pepper, seeded and diced

1 cup chopped fresh parsley

¾ cup Kalamata or green olives, pitted and chopped

3 shallots, 1 medium red onion or 6 scallions, white parts only, chopped

6 to 8 cloves garlic, minced

Juice of 3 lemons (about ½ cup), or to taste

½ teaspoon crushed red pepper (optional)

Tomato Salad

SALATET BANDOORA

This is one of the most popular salads on the Palestinian table. You would be hard pressed to find a single household in the region that doesn't serve a tomato salad with every dinner during the summer months. I prepare it the traditional and very simple way: tomatoes, onions and chile peppers. However, it is not unusual to find diced cucumber and chopped parsley in some preparations. It is a colorful addition to the mezze table and is also eaten with anything grilled, Whole Fried Fish, page 145, and Lentil Pilaf, page 198. For the best results, use ripe summer tomatoes at their peak.

In a medium serving bowl, combine the tomatoes, onions and chile pepper with the mint, garlic, oil, lemon juice and salt. Toss thoroughly. Taste and adjust the oil, lemon juice and salt.

SERVES 4 TO 6

3 to 4 beefsteak or Jersey tomatoes, or 8 plum tomatoes, peeled and diced, at room temperature

2 small red or yellow onions, diced

1 chile pepper (poblano, jalapeño or long hot), seeded and cut into small cubes

4½ teaspoons chopped fresh mint or 1 tablespoon dried

½ teaspoon finely chopped garlic

½ cup extra-virgin olive oil or more to taste

4 to 6 tablespoons fresh lemon juice or more to taste

½ teaspoon sea salt or more to taste

Beet Salad

SALATET SHAMANDAR

In the Middle East, the most popular ways to prepare beets are pickled with turnips, page 210, or as my father used to do, boiled with carrots and dipped in sugar for a quick, old-style dessert. The beet salad I created at Tanoreen is the perfect example of how travel has influenced my palate over the years—in this case, time spent in Italy. I add a cheese-free basil pesto and roasted slivered almonds and walnuts to the beets. Sometimes I dot the top with some goat cheese just before serving.

Place the beets in a large pot with enough cold water to cover. Bring to a boil, reduce the heat and simmer until fork tender, 20 to 40 minutes. Transfer the beets to a colander to drain and cool. When cool enough to handle, slice the beets crosswise into ¼-inch-thick slices.

Meanwhile, in a large bowl, pour in the oil, lemon juice and pesto with the garlic, basil, mint, walnuts, almonds and salt. Whisk to combine.

Add the beets to the bowl and toss to coat. Transfer to a rimmed dish and serve.

SERVES 6

2 pounds medium beets, scrubbed and peeled

½ cup extra-virgin olive oil

⅓ cup fresh lemon juice

⅓ cup Basil Pesto (page 215)

1½ teaspoons finely chopped garlic

½ cup chopped fresh basil

½ cup chopped fresh mint

½ cup chopped walnuts, toasted

⅓ cup slivered almonds, toasted

1½ teaspoons sea salt

Fattoush

This superb salad is very popular throughout the Middle East, but especially throughout the Levant. Every country has its own version, but, honestly, I think the most delicious version comes from Lebanon. Some won't consider fattoush the real thing without sumac; others say purslane is the essential ingredient. I agree that both are important components (but don't worry about the purslane if you can't find it), however, the one ingredient that makes fattoush, well, fattoush, is plenty of toasted Arabic bread!

> **INGREDIENT NOTE** In my mind, the fattoush my mother composed was the best: She just tossed in whatever the garden yielded. The ingredients must all be cut into the same size pieces—about ¼-inch cubes—and tossed with sumac, dried mint and toasted pita. Otherwise, the sky is the limit! I add fresh pomegranate seeds when they are readily available or finely chopped Granny Smith apples. If heirloom tomatoes are in season, I use them. You can use whatever fresh greens are on hand, too. You see where this is going!

In large salad bowl, throw in the romaine, tomatoes, cucumbers, onion, scallions, garlic and mint. Gently toss together.

In a lidded jar, combine the lemon juice, oil, sumac, garlic, mint and salt. Cover the jar tightly and shake to mix.

Just before serving, drizzle the dressing over the salad and serve with the Arabic bread.

VARIATION *One of my favorite versions of fattoush is a mix of arugula, cilantro, scallions and radishes tossed with toasted pita chips and the dressing above.*

SERVES 8

3 cups chopped romaine lettuce
3 plum tomatoes, chopped
3 small Kirby cucumbers, chopped
1 medium red onion, chopped
3 scallions, chopped
1 clove garlic, minced
8 fresh mint leaves, chopped
Arabic Bread (page 61), toasted

For the Dressing

¾ cup fresh lemon juice
½ cup extra-virgin olive oil
2 tablespoons sumac
1 clove garlic, minced
2 teaspoons dried mint
1½ teaspoons sea salt

DRYING HERBS

If you grow your own leafy herbs (mint, parsley, oregano, thyme, or basil) or have bought more than you can use immediately, you can dry them. Pick the leaves off the stems and wash them thoroughly in several changes of cold water, each time lifting the herbs out of the water (don't pour them out or you won't get rid of the dirt). Dry completely in a cloth towel you reserve for herbs. Spread on a cookie sheet and slide into a 75°F to 100°F oven for 1 hour, turning once to ensure even drying. Alternatively, set them out in full sun for a full day, turning once to ensure even drying. Store the dried herbs in a mason jar or other glass container with a tight-fitting lid. The herbs should keep their aroma and flavor for many months.

Feta Salad

SALATET FETA

Fresh green za'atar, also known in the Middle East as wild thyme, has been a staple in the region's cuisine since medieval times. It is rare to find it here in the States, though I have noticed it showing up in some of the larger produce markets around New York City. Though the flavor of the salad will be different if you use dried za'atar, which is available in Middle Eastern markets and online, it is no less delicious. This salad started out as a classic za'atar salad—tomatoes, za'atar, lemon juice and olive oil—which I made for my daughter, Jumana, throughout her childhood. But I took a cue from the Lebanese, who often add feta, which lends a salty flavor and creamy texture.

> **COOKING TIPS** I use domestic feta whenever possible; it's firmer and easier to cut into clean dice than the creamier, French version. Garnish with the onions rather than tossing them into the salad. That way, when you are storing leftovers or making the dish ahead, simply remove the onions from the top and keep the salad tightly covered, in the refrigerator, for up to three days.

In a medium serving bowl, combine the feta and tomatoes with the za'atar, red pepper flakes, if using, oil, lemon juice and salt. Gently toss to combine.

Taste and adjust the oil, lemon juice and salt. Scatter the onions on top, if desired, and serve with warm Arabic bread.

SERVES 6 TO 8

1 pound feta, preferably domestic, cut into ½-inch cubes
8 plum tomatoes, or 4 to 5 beefsteak tomatoes, diced
1 cup chopped fresh green za'atar or fresh oregano leaves, or ½ cup dried za'atar or oregano
½ teaspoon crushed red pepper flakes (optional)
½ cup extra-virgin olive oil or to taste
Juice of 1½ lemons or to taste
Sea salt to taste
1 small red onion, chopped (optional)
Arabic Bread (page 61) for serving

Tabouleh

Tabouleh is an essential part of a classic mezze spread, but it is also a very popular lunch dish. When I was growing up, tabouleh was only prepared by women and eaten by women. Of course, these days you will find everyone—men, women, children—eating tabouleh—not only in the Middle East but all over the West. It is synonymous with a healthy diet, touted for parsley's nutritious profile. Stateside, it is often served with Arabic bread, a pairing you will never find in the Middle East. Instead, try eating tabouleh in lettuce cups or wrapped in fresh off-the-vine grape leaves if you are lucky enough to have access to them. As with many classic dishes, every region has its own version of tabouleh; Nazarenes put a pinch of cumin, Lebanese add extra bulgur (you can double or triple the amount used below if you like). Tabouleh should be tossed just before serving, as it has a tendency to wilt rather quickly. I don't recommend making it ahead or planning for leftovers.

> **COOKING TIP** There's nothing quite like freshly made tabouleh prepared with the fluffiest parsley and top-quality olive oil. The trick to featherweight parsley is not only to make sure it is thoroughly dry before chopping, but to resist over chopping, which bruises the soft herb. I prefer Italian parsley to its curly-leaved cousin, which, though easier to chop, is not as soft or flavorful as flat-leaved.

In a large bowl, combine the parsley with half the tomatoes, the onion, fresh and dried mint, salt, lemon juice, oil and cracked wheat. Gently toss to evenly distribute the ingredients. Taste and adjust the lemon juice and salt.

Transfer to a serving bowl and garnish with the remaining tomatoes. Serve over the romaine, cabbage leaves or grape leaves.

VARIATIONS *To make tabouleh the Nazarene way, add ½ cup peeled, chopped cucumber and 1 teaspoon ground cumin. If you are allergic to wheat, skip the bulgur altogether and add a chopped cucumber and chile pepper to give the salad both crunch and a sharp bite.*

MAKES 4 SERVINGS

4 cups fresh flat-leaf parsley

2½ plum tomatoes, or 2 medium Jersey tomatoes, chopped

1 medium red onion, or 6 scallions, chopped

2 tablespoons chopped fresh mint

1 tablespoon dried mint

½ tablespoon sea salt or to taste

Juice of 2 lemons or to taste

⅓ to ½ cup good-quality extra-virgin olive oil

3 to 4 tablespoons fine bulgur (#1), picked over and rinsed

Romaine lettuce, cabbage leaves or grape leaves for serving

Armenian Tabouleh

There was a small Armenian Orthodox community in my mother's village of Rameh, in the north of Palestine. An Armenian priest and his family lived right next to my grandmother's home, and their kitchen always filled the air with incredible aromas. Every summer, I'd find myself drawn to their house to ask what was cooking, and they were always generous, letting me taste whatever they were making.

It wasn't until I came to the United States that I discovered Armenian tabouleh. The moment I tasted it, I knew exactly how to make it—it brought back vivid memories of our Armenian neighbor's kitchen, like déjà vu.

Rinse and drain the bulgur. Put it in a bowl and just cover with cold water. Set aside to soak for 30 minutes, to absorb the water.

Heat 2 tablespoons of olive oil in a frying pan over medium heat. Add the diced onion and shallot, and sauté until golden brown, about 10 minutes.

Stir the tomato paste and harissa or chile paste into the onion mixture. Mix in 2 tablespoons of the lemon juice to help blend the mixture. Set aside to cool.

Check the bulgur has absorbed the water. Once the paste has cooled, add it to the bulgur and mix thoroughly until the bulgur is evenly coated and takes on a red color from the paste. Mix in the parsley, mint, tomatoes, scallions, cilantro, and chopped hot pepper, if using, until combined.

In a small bowl, mix the remaining olive oil, lemon juice, and a pinch of sea salt. Drizzle this dressing over the tabouleh and toss to coat. Taste and season to your liking.

Serve with warm bread or, for a lighter option, use romaine lettuce or cabbage leaves as wraps.

SERVES 4 TO 6

1 cup fine bulgur (#1)
½ cup olive oil, plus 2 tablespoons
1 onion, diced
1 shallot, diced
1 tablespoon tomato paste
1 tablespoon harissa or chile paste
1 cup lemon juice
4 packed cups chopped parsley
½ cup chopped mint
2 cups chopped tomatoes
1 cup chopped scallions
1 cup chopped cilantro
1 long hot pepper or jalapeño, chopped (optional, depending on heat preference)
Sea salt
Arabic Bread (page 61), or romaine or cabbage leaves for serving

Savory and Sweet: Carrots Two Ways

Warm Carrot Salad

Sweet and crunchy when raw, flavor sponges when cooked, carrots were a staple on our table growing up. They were readily available and could always bulk up a meal. Since we were a family of seven on a tight budget, my mom got creative with how to use them. This carrot salad is simple, delicious and is the perfect side dish for a sit-down dinner or even a buffet-style gathering.

In a large pan, steam the carrots whole until just tender, 8 to 10 minutes. Drain and slice the carrots into rounds or half-moons, each about ¼ inch thick. Transfer to a serving bowl.

In a small bowl or jar, combine the garlic, lemon juice, olive oil, parsley or cilantro, and cumin, and season with salt and black pepper. Mix well to combine.

Drizzle the dressing over the carrots and toss to coat them evenly. This will keep in the refrigerator for up to a week.

SERVES 4 TO 6

6 large carrots, or 10 small carrots, peeled
3 garlic cloves, chopped
Juice of 1½ lemons
4 to 6 tablespoons olive oil
½ packed cup chopped parsley or cilantro
1 teaspoon cumin
Sea salt and freshly ground black pepper

Sweet Carrot Salad

My father, a former nurse and health inspector, was passionate about nutrition. So, instead of sugary desserts, he would often eat something simple like carrots or citrus as a sweet treat. This crunchy, juicy, shredded carrot salad is a great palate cleanser after a rich or heavy meal.

In a large bowl, combine the grated carrots, orange juice, orange zest, and orange blossom water, and mix well. Taste; depending on the sweetness of your oranges, you may wish to add up to 2 tablespoons honey. Mix well, then refrigerate the salad for about 1 hour before serving, to allow the carrots to absorb the flavors.

For a unique presentation, serve the salad in halved avocados.

SERVES 4 TO 6

6 large carrots, peeled and grated
Juice of 3 oranges
Zest of 1 orange
1 tablespoon orange blossom water
1 to 2 tablespoons honey (optional)
2 to 3 avocados, halved and pitted, to serve (optional)

Cauliflower Salad

SALATET ZAHRA

In Nazareth, cauliflower is prepared and eaten simply: fried and tucked into Arabic bread, spritzed with lemon juice and sprinkled with sea salt. That elemental sandwich inspired this dish, which is dressed with a pomegranate molasses–spiked tahini sauce. It's a beloved mezze on the Tanoreen menu, and I also serve it as an entree with meat or chicken.

Place the cauliflower in a large pot with enough water to cover. Bring the water to a boil and continue to boil for 2 minutes. Transfer to a colander to drain.

In a large skillet, heat ½ to ¾ inch oil over high until hot. Working in batches, fry the cauliflower until golden brown, about 2 minutes per side. Using a slotted spoon, transfer to paper towels to drain. Alternatively, preheat the oven to 500°F. Spread the cauliflower on a sheet pan and brush all over with oil. Roast until golden and fork tender, about 15 minutes. Or, grill the cauliflower directly over medium heat.

Arrange the cauliflower on a serving platter. Drizzle with the tahini sauce followed by the pomegranate molasses. Garnish with the parsley and serve.

SERVES 6 TO 8

2 heads cauliflower, cut into 2-inch florets
Corn oil for frying
1 cup Thick Tahini Sauce (page 221)
¼ cup pomegranate molasses
2 tablespoons chopped fresh parsley

Tanoreen Potato Salad

SALATET BATATA

This is made dozens of ways back home—dressed with mayonnaise or tahini or, in this case, with a garlic-and-lemon combination warmed with cumin and cooled with mint. It's a hybrid of the way my mother used to make potato salad and the version I created for Tanoreen. The traditional recipe, made all over Palestine, Lebanon and Syria features the first six ingredients below. I love the addition of olives; they lend a wonderful sea salty, briny kick.

Place the potatoes in a large pot with enough water to cover. Bring to a boil and cook over medium-high heat until a toothpick slides easily into a piece but doesn't cause the potato to fall apart, 7 to 10 minutes. Transfer to a colander to drain, then rinse under cold water. Spread the potatoes on a baking sheet to cool.

Combine the garlic and salt in the bottom of a mixing bowl. Using a fork, mash the garlic into a paste. Pour in the oil and lemon juice with the parsley, scallions, green and red peppers, mint, cumin, paprika and black pepper; mix to combine. Add the potatoes and, using a wooden spoon, toss gently until thoroughly coated with the dressing. Transfer to a serving platter and garnish with the olives and cilantro.

SERVES 6

6 to 7 Idaho potatoes, or 15 small red potatoes, peel on if preferred, cut into 1-inch cubes
2 tablespoons chopped garlic
1 tablespoon sea salt
½ cup extra-virgin olive oil
Juice of 2 lemons
1 packed cup chopped fresh parsley
6 scallions, green parts only, chopped
¼ cup finely diced green pepper
¼ cup finely diced red pepper
2 tablespoons chopped fresh mint
1 teaspoon ground cumin
1 teaspoon ground paprika
1 teaspoon freshly ground black pepper
½ cup chopped green olives
3 tablespoons chopped fresh cilantro

Tanoreen Green Salad

SALATA KHADRA

I created this Tanoreen specialty for my customers who were looking for a tossed green salad option. Here, a mix of baby greens is tossed with a dressing that borrows flavorful ingredients from all over the world: sesame oil, ginger, and pomegranate molasses. It is an unusual combination that really hits the mark. You can mix and match your greens, but I find peppery arugula is essential here.

In a large serving bowl, combine the arugula, spinach, lettuce and kale with the tomatoes, onion, and mint leaves; toss to mix.

Make the dressing: In a large bowl, whisk together the lemon juice, sesame oil, pomegranate molasses, if using, olive oil, garlic and ginger.

When ready to serve, pour the dressing over the salad and toss to coat the greens evenly. Season with salt and sprinkle the olives and walnuts, if using, on top.

SERVES 6 TO 8

3 packed cups baby arugula
1 packed cup baby spinach
1 packed cup baby lettuce
1 packed cup finely chopped kale
2 plum tomatoes, diced, or 12 grape or cherry tomatoes, halved
1 red onion, diced
8 to 10 fresh mint leaves
Sea salt to taste
½ cup chopped green olives
½ cup chopped walnuts (optional)

For the Dressing
1 cup fresh lemon juice or to taste
3 tablespoons toasted sesame oil
2 tablespoons pomegranate molasses (optional)
3 tablespoons extra-virgin olive oil
3 cloves garlic, finely chopped
1 teaspoon freshly grated ginger

SOUPS & STEWS

Family Meals

Soups and stews, or *yakhani* as they are known in the Middle East, are synonymous with family meals. When I was growing up in Nazareth, dishes centered around beef or lamb were generally reserved for special celebrations, holidays and weddings, as meat was too expensive to serve a family of seven every night. Let's face it, it still is.

My mother was masterful at creating hearty, healthy soups and stews made primarily with vegetables; meat was always a secondary ingredient. She could turn such humble garden bounty as cauliflower, string beans, okra and potatoes into soups and stews that always seemed special. Her secret was actually quite simple: fresh ingredients, seasoned well and cooked with care. I have very fond memories of her grinding down the freshly harvested freekah (smoked and cracked green wheat) into coarse crumbs and turning it into a hearty soup with chicken or lamb. Whenever I make Freekeh Soup, page 101, the aroma of warm spices and smoky grains never ceases to lift my spirits.

I cook for my family here in the States much the same way my mother did, with soups and stews routinely simmering on the stovetop. They make sense not just for a large family like the one I grew up in, but for my decidedly smaller family of four. Indeed, my son, Tarek, would rather eat stew than anything else for any meal, especially breakfast. When he visits, I make sure to have the refrigerator fully stocked with his favorites: Cauliflower and Lamb Stew, page 108, and Chopped Mlookhia Stew, page 109.

The soups in this chapter are ideal for preparing in big batches and freezing. What's more, once all of the ingredients make it into the pot, they will cook slowly to allow the flavors of the seasoned broth, vegetables and, in some cases, meat or chicken, to meld. The active cooking time in these recipes is actually quite short. As with most stews and soups, they taste better the day after, making them ideal make-ahead meals.

In the beef- and chicken-based soups, it is ideal to use Seasoned Chicken with Stock, page 100, and Seasoned Lamb or Beef with Stock, page 112. Both are fragrant of cardamom, nutmeg and allspice, which lends a distinct Middle Eastern flavor to any dish that calls for them. Of course, if time is not on your side, good-quality purchased stocks are fine.

All of the soups in this chapter are hearty enough to be meals in themselves. Ladle the stews over Rice and Vermicelli Pilaf, page 204, or serve bowls of the soups or stews with warm Arabic Bread, page 61, and some olives, pickles and fresh sliced jalapeños on the side. At Tanoreen, come fall and winter, I always make sure to offer a few more of these robust options on my menu, as they warm up my diners on those infamously cold New York City winter nights.

> "I cook for my family here in the States much the same way my mother did, with soups and stews routinely simmering on the stovetop. They make sense not just for a large family like the one I grew up in, but for my decidedly smaller family of four."

Tanoreen's Leek and Potato Soup

I had never tasted leeks until I arrived in New York—we didn't grow them in Nazareth, but instead used scallions or spring onions. Cooking with these mild members of the onion family seemed like an interesting prospect, but as you probably know by now, I am hard pressed to make anything with too mellow a flavor. So I punched up this classic soup with elements from the earthy Middle Eastern flavor profile. To give the soup a little bite, add the chopped white parts of six scallions.

> **COOKING TIP** Take care not to allow the shallots and garlic to burn or they will darken this white soup.

In a medium pot, heat the oil over medium heat. Toss in the shallots and saute until tender but still pale, 4 to 5 minutes. Add the garlic and saute, stirring, until fragrant but still pale, about 2 minutes. Sprinkle in the pepper, nutmeg and cardamom (if using) and stir until fragrant, about 30 seconds. Mix in the potatoes and leeks until thoroughly combined and season with the salt. Reduce the heat to medium-low, cover and cook, stirring occasionally, until the potatoes are fork-tender, about 15 minutes.

Pour in the milk and cream, if using, raise the heat to high and bring to a boil. Reduce the heat and simmer for 15 minutes, scraping the sides of the pot frequently with a rubber spatula. Add the ghee and sage, if using, and stir for 2 minutes. Turn the heat off and puree the soup with an immersion blender.

Ladle into bowls and garnish with the nutmeg. Serve with toasted Arabic bread.

SERVES 6 TO 8

½ cup extra-virgin olive oil
4 shallots, chopped
1 tablespoon finely chopped garlic
½ teaspoon white or black pepper
½ teaspoon ground nutmeg, plus more for garnish (optional)
⅓ teaspoon ground cardamom (optional)
6 baking potatoes, peeled and diced
6 to 8 leeks, light green and white parts only, thoroughly rinsed, dried and chopped
1 tablespoon sea salt
8 cups whole or skim milk
1 cup heavy cream (optional)
3 tablespoons ghee or butter
1 fresh sage leaf (optional)
Arabic Bread (page 61), toasted

Pureed Lentil Soup

SHORABIT ADDAS MAJROOSH

A staple in the Palestinian region, this soup could not be more comforting, healthy, and simple to make. Because the lentils are rich in protein and fiber, and the soup is thick, I have served it for dinner with only a side salad to complete the meal.

In a medium pot, heat the oil over medium heat. Toss in the onions and garlic and saute until golden brown, about 4 minutes. Stir in the coriander, cumin, and pepper and cook for 1 minute. Add the carrots and cook until soft, about 5 minutes. Pour in 12 to 15 cups water and the lentils and bring to a boil. Reduce the heat and bring to a simmer for 30 minutes, or until the lentils are easily crushed when pressed against the side of the pot.

Stir in the lemon juice, season with the salt and remove from the heat. Serve hot as is, or puree to your desired texture using an immersion blender.

SERVES 6 TO 8

½ cup extra-virgin olive oil
2 yellow onions, diced
3 cloves garlic, finely chopped
2 tablespoons ground coriander
1 tablespoon ground cumin
½ teaspoon freshly ground black pepper
2 large carrots, peeled and diced
1½ pounds small red lentils (3 cups), picked over
Juice of 1 lemon
1 tablespoon sea salt

Harira

Harira was the soup of kings in Morocco during the Ramadan holidays. It was always offered in a covered pot, into which an egg would be cracked while the king looked on. If the soup was hot enough to poach the egg, then it was heated to his liking. This traditional soup requires some time and patience, but it's worth preparing an extra-large batch because it gets better over the course of a few days. The exact translation of *harira* is "silky"—an apt description.

> **COOKING TIP** Make sure the soup is very hot before you crack the egg into it; the white and yolk should firm up within a minute or two. *Harira* will keep, covered and refrigerated, for up to 1 week or in resealable bags in the freezer for up to 2 months.

Combine the allspice, 1 tablespoon of the salt, pepper, turmeric, nutmeg, saffron and cardamom in a small bowl. Place the meat in a bowl and pour half the spice mixture over it. Using your hands, toss the spices and meat together to coat it all over.

In a large pot, heat the olive oil over high heat. Brown the meat all over, turning occasionally. Toss in the shallots and saute until soft and fragrant, about 3 minutes. Add the garlic and cook until golden and fragrant, about 30 seconds. Stir in the tomato paste to coat the meat and vegetables and saute for 3 to 5 minutes. Add the fresh tomatoes and cook until they release their juices, about 5 minutes. Toss in the carrots and celery and saute until softened, about 3 minutes. Sprinkle in the cilantro, parsley and the remaining spice mixture and cook until fragrant, 1 to 2 minutes. Pour in 8 cups water and bring to a boil for 3 to 5 minutes. Reduce the heat to low, add the remaining 1 tablespoon of salt, lentils and chickpeas, bay leaves, cloves and cinnamon sticks, cover and cook until the meat falls apart, 1½ to 2 hours, stirring occasionally. Stir in the vermicelli during the last 5 minutes of cooking.

Meanwhile, carefully crack the egg, if using, into a small bowl. Do not break the yolk. Squeeze the lemon juice over it. Turn the heat off and slide the egg into the soup; the egg should set rather quickly. Serve immediately.

SERVES 8 TO 10

1 tablespoon ground allspice
2 tablespoons sea salt or to taste
1 teaspoon freshly ground black pepper
1 teaspoon turmeric
¾ teaspoon ground nutmeg
½ teaspoon saffron threads
½ teaspoon ground cardamom
2 pounds lamb shoulder, cut into 1½-inch pieces, or one (2-pound) chicken, cut into eight pieces
⅓ cup extra-virgin olive or corn oil
4 shallots, chopped
3 cloves garlic, chopped
2 tablespoons tomato paste
4 plum tomatoes, chopped
2 carrots, peeled and chopped
2 celery stalks, diced (about 1 cup)
1 cup chopped fresh cilantro
½ cup chopped fresh parsley
⅔ cup brown lentils
½ cup red lentils
1 (12-ounce) can chickpeas, drained
3 bay leaves
3 whole cloves
2 cinnamon sticks
1 cup broken vermicelli
1 large egg (optional)
Juice of 1 lemon (optional)

Pureed Split Pea Soup

SHORABIT BAZZELA

This beautiful hearty soup makes a great vegetarian meal. I prefer using dried green split peas rather than the yellow variety, which customers at the restaurant often mistake for lentils. Of course, you can substitute any color—yellow, orange or brown—and it won't noticeably change the taste, nor will leaving it chunky if you prefer it that way. If you want more intense flavor, stir in some garlicky *Teklai*, page 222, at the very end. I serve this soup with toasted Za'atar Bread, page 62, and Homemade Hot Sauce, page 220.

In a large pot, heat ⅔ cup of the olive oil over medium heat. Toss in the onions and saute until soft and fragrant, about 3 minutes. Add the shallots and saute for 3 minutes more. Stir in the garlic and cook until fragrant, 3 to 5 minutes. Sprinkle in the coriander, cumin, salt and pepper and saute until fragrant, about 30 seconds. Add the cilantro and cook for 2 to 3 minutes. Add the carrots and cook until softened, about 3 minutes. Throw in the spinach, if using, and cook until it begins to wilt. Toss in the split peas and 5–7 cups water and bring to a boil. Reduce the heat, cover, and simmer for 30 minutes.

Remove the soup from the heat and drizzle with the remaining olive oil. Puree using an immersion blender. Ladle into bowls, add a dollop of *teklai*, if using, and garnish with the parsley. Serve with the za'atar bread, hot sauce and lemon wedges.

VARIATION *Teklai is a wonderful flavoring, but herbed* teklai *takes this soup right over the top: Simply saute ½ cup chopped fresh cilantro and 1 chopped chile pepper after cooking the garlic in basic* teklai.

SERVES 6 TO 8

1 cup olive oil
1 cup chopped yellow onions
2 shallots, chopped
8 cloves garlic, finely chopped (about 2 tablespoons)
2 tablespoons ground coriander
½ tablespoon ground cumin
½ teaspoon sea salt or to taste
½ tablespoon freshly ground black pepper
1 packed cup chopped fresh cilantro
1 cup peeled and chopped carrots
½ packed cup chopped spinach (optional)
2 cups dried green split peas, picked over
1 tablespoon *Teklai* (page 222), optional
½ cup chopped fresh parsley for garnish
Za'atar Bread (page 62), Homemade Hot Sauce (page 220) and lemon wedges for serving

Simple Chicken Soup

SHORABIT DJAJ

Every cook needs a restorative chicken soup in his or her repertoire. This Palestinian version is typically made when preparing the Seasoned Chicken with Stock below. If you have the stock on hand, it can be made in a matter of minutes —there's no sauteing vegetables or simmering necessary. My grown-up kids still request this soup, whether they're under the weather or not. Serve with warm Arabic bread.

Put the stock in a large pot over high heat. Bring to a boil and add the shredded meat from ½ to 1 whole chicken and the vermicelli or rice. Reduce the heat, cover and cook until the noodles are al dente or the rice is tender but not mushy.

Ladle into bowls, squeeze in some lemon juice and garnish with the parsley. Serve with bread.

SERVES 6 TO 8

10 cups stock plus some meat from Seasoned Chicken with Stock (recipe follows)
1½ cups vermicelli, or ¾ cup Egyptian rice
Lemon wedges for squeezing
Chopped fresh parsley for garnish
Arabic Bread (page 61) for serving

Seasoned Chicken with Stock

In a small bowl, combine the allspice, salt, pepper, cardamom and nutmeg. Rub half of the spice mixture all over the chicken pieces and set the remaining mixture aside.

In a large pot, heat the oil over medium-high heat. Working in batches if necessary, sear the chickens all over, about 3 minutes per side. Add the cinnamon stick, onion, bay leaves, cloves and 15 to 20 cups water. Bring to a boil for 5 minutes, skimming the surface with a spoon. Sprinkle in the remaining spice mixture, reduce the heat and simmer, partially covered, for 1 hour.

Strain the stock into a bowl, let cool then transfer the chickens to a plate with a slotted spoon. Remove the meat from the bone and use as desired.

Allow the stock to cool, then store in resealable freezer bags for up to 2 months.

> **COOLING STOCK** It is essential to bring the temperature of stock down quickly to avoid the risk of bacterial growth. To cool quickly, place the bowl or pot, uncovered, into a cold-water bath, ideally a sink full of ice water. Stir the stock often. Once it's cooled to lukewarm, pour into resealable freezer bags and freeze up to 2 months.

MAKES 5 TO 6 QUARTS STOCK AND 6 POUNDS OF MEAT

2 tablespoons ground allspice
1 tablespoon sea salt
1 tablespoon freshly ground black pepper
½ teaspoon ground cardamom
½ teaspoon ground nutmeg
2 chickens (2 to 3 pounds each), cut into 6 to 8 pieces each, washed and patted dry
½ cup extra-virgin olive oil or corn oil
1 cinnamon stick
1 yellow onion, halved
5 bay leaves
5 whole cloves

Freekeh Soup

SHORABIT FREEKAH

My mother always made this soup with turkey necks because she believed they had a different flavor than whole chickens. My version, made with seasoned poached chicken and stock, is every bit as delicious—and very simple to prepare. I used to make this for my kids a lot; if you have the stock prepared, all it requires is quickly sauteing some shallots and combining a few ingredients in a pot. Look for freekeh (smoked and cracked green wheat berries) that is chopped into very fine pieces; if you can't find it, put the larger-grained version in the food processor and pulse until it has the consistency of coarse grain. Serve this soup with toasted Arabic bread.

Heat the oil in a soup pot over medium-high heat. Add the shallots and saute until soft and fragrant, about 3 minutes. Pour in 10 cups stock with the parts of 1 whole chicken or half of the lamb and the freekeh and bring to a boil. Boil for 10 minutes, then reduce the heat, cover and simmer until the freekeh is cooked to desired consistency, about 30 minutes.

Ladle the soup into bowls. Garnish with the parsley and serve hot, with the lemon wedges and Arabic bread on the side.

VARIATION *To make this the way my mother did, substitute turkey necks for the chicken, about 4 pounds total, when preparing the stock. Put one cooked neck in each bowl of broth and serve.*

MAKES 6 TO 10 SERVINGS

¼ cup corn oil
2 shallots, diced
Seasoned Chicken with Stock (see opposite) or Seasoned Lamb with Stock (page 112)
1 cup fine-grain freekeh (smoked and cracked green wheat berries)
4 teaspoons chopped fresh parsley
Lemon wedges for serving
Arabic Bread (page 61) for serving

Lamb and Vegetable Soup

SHORABAT KHOUDRAH

My mother loved making hearty vegetable soups and always used more vegetables than we could count! She happily mixed root vegetables with the classic trio of squash, tomatoes and celery, and of course, she chopped her vegetables into small, perfect squares. I suspect chopping was a form of meditation for her. I, however, am a bit looser in my methodology (and I won't hold you to including all of the vegetables in the ingredients list), but I still prepare this soup the day before I want to serve it, the way my mother did. She insisted it was better the second day. It most certainly is.

> **COOKING TIP** Of course, you can omit the lamb and use vegetable broth instead of lamb stock to make a vegetarian version.

Heat the oil in large pot over medium heat. Toss in the shallots and saute until golden brown, 5 to 8 minutes. Sprinkle in the cardamom and pepper and cook until fragrant, about 30 seconds. Add the celery, potatoes and carrots and saute until the vegetables begin to soften, 5 to 8 minutes. Toss in the zucchini, corn and artichoke hearts and cook for 5 minutes more. Add the tomatoes and cilantro, if using, and saute for 2 minutes to soften the tomatoes.

Cut 1 pound of the lamb meat into ½-inch pieces and throw into the pot with 10 to 12 cups of the stock. Season with salt. Bring to a boil, reduce the heat, cover, and simmer for 5 minutes. Serve hot.

SERVES 6

2 tablespoons extra-virgin olive oil
1 cup chopped shallots or yellow onion
½ teaspoon ground cardamom
½ teaspoon freshly ground black pepper
4 celery stalks, chopped
2 white potatoes, peeled and coarsely chopped
2 carrots, peeled and coarsely chopped
4 baby zucchini, coarsely chopped or cut into ½-inch-thick half moons
1 to 1½ cups fresh corn kernels (from 2 cobs)
7 fresh or frozen artichoke hearts, chopped
2 plum tomatoes, chopped
½ cup chopped cilantro (optional)
Seasoned Lamb with Stock (page 112)
Sea salt

Seafood Soup

SHORABIT AKL BAHRI

I created this soup for my son, Tarek, who loves seafood above all else. There's nothing quite like the flavor of the very freshest fish and shellfish cooked in an herbed broth; I use as many fresh, fragrant herbs as I can get my hands on. Of course, it's okay to substitute more of one for another, but the combination of fresh cilantro, basil, dill and oregano is ideal. It is unusual to find cumin in a seafood soup, but I find a touch subtly warms the broth. The beauty of this soup is in its versatility: you can use whatever firm fish you like. Sometimes I prepare it with root vegetables, other times, I add more chopped tomatoes to make the soup resemble a classic bouillabaisse. The recipe can be halved, if desired.

Combine the salt, pepper and cumin, if using, in a small bowl. Sprinkle a third of the seasoning mixture over the snapper and set the remaining two-thirds aside.

In a large pot, heat the oil over medium heat. Add the snapper and saute, turning once, until golden brown, 3 to 4 minutes per side. Using a fish spatula, transfer the fish to a paper towel–lined platter.

Add the shrimp and calamari to the same pot and cook, stirring occasionally, 3 to 5 minutes. Using the fish spatula, transfer the calamari and shrimp to the paper towel–lined platter.

Toss the shallots in the pot and cook until soft and fragrant, about 5 minutes. Add the potatoes, carrots and celery, and cook, stirring once or twice, for 5 minutes more. Stir in the cilantro, basil, dill and oregano and cook until fragrant, about 3 minutes. Pour in the stock or water and bring to a boil. Reduce the heat, add the bay leaves, cover and simmer until the vegetables are soft and the stock thickens slightly, 15 to 20 minutes.

In the meantime, debone the fish and add it, along with the reserved shrimp and calamari, sage leaf and tomatoes, to the pot; cook for 5 minutes more. For a more intense flavor, include the fish head. Turn off the heat, remove the sage leaf and the bay leaves and stir in the lemon juice. Spoon into soup bowls and garnish each serving with some parsley.

SERVES 10

1 tablespoon sea salt

1½ teaspoons freshly ground black pepper

1½ teaspoons ground cumin (optional)

1 whole red snapper (about 1 pound)

1 cup extra-virgin olive oil

10 medium shrimp, peeled, deveined and cut into 2- to 3-inch pieces

8 ounces calamari, cut into thin rings

3 shallots, chopped

2 baking potatoes, peeled and diced

2 medium carrots, peeled and diced

2 stalks celery, diced

½ cup chopped fresh cilantro

½ cup chopped fresh basil

1 tablespoon chopped fresh dill

1 tablespoon chopped fresh oregano

16 cups (4 quarts) low-sodium chicken stock or water, or 4 cups clam juice mixed with 8 cups water

3 bay leaves

1 fresh sage leaf

4 plum tomatoes, chopped

Juice of 1 lemon

2 tablespoons chopped fresh parsley for garnish

Cauliflower and Lamb Stew

YAKHNIT ZAHRA

When I was eighteen, I taught fifth-grade students in Haifa. On the weekends, I would return home to Nazareth, where this soothing stew routinely awaited me. My mother knew it was a favorite of mine—and it still is. I've added my own flourishes to intensify its flavor: the fresh cilantro and pomegranate molasses are transformative. This recipe is perfect for vegetarians, as it doesn't rely on the meat for its flavor; simply use vegetable broth, omit the meat and enjoy it just the same, ladled over fragrant basmati rice.

> **COOKING TIP** If you are preparing this in advance, keep the meat and cauliflower separate until just before you plan to heat and serve the stew.

Heat the corn oil over high heat in a high-sided skillet. Fry the cauliflower in batches, turning occasionally, until it is golden brown all over. Using a slotted spoon, transfer the cauliflower to a paper towel–lined platter and set aside. Alternatively, preheat the oven to 500°F. Arrange the cauliflower florets on a sheet pan and brush all over with the ½ cup olive oil. Roast until deep golden, about 25 minutes. Set aside.

In a small bowl, combine the allspice, salt, pepper, cumin and nutmeg. In a large soup pot, heat the ¼ cup olive oil over medium-high heat. Add the garlic and cook, stirring, until soft and golden, 3 to 5 minutes. Sprinkle in the spice mixture and cook, stirring, until fragrant, about 30 seconds. Stir in the cilantro. Pour in 7 cups stock and the lemon juice and bring to a boil. Stir in ¼ cup of the *teklai*—it will make a wonderful swishing sound. Add the pomegranate molasses, if using, the lamb and cauliflower and stir to combine. Bring to a boil, then reduce the heat and simmer for 10 minutes.

Ladle into soup bowls and serve with the remaining *teklai* on the side, along with either of the rice options.

VARIATION Add the juice of 1 lemon to the remaining *teklai to make a delicious sauce for spooning over the stew and rice.*

SERVES 6 TO 8

2 cups corn oil, or ½ cup olive oil

3 large or 4 small heads cauliflower, cored and cut into large florets

1 tablespoon ground allspice

1½ teaspoons sea salt

1 teaspoon freshly ground black pepper

1 teaspoon ground cumin

⅓ teaspoon ground nutmeg

¼ cup extra-virgin olive oil

5 cloves garlic, minced

1 packed cup chopped fresh cilantro

Seasoned Lamb with Stock (page 112)

Juice of 1½ lemons or to taste

Teklai (page 222)

3 tablespoons pomegranate molasses or to taste (optional)

Basmati Vegetable Rice (page 205) or Rice and Vermicelli Pilaf (page 204)

Chopped Mlookhia Stew

MLOOKHIA NAAMEH

Literally translated, *mlookhia* means "the food of kings" because at one time, the spinach-like leaf, a member of the jute family, required very special attention to grow and to prepare, thus making it available only to the wealthy. These days, everyone in the Middle East eats the earthy, herbaceous green, which boasts a higher iron content than spinach. Fresh green *mlookhia* is nearly nonexistent in America, though I have discovered that some farms in New Jersey and California grow it. The frozen greens are far more readily available in the States, so I call for them along with the dried version, both of which are widely available at specialty and Middle Eastern markets.

The preparation of this stew varies from one country to another—in Lebanon and Syria, it is topped with chopped raw onion, red or white wine vinegar and toasted Arabic bread, as it is here. Egyptians stir in garlicky *Teklai*, page 222, and squeeze a bit of lemon juice into the stew just before serving. I like to serve it with Rice and Vermicelli Pilaf, page 204.

Preheat the oven to 450°F.

In a large pot, heat the oil over medium heat. Toss in the onion and saute until fragrant, about 3 minutes. Add the tomato, salt, pepper and nutmeg and saute for 3 minutes more. Pour in 11 cups of the stock and bring to a boil. Sprinkle in the dried *mlookhia* and return the stew to a boil, stirring occasionally, for 5 minutes more. Add the frozen *mlookhia* and return to a boil. A thick white foam will appear on the top. Using a large spoon, skim off the foam from the surface until it no longer appears. Stir 3 tablespoons of the *teklai* into the boiling stew; it should make a sizzling sound as it hits the hot broth. Turn off the heat.

In a medium bowl, combine the lemon juice, ghee and remaining 1 cup chicken stock and 1 tablespoon *teklai*. Arrange the seasoned chicken pieces in a large baking dish. Drizzle the lemony broth all over the chicken and roast, uncovered, until the chicken is slightly crispy on top, about 30 minutes. Set aside to cool. When cool enough to handle, remove the chicken from the bone.

To serve, divide the toasted bread among individual soup bowls, top with the rice pilaf, then ladle the *mlookhia* over it all. Top each serving with chicken and 2 to 3 tablespoons diced onion. Serve the vinegar on the side.

SERVES 6 TO 8

6 tablespoons corn oil
1 small yellow onion, finely chopped
1 plum tomato, finely chopped
½ teaspoon sea salt
½ teaspoon freshly ground black pepper
¼ teaspoon ground nutmeg
12 cups stock from Seasoned Chicken with Stock (page 100), plus the meat
½ cup chopped dried *mlookhia*
4 (16-ounce) bags frozen chopped *mlookhia*
¼ cup *Teklai* (page 222)
Juice of 3 lemons
¼ cup ghee or butter or olive oil
Arabic Bread (page 61), toasted
Rice Vermicelli Pilaf (page 204)
1 large yellow onion, diced (about 1½ cups)
Red or white wine vinegar for serving

String Bean and Tomato Stew

FASOOLYA KHADRA

I prefer making this very basic stew with fresh string beans. Obviously, fresh produce always tastes better, but if you are in a pinch, frozen vegetables make a fine substitute. I do draw the line at canned vegetables. Always mushy. Never good. This recipe can be a staple on your weekday menu—when beans are in season, you can use any variety: wax (I prefer these over all others), yellow, haricot vert or flat beans. And, as with most Middle Eastern soups, this one is even better the next day! Serve with Arabic Bread, page 61, and Rice and Vermicelli Pilaf, page 204.

In a large pot, heat the oil over high for 30 seconds until hot but not smoking. Toss in the shallots and cook until soft and fragrant, about 3 minutes. Add the garlic and cook until golden, 3 minutes more.

In a small dish, combine the coriander, allspice, and black pepper. Sprinkle the spice mixture into the pot and cook until fragrant. Stir in the string beans and salt. Reduce the heat to medium, cover and cook for 10 minutes or until the string beans are tender. Toss in the plum tomatoes, cover and cook until the tomatoes begin to soften, 4 to 5 minutes. Add the crushed tomatoes and lemon juice and cook for 3 to 5 minutes more. Stir in the *teklai*, add the chile pepper, if using, and serve hot.

VARIATION To make this a beef or lamb stew, prepare Seasoned Beef or Lamb with Stock, page 112. Add 2 cups of the beef or lamb stock plus the boiled meat to the pot after adding the lemon juice. Raise the heat to high, cover and bring to a boil; cook 3 minutes. Uncover and cook 15 minutes more to allow the mixture to thicken slightly. Stir in the *teklai* and chile pepper, if using. Remove from the heat.

SERVES 8 TO 10

1 cup extra-virgin olive oil
2 shallots, diced
10 cloves garlic, finely chopped
2 heaping tablespoons ground coriander
1 teaspoon to ½ tablespoon allspice
1 teaspoon freshly ground black pepper
5 pounds string beans, both ends trimmed and cut into 1½-inch pieces
1 tablespoon sea salt or to taste
6 plum tomatoes, chopped, with their juices
1 (16-ounce) can crushed tomatoes
Juice of ½ lemon, or 3 tablespoons lemon juice
1 tablespoon *Teklai* (page 222)
1 chile pepper, finely diced (optional)

Spinach Stew with Beef or Lamb

YAKHNIT SABANIKH

In the past, Palestinian cooks were more likely to cook this iron-rich, healthy stew when spinach was abundant in their gardens, but now that spinach is available throughout the year, it is made whenever the desire strikes. Pickled Jalapeños and Carrots, page 210, make a delicious accompaniment. Serve with Rice and Vermicelli Pilaf, page 204, or with Arabic Bread, page 61.

In a medium pot, heat the oil over high heat. Add the garlic and saute until golden brown, 2 to 3 minutes. Stir in the coriander and pepper and cook until fragrant, about 1 minute. Toss in the spinach and saute, stirring, until the spinach wilts, 2 to 3 minutes. Add the boiled meat, 6 cups of the broth and the split peas to the pot; turn the heat to high and bring to a boil for 5 minutes. Reduce the heat and simmer for 10 minutes.

Ladle into bowls and drizzle each serving with the lemon juice and, if desired, the pomegranate molasses.

SERVES 6 TO 8

½ cup extra-virgin olive oil
10 cloves garlic, finely chopped
2 tablespoons ground coriander
1½ teaspoons freshly ground black pepper
3 pounds fresh baby spinach, roughly chopped
Seasoned Lamb or Beef with Stock (see below)
1 cup split peas, boiled for 10 minutes and drained
Juice of 2 lemons
2 tablespoons pomegranate molasses (optional)

Seasoned Lamb or Beef with Stock

In a small bowl, combine the allspice, salt, pepper and nutmeg. Place the lamb or beef in a medium bowl and dump half of the spice mixture into it. Using your hands, rub the spice mixture into the meat, coating all sides thoroughly. Set the remaining spice mixture aside.

In a large pot, heat the oil over high until hot. Toss in the meat and sear on all sides, about 3 minutes. Add the cardamom seeds, bay leaves, cloves, cinnamon stick, onion, the remaining spice mixture, and enough water to cover by 3 inches. Bring to a boil for 5 minutes. Reduce the heat to medium-low and simmer, skimming the fat from the surface with a slotted spoon, for 40 to 60 minutes for lamb and 60 to 90 minutes for beef, or until the meat is fork-tender. Strain the stock into a bowl to let cool. Use the meat as desired or place in resealable plastic bags and refrigerate up to 3 days or freeze up to 2 months.

MAKES 5 TO 6 QUARTS OF STOCK AND 3 POUNDS OF MEAT

1 tablespoon ground allspice
1 tablespoon sea salt
1½ teaspoons freshly ground black pepper
⅓ teaspoon ground nutmeg
3 pounds lamb meat from the leg or beef sirloin, cut into 1½-inch cubes
½ cup corn oil
5 whole cardamom seeds
3 bay leaves
2 whole cloves
1 cinnamon stick, halved lengthwise, or ⅓ teaspoon ground cinnamon
1 yellow onion, cut in half

> **COOLING STOCK** It is essential to bring the temperature of stock down quickly to avoid the risk of bacterial growth. To cool quickly, place the bowl or pot, uncovered, into a cold-water bath, ideally a sink full of ice water. Stir the stock often. Once it's cooled to lukewarm, pour into resealable freezer bags and freeze up to 2 months.

Sweet Pea and Kafta Stew

YAKHNIT BAZELLA BELKAFTA

Most Palestinian cooks make this with cubes of lamb and serve it with rice, but my mother made it with *kafta* (ground lamb mixed with parsley and onion and shaped into small kebabs) and served it with mashed potatoes. When tender whole snap peas in the pod are in season, I use them in place of the frozen sweet peas. If you don't want to use kafta here, add the lamb or beef from the Seasoned Stock with Lamb or Beef, page 112, during the last 5 minutes of simmering.

Shape the *kafta* into 1½-inch-long by 1-inch-thick fingers. Heat the oil in a large skillet over medium heat. Working in batches if necessary, sear the *kafta* just until golden brown, turning once, about 3 to 4 minutes total. Using a slotted spatula, transfer the *kafta* to a paper towel–lined platter to drain.

To the same skillet, toss in the shallots and garlic and saute until lightly browned, 3 to 4 minutes. Add the coriander, allspice, salt, pepper, nutmeg and cardamom, if using, and stir until fragrant, about 2 minutes. Reduce the heat, add the peas and carrots and saute until just softened, about 5 minutes. Tip in the fresh and crushed tomatoes and the stock. Raise the heat, bring to a boil, then reduce the heat and simmer for 15 to 20 minutes. Add the reserved *kafta* fingers and simmer for 5 minutes more. Serve hot.

SERVES 8

Kafta (page 174)
½ cup corn oil
3 shallots, diced
8 cloves garlic, crushed or finely chopped
1 tablespoon ground coriander
1 teaspoon ground allspice
1 tablespoon sea salt
½ tablespoon freshly ground black pepper
⅓ teaspoon ground nutmeg
⅓ teaspoon cardamom (optional)
4 (16-ounce) bags frozen baby sweet peas
2 carrots, peeled and diced
4 fresh plum tomatoes, chopped (optional)
1 (28-ounce) can crushed tomatoes
4 cups stock from Seasoned Lamb or Beef with Stock (page 112) or low-sodium beef stock or water

Red Lentil and Butternut Squash Stew

If you make this stew once, there is no going back. Growing up, I loved my lentil soup pureed, but in this recipe I leave the lentils whole. The butternut squash adds a mellow sweetness that gives the stew another flavor dimension, but it is also delicious with chunks of yams or even pumpkin. Use one of these vegetables or a mix to make this stew, which can be served piping hot, warm or chilled. This recipe is inspired by a dish in *The Gaza Kitchen* by Laila El-Haddad and Maggie Schmitt.

Heat the olive oil in a deep skillet over medium-high heat until hot. Toss in the shallots and onion and saute until soft and golden, 3 to 4 minutes. Add the garlic and saute, stirring until fragrant, about 30 seconds. Sprinkle in the chile peppers, cilantro, coriander, cumin, black pepper and stir, about 1 minute. Stir in the squash. Reduce the heat and cook, covered, about 10 minutes.

Add the lentils and 6 cups water, cover and cook for about 12 minutes. If the squash has not softened, pour in 1 cup additional water, cover and cook for 10 minutes more. Ladle the stew into serving bowls, drizzle with olive oil and serve.

SERVES 6 TO 8

6 tablespoons olive oil, plus more for drizzling
4 shallots, chopped
1 white onion, chopped
8 cloves garlic, crushed
2 chile peppers, such as long hots, jalapeños or poblanos
1 cup chopped fresh cilantro
2 tablespoons ground coriander
1 tablespoon ground cumin
1 tablespoon freshly ground black pepper
2 butternut squash, peeled and diced to make 5 to 6 cups
1½ cups red lentils, picked over

White Bean and Beef Stew

YAKHNIT FASOOLYA BAIDA

As a child, I remember watching some of my schoolmates bite into whole raw garlic cloves or onions in between spoonfuls of this extra-hearty stew. Popular throughout the Levant, this rather old recipe was commonly prepared in winter, when fresh vegetables were spare and beans were in every pantry. It is invariably served with olives and pickles to add salty, briny flavor. Serve with Rice and Vermicelli Pilaf, page 204, or Basmati Vegetable Rice, page 205.

Heat the oil in a soup pot over medium heat. Toss in the shallots and saute until golden brown, about 3 minutes. Add the garlic and saute until fragrant, about 1 minute. Sprinkle in the chile peppers, coriander, cumin, pepper and allspice and stir until fragrant, about 30 seconds. Add the celery and carrots and cook until the vegetables soften, stirring frequently, about 5 minutes. Add the cilantro and saute to mellow its flavor, about 2 minutes. Toss in the plum tomatoes and stir until they release their juices, 2 to 3 minutes. Stir in the tomato paste and chile paste and stir continuously for 3 minutes.

Add 2 to 3 pounds of the meat with 6 cups of the stock and the crushed tomatoes. Bring to a boil. Add the beans and sugar or lemon salt. Return to a boil until the liquid thickens slightly, 10 to 15 minutes. Stir in the hot *teklai* and listen for the swoosh. Remove from the heat and serve with a rice dish on the side.

VEGETARIAN VARIATION *In Nazareth, white beans and beef always went together; you never served the beans without the meat. But once I opened my restaurant, I learned from some of my staff that beans themselves can carry a dish, particularly when a mix of spices and the teklai are added to the pot. To make the vegetarian version of this stew, simply omit the meat and use vegetable broth in place of the stock.*

SERVES 8 TO 10

1 cup olive oil

3 shallots, cut into small cubes

2 tablespoons finely chopped garlic

2 long hot or jalapeño chile peppers, seeded and finely chopped (seeds reserved if desired)

1½ tablespoons ground coriander

1 tablespoon ground cumin

1 tablespoon freshly ground black pepper

1 tablespoon ground allspice

2 stalks celery, diced

2 small carrots, peeled and diced

1 cup chopped fresh cilantro

4 plum tomatoes, diced

3 tablespoons tomato paste

1 tablespoon seedless Middle Eastern or Turkish chile paste

Seasoned Lamb or Beef with Stock (page 112)

1 (28-ounce) can crushed tomatoes

2 pounds small dried white beans, soaked and boiled (see page 21), or 6 (15-ounce) cans great northern or cannellini beans, drained and rinsed

1 teaspoon sugar, or ½ teaspoon lemon salt

3 tablespoons *Teklai* (page 222), hot

Rice and Vermicelli Pilaf (page 204) or Basmati Vegetable Rice (page 205) for serving

Beef and Potato Stew

YAKHNIT BATATA

It is a rare Palestinian pantry that doesn't have a basket filled with potatoes in it. They are used in so many traditional Middle Eastern dishes, including this "peasant" stew, a combination of beef and potatoes seasoned with allspice, coriander, nutmeg and cardamom. I prefer using beef sirloin in this recipe, but you could use a less expensive cut and allow the soup to simmer until the meat is fork-tender.

In a large pot, heat the oil over medium heat. Add the onion and cook until golden brown, 4 to 5 minutes. Sprinkle in the garlic, chile peppers, if using, allspice, pepper, coriander, cumin, nutmeg and cardamom, if using, and saute until fragrant, about 1 minute. Toss in the carrots and the beef and cook, stirring, until the beef is seared on all sides. Add the tomatoes, cilantro and the beef stock and stir with a wooden spoon, scraping up the crispy bits from the bottom of the pot. Cover and let simmer until the meat is tender, 60 to 90 minutes.

Meanwhile, in a large, deep skillet, heat 2 cups of the corn oil over medium-high heat. Working in batches if necessary, fry the potatoes, turning occasionally, until they are golden brown all over. Using a slotted spoon, transfer to a paper-towel lined platter and set aside. The potatoes can be made one day in advance and stored in a container with a tight-fitting lid in the refrigerator. Alternatively, brush the potatoes liberally with the oil and arrange in a single layer on a baking sheet or in a roasting pan. Roast in a 350°F oven until golden and crispy, about 30 minutes. Repeat this same step with the pearl onions and 2 more cups of corn oil if roasting.

Uncover the pot and add the potatoes, pearl onions and lemon juice and season with salt. Simmer 5 minutes before serving hot.

VARIATIONS *Chicken may be substituted for the beef: use 1 whole chicken cut into 8 pieces or 2 pounds boneless chicken breasts cut into 1- to 2-inch cubes. Season with salt and pepper, then sear the chicken on all sides in a skillet slicked with olive oil over medium-high heat.*

If you can find tamarind paste, use it in place of the lemon juice. Soak 8 ounces tamarind paste in 2 cups boiling water and let it dissolve. Pass the liquid through a sieve and use in the same proportion as the lemon juice. The tamarind liquid will keep, tightly covered, in the refrigerator for up to 2 weeks. Alternatively, substitute store-bought liquid tamarind for the lemon juice.

SERVES 6 TO 8

½ cup olive oil
1 red onion, chopped
10 cloves garlic, crushed
2 chile peppers, seeded and diced (optional)
1 tablespoon ground allspice
1 tablespoon freshly ground black pepper
1 tablespoon ground coriander
½ tablespoon ground cumin
⅓ teaspoon ground nutmeg (optional)
⅓ teaspoon ground cardamom (optional)
2 carrots, peeled and diced or thinly sliced
2 pounds beef sirloin, cut into
    1- to 2-inch cubes
2 plum tomatoes, chopped
1 bunch fresh cilantro, chopped
11 cups beef stock or water
2 to 4 cups corn oil
6 baking potatoes, peeled, each cut into
    8 to 10 pieces
1 pound pearl onions, peeled
½ cup fresh lemon juice
Sea salt

Okra Stew with Lamb and Pomegranate Molasses

YAKHNIT BAMYA

When I first found okra in the markets in the U.S., I was dumbstruck by its size. In fact, I brought it home and, like any good Middle Eastern cook, I tried to stuff it! Okra is traditionally cooked with tomato (see page 202), but my mom always made hers with lemon juice and pomegranate molasses—her way of working around the exorbitant number of tomato-based dishes in Middle Eastern cuisine. Of course, I couldn't leave well enough alone, so I added cilantro and chile pepper to her recipe. I love the assertive seasonings in this stew; the sweet-sour pomegranate molasses and the herby cilantro pair well with the rich flavors of the lamb and okra. Serve this stew with Rice and Vermicelli Pilaf, page 204, or scoop it up with warm Arabic Bread, page 61.

> **COOKING TIP** I find fresh okra generally too big to use in this stew—it is filled with seeds and produces an unappealing texture when cooked—but if you find it in diminutive form, then by all means use it. Be sure to cut the stems away first.

In a medium skillet, heat ½ cup oil over medium-high heat. Working in batches, fry the okra, turning so that it takes on color all over, 6 to 8 minutes. Using a slotted spoon, transfer to a paper towel–lined plate. Alternatively, pat dry the okra and arrange in a single layer on a baking sheet or in a roasting pan. Brush liberally with the oil and roast in a 500°F oven until light golden.

In a medium pot, heat ⅓ cup oil over medium heat. Toss in the garlic and saute until golden brown, about 3 minutes. Sprinkle in the coriander and saute until fragrant, about 30 seconds. Stir in the allspice, black pepper, cumin, nutmeg and 10 cups of the lamb stock; bring to a boil. Add the fried okra and lamb. Season with salt and continue to boil until the okra softens, about 10 minutes. Add the pomegranate molasses and simmer for 2 minutes more. Remove from the heat and stir in the lemon juice. Serve with the rice pilaf and hot peppers.

SERVES 8

½ cup plus ⅓ cup extra-virgin olive oil

6 (1-pound) bags frozen baby okra, rinsed and thoroughly drained

3 tablespoons finely chopped garlic

2 tablespoons ground coriander

1 tablespoon ground allspice

1 teaspoon freshly ground black pepper

½ teaspoon ground cumin

½ teaspoon ground nutmeg

Seasoned Lamb with Stock (page 112)

Sea salt

¼ cup pomegranate molasses

Juice of 1 large lemon

Rice and Vermicelli Pilaf (page 204)

Long hot chile peppers for serving

MAIN COURSES

Big Dishes

The idea of eating the biggest meal of the day at dinnertime was foreign to me until I moved to New York. Back home in Nazareth, lunch, or *ghada*, was the grand meal and it was always served in the late afternoon. In the evening, we generally ate a variation of breakfast. Admittedly, there are times when I still like to eat this way, but after 30 years of living in the States, I've made the transition!

In this chapter, there is a wonderful mix of classic Middle Eastern dishes and others of my own invention. Many are straightforward, simple recipes that can be prepared for weeknight dinners—Shrimp in Garlic Sauce (page 146) and *Mhammar* (page 160), the classic chicken and potato dish, and *Shakshuka* (page 125), a comforting combination of seasoned tomato sauce and eggs, also known as Eggs in Purgatory. Others are meant to be prepared for special occasions and celebrations or on a leisurely Sunday when the day revolves around preparing a big meal. The traditional dishes are here—*Mansaaf* (page 173), a classic combination of Egyptian rice, lamb and pine nuts; *Sayadiyya* (page 139), the fisherman's dish; and both Chicken and Fish Tagines (page 161 and page 140) along with a handful of Tanoreen specialties in which I have tinkered with tradition—Eggplant Napoleon (page 129) and Tanoreen Baked Fish (page 135) among them. In fact, my customers are increasingly looking for meatless main courses, to which I have responded by modifying several traditional Middle Eastern recipes into *siyami*, or vegetarian style meals. I've included them here because to my mind, they've earned their place in the Tanoreen repertoire.

As you flip through these pages, you will notice that I am not shy when it comes to using warm, fragrant spices in my cooking, particularly when I am making a slow-cooked dish. I reach for smoky cumin, sweet cinnamon and earthy allspice almost reflexively when I step into the kitchen. After years of seasoning my dishes with one spice at a time, I created a custom blend for using at the restaurant. In the dishes that follow, I offer as close to those measurements as possible. Fresh herbs, too, are an essential part of my generously seasoned dishes. Basil, cilantro and parsley all brighten the flavor of a warmly scented dish and also add a wonderfully herbaceous green note. At Tanoreen, I am quite heavy-handed with the parsley (a source of endless teasing by my daughter Jumana) because I like my platters to look like a garden. You will also notice that I cook primarily with olive oil. Traditionally, all dishes featuring meat are prepared with ghee or butter, but I do as my mother did. How could she not? She grew up in an olive-growing family!

The following pages are filled with what I call big dishes— big flavors, generous servings and storied origins. I like to think of it as the chapter in which you will spend time reading the recipes, enjoying the stories, and cooking and eating with people you truly care about. That's what I do—every day—and I can't think of a more pleasurable way to spend my time.

> *"Back home in Nazareth, lunch, or ghada, was the grand meal and it was always served in the late afternoon. In the evening, we generally ate a variation of breakfast. Admittedly, there are times when I still like to eat this way, but after 30 years of living in the States, I've made the transition!"*

VEGETARIAN

Baked Eggplant

SINIYAT EL FOKRRA

Siniyat el fokrra, which means "a tray for the poor," is this dish's name because it makes use of whatever leftover vegetables are in the house. My mother's preparation didn't feature herbs or nuts, which were unaffordable for home cooks at the time. I thought it needed a bit of brightening and some crunch, so I sprinkled both in. It is a forgiving dish; use eggplant entirely if you don't have or like squash. Serve with pickles and sliced chile peppers.

> **COOKING TIP** Leftover baked eggplant freezes beautifully. Cut it into individual servings, wrap well and freeze up to 2 months. Simply defrost and reheat in a 350°F oven.

In a large skillet over medium-high heat, heat ¼ cup oil. Toss in the onions and saute until amber, 7 to 8 minutes. Add the garlic and saute until fragrant, 1 to 2 minutes. Sprinkle in the allspice, coriander, pepper, cumin and paprika, if using, and cook, stirring, until fragrant, about 30 seconds. Stir in the basil and cilantro and cook until the herbs change color slightly, 1 to 1½ minutes. Add the chopped tomatoes and lemon juice, bring to a boil and cook for 3 to 4 minutes more. Remove from the heat and stir in the almonds. Set aside.

Preheat the oven to 450°F. In a 3-quart baking dish or 16-inch round dish, arrange the potato slices in a single layer. Spread a thin layer of the tomato-onion mixture over the potatoes. Top with a single layer of the eggplant, followed by a thin layer of the tomato-onion mixture. Arrange a single layer of squash over the tomato-onion mixture. Repeat the layering, ending with the eggplant. Arrange the fresh tomato slices on top. Add 2 cups water to the remaining tomato-onion mixture and stir to incorporate. Drizzle the tomato sauce all over the tomato slices. Drizzle the remaining ¼ cup olive oil on top. Cover with foil and bake until all of the liquid has evaporated, 40 minutes to 1 hour. Serve with the rice and vermicelli pilaf or Arabic bread.

VARIATION *Split open a baguette or loaf of Italian bread and stuff with cold baked eggplant for a wonderful summer sandwich.*

SERVES 6 TO 8

½ cup extra-virgin olive oil

2 medium yellow onions, chopped

4 to 5 cloves garlic, finely chopped

1 tablespoon ground allspice

1 tablespoon ground coriander

1 tablespoon freshly ground black pepper

1 teaspoon ground cumin (optional)

½ teaspoon hot or sweet paprika (optional)

½ cup chopped fresh basil

½ cup chopped fresh cilantro

4 plum tomatoes, chopped, plus 5 plum tomatoes or 2 beefsteak tomatoes, thinly sliced

½ cup fresh lemon juice

1 cup slivered almonds, toasted

3 baking potatoes (about 2½ pounds total), peeled and cut lengthwise into ¼-inch-thick slices

3 Italian eggplants (2½ to 3 pounds total), sliced lengthwise into ⅓-inch-thick slices, fried or baked (see page 43)

8 Arabic squash or zucchini, or 5 small seedless zucchini, cut lengthwise into ½-inch-thick slices

Rice and Vermicelli Pilaf (page 204) or Arabic Bread (page 61) for serving

Eggs in Purgatory

SHAKSHUKA

Most Middle Eastern countries, from Israel and Palestine to Algeria, Morocco and Tunisia, make a variation of this delicious peasant dish. It is an ideal option when you don't have anything in the cupboard—you break a few eggs into a simmering seasoned tomato sauce and it's time to eat. Stir in cooling plain yogurt and serve with Arabic bread for scooping up the sauce. It is delicious for breakfast, lunch or dinner, or as at Tanoreen, for Sunday brunch.

In a large skillet, heat the oil over medium-high heat. Toss in the garlic and shallots and saute until they begin to take on color, about 3 minutes. Add the red and green peppers and saute for 3 minutes more. Stir in the tomato paste and hot sauce and mix until incorporated, about 3 minutes. Sprinkle in the cumin, coriander, salt and caraway, if using, and stir for 1 minute. Add the tomatoes, reduce the heat and cook until the liquid is reduced and the sauce has thickened, 10 to 12 minutes.

Add the eggplant, if using, and lemon juice, raise the heat and bring to a boil. Break the eggs into the skillet in a single layer, pushing the whites toward the yolk with a wooden spoon to keep them intact. Cook until the whites are opaque and the middle of the yolk is still slightly runny. Scoop the eggs and tomato sauce into bowls and serve with the bread and yogurt.

SERVES 6

6 tablespoons extra-virgin olive oil
6 cloves garlic, finely chopped
2 shallots, finely chopped
1 red pepper, cored and cut into small cubes
1 green pepper, cored and cut into small cubes
3 tablespoons tomato paste
3 tablespoons Homemade Hot Sauce (page 220) or store-bought or seedless Middle Eastern or Turkish chile paste
1 tablespoon ground cumin or to taste
1 teaspoon ground coriander
1 teaspoon sea salt
¼ teaspoon ground caraway (optional)
6 ripe beefsteak tomatoes (about 4 to 5 pounds total), peeled and chopped
1 medium eggplant, about 1 pound, peeled, cut into 1-inch dice and roasted or fried (see page 43; optional)
Juice of ½ lemon
6 large organic eggs
Arabic Bread (page 61) and plain yogurt for serving

Vegetarian Stuffed Vegetables

KHUDRA MAHSHI

If a vegetable can be stuffed, an Arab cook will stuff it! It may seem odd when it comes to potatoes, but it is second nature to me since my mother never missed a chance to use them. This stuffing is rather traditional—feel free to play with the spices and herbs to suit your taste. But keep in mind that the softer the vegetable, the more loosely packed with stuffing it should be; if a vegetable like Arabic summer squash is overfilled, the vegetable will burst during cooking. To serve, either arrange the whole vegetables on dinner plates with the sauce on the side, or split them lengthwise and drizzle the sauce over the top.

> **COOKING TIP** If you're not going to serve the vegetables right away, remove them from the sauce to prevent the rice mixture from overcooking. It continues to cook for about 15 minutes after it is removed from the heat.

Using an apple corer, remove the insides of the eggplant, squash, tomatoes and potatoes, reserving only the insides of the squash. Place the cored vegetables in a large bowl of cold salted water and set aside.

Prepare the stuffing: In a large skillet, heat ½ cup olive oil over medium-high heat. Toss in the onions and saute until soft and fragrant, about 3 minutes. Add the garlic, if using, and saute until fragrant, 1 minute. Sprinkle in the allspice, black pepper, nutmeg and cumin, if using, and saute until fragrant, about 30 seconds. Add the parsley, cilantro, dill and mint and stir until the cilantro changes color, about 1 minute. Stir in 2 tablespoons tomato paste, the reserved squash flesh, the chile pepper, if using, tomatoes, and 2 tablespoons pomegranate molasses. Raise the heat and bring the mixture to a boil. Season with salt. Remove from the heat and stir in the rice until thoroughly combined. Stir in half of the lemon juice and the remaining ½ cup olive oil. Taste and adjust the seasonings.

Drain the vegetables soaking in cold water. Working with one vegetable at a time, pat it dry and spoon the stuffing to within ½ inch of the opening. Place the vegetables, vertically with the open end up, in a 5-quart pot. Repeat with remaining vegetables. Replace the reserved trimmed end to each vegetable. Add enough water to cover, the remaining 2 tablespoons each of tomato paste and pomegranate molasses, and the remaining half lemon juice to the pot. Cover the vegetables with a heatproof plate, cover the pot and bring to a boil over high heat. Reduce the heat and simmer until the rice is tender, 35 to 40 minutes.

Using a slotted spoon, remove the vegetables to a platter and spoon the sauce in the pot on the side.

MAKES 4 SERVINGS

4 baby eggplants, rinsed, stem end trimmed and reserved

4 Arabic squash or zucchini, rinsed, stem end trimmed and reserved

4 plum tomatoes, rinsed, stem end trimmed and reserved

4 baking potatoes, rinsed, narrow end trimmed and reserved

For the Stuffing

1 cup extra-virgin olive oil

2 medium yellow or red onions, cut into small cubes

1 clove garlic, finely chopped (optional)

4½ teaspoons ground allspice

1 tablespoon freshly ground black pepper or to taste

½ teaspoon ground nutmeg

1 teaspoon ground cumin (optional)

1 cup chopped fresh parsley

½ cup chopped fresh cilantro

2 tablespoons chopped fresh dill

1 tablespoon dried mint

¼ cup tomato paste

1 jalapeño or long hot chile pepper, cored, seeded and cut into small cubes (optional)

6 plum tomatoes, diced

¼ cup pomegranate molasses

Sea salt to taste

3 cups Egyptian rice or bulgur

Juice of 2 lemons

Eggplant Napoleon

One of the most popular items on the Tanoreen menu, this tower of crispy pesto-marinated eggplant slices spread with smoky baba ghanouj, just might be the dish that inspired me to write this cookbook. It draws on the flavors of the Middle East and the Mediterranean, but the truth is, I created it to encourage my son to eat eggplant. He always loved fried zucchini sticks, so I cut eggplant in the same shape and he was none the wiser (although here they're cut in rounds). This is a good example of how I have taken advantage of ingredients that are available to me in the States and married them with the classic preparations from my childhood.

Arrange the eggplant slices on two sheet pans, sprinkle with salt and set aside for 30 minutes or until they begin to sweat. Using a paper towel, pat the slices dry and set aside.

In a large bowl, whisk together the pesto, olive oil, garlic and lemon juice. Toss in the eggplant to coat and let marinate at room temperature for at least 1 hour or overnight in the refrigerator.

Dump the flour onto a shallow rimmed plate. In a medium bowl, whisk together the egg whites and 1 cup water. Combine the panko, Parmigiano-Reggiano, parsley and pepper on a second shallow rimmed plate.

Spread a sheet of waxed paper on a clean work surface. Working with one slice of eggplant at a time, dredge it in the flour first, shaking off the excess, and then dip it in the egg mixture followed by the breadcrumbs. Gently press the breadcrumbs onto both sides of the eggplant and place on the waxed paper. Repeat with the remaining eggplant slices.

Pour at least 2 inches of corn oil into a small, deep pot. Heat the oil over high until hot but not smoking. Working in batches, fry the eggplant slices until golden, turning once, 3 to 5 minutes. Do not crowd the pot. Using a slotted spoon, transfer the eggplant slices to a paper towel–lined platter to drain.

Place an eggplant slice on a small plate. Spread with 2 tablespoons of the baba ghanouj, top with a second eggplant slice and spread 1 tablespoon of baba ghanouj on top. Repeat layering in this order with the remaining eggplant slices and baba ghanouj to make eight to ten eggplant stacks.

Just before serving, toss together the salad: In a medium bowl, combine the tomatoes and onion. In a small bowl, whisk together the pesto, lemon juice, olive oil and salt. Drizzle just enough of the pesto mixture over the tomato-onion mixture to thoroughly coat. Spoon some salad around each napoleon and drizzle the napoleons with some of the dressing left in the bottom of the bowl. Serve immediately.

SERVES 8 TO 10

3 medium eggplants (2½ to 3 pounds total), stem and root ends trimmed and discarded, sliced into ½-inch-thick rounds
Sea salt for sprinkling
¼ cup Basil Pesto (page 215)
½ cup extra-virgin olive oil
6 cloves garlic, finely chopped
Juice of 3 lemons
½ cup all-purpose flour
2 egg whites, beaten
2 cups panko (Japanese breadcrumbs)
2 tablespoons grated Parmigiano-Reggiano cheese
2 tablespoons dried parsley
½ teaspoon freshly ground black pepper
Corn oil for frying
3 cups Baba Ghanouj (page 44) or *Mutabal* (page 45)

For the Salad

8 plum tomatoes, chopped
1 medium red onion, chopped
7 tablespoons Basil Pesto (page 215)
Juice of 2 lemons
¾ cup extra-virgin olive oil
Pinch sea salt

MAIN COURSES: VEGETARIAN

Vegetarian Stuffed Cabbage

MALFOOF BELZAIT

I make these delicious rolls my mother's way, with cracked wheat rather than rice, which is what everyone back home uses. If you're gluten sensitive, rice is a nice alternative. I prefer using #4 bulgur, which is the coarsest, but #2 or #3 will work just fine. These rolls can be wrapped tightly and refrigerated up to ten days but they do not freeze well. Eat them at room temperature, or reheat them with a little water in a covered pot over low heat. We never made just one meal's worth of these delicious stuffed leaves; they are delicious stuffed into Arabic Bread, page 61.

In a large bowl, combine the bulgur with the parsley and all but 1 tablespoon of the garlic, the shallots, tomatoes, 1 tablespoon of the chile peppers, if using, half of the lemon juice, the oil, chile paste, if using, cumin, salt, pepper and allspice. Stir with a wooden spoon until thoroughly combined. Trim the tough ribs from the cabbage and stack the leaves on top of each other.

Line a 4-quart pot with a single layer of the potato slices. Arrange the ribs of the cabbage on top of the potatoes. Working with one cabbage leaf at a time, place a leaf on a clean work surface with the stem end facing you. Spoon 2 tablespoons of the bulgur filling into the center of the leaf. Roll the leaf away from you, tucking in the sides as you go. Arrange the rolls in the pot in concentric circles, beginning from the outer rim and working in. Stack them, one atop another, to make a second layer.

Place a heatproof plate on top of the rolls. Add enough water to the pot to barely cover the rolls, about 3 to 4 cups water, along with a pinch of salt. Cover the pot and bring to a boil over high heat. Reduce the heat, bring to a simmer and cook for 35 to 40 minutes.

Remove the pot from the heat, uncover, and, wearing an oven mitt, press the plate firmly against the cabbage and upend the pot to drain the cooking water into a large bowl. Stir the remaining 1 tablespoon garlic and the remaining lemon juice and chile peppers into the cooking water to create a broth. Remove the plate from the pot and pour the seasoned broth back into the pot. Cover the pot and return to a boil over high heat; boil for 1 minute more. With a slotted spoon, transfer the rolls to a platter and serve.

VARIATION *Cabbage Lasagna* *If you don't have time to roll the stuffing into the cabbage leaves, prepare this dish as you would lasagna. Arrange a single layer of cabbage leaves on the bottom of an ungreased 3-quart baking dish and spread a third of the stuffing over the leaves. Toss a few garlic cloves over it. Cover the stuffing with a second layer of cabbage leaves. Continue layering the cabbage, stuffing and garlic cloves, ending with a layer of cabbage. Pour enough vegetable stock into the pan to just cover the top layer (about 4 cups) and bake at 350°F until the broth is absorbed, 35 to 40 minutes. Squeeze some fresh lemon juice over the cabbage lasagna and serve.*

SERVES 6 TO 8 (WITH LEFTOVERS)

1½ cups coarse bulgur (#4), rinsed under warm water, or 2 cups Egyptian short-grain rice

1 cup chopped fresh parsley

6 cloves garlic, finely chopped

5 shallots, finely chopped

3 plum tomatoes, chopped

1 jalapeño, or 2 long hot chile peppers, finely chopped (optional)

Juice of 3 lemons

½ cup extra-virgin olive oil

2 tablespoons seedless Middle Eastern or Turkish chile paste (optional)

1 teaspoon ground cumin or to taste

1 tablespoon plus 1 pinch sea salt

1 tablespoon black pepper

1 tablespoon ground allspice

1 large cabbage (about 4 pounds), boiled (see page 172)

1 baking potato, or 2 tomatoes or carrots, sliced into ¼-inch thick slices

Spicy Vegan Swiss Chard Rolls

SILIK MALFOOF

Growing up, chard grew wild and was often used to make savory *fatayer* pies, a regional favorite in northern Galilee. My mom used to make Swiss chard rolls exactly like classic stuffed cabbage leaves, with meat and rice, but as we grew older and some of us became vegetarian, she adapted and came up with a whole new dish that I love! It's a spicy vegan alternative made with Swiss chard and substituting rice for smoky freekeh. This vegan version is meant to be spicy! If you are not a fan of heat, feel free to reduce the amount of pepper and harissa to your liking, but I think the spice takes the dish to another level. It has earned a permanent spot in my specials rotation at Tanoreen.

In a large bowl mix together all of the stuffing ingredients. Taste the mixture to ensure the flavor profile works for you, and adjust the seasoning as needed.

In a large pot, bring 6 cups of salted water to a boil. Working in batches, plunge the Swiss chard leaves into the boiling water for 1 to 2 minutes, just until the stems are tender. Transfer the leaves to a colander to drain, and reserve the blanching water.

Remove any hard, thick stems from the chard. Place one leaf in front of you horizontally. Place about 1 tablespoon of filling at the edge of the leaf closest to you. Fold either side of the leaf over the stuffing and tightly roll the leaf up to the end, like a cigar. Repeat, arranging the rolls in concentric circles in the base of a 5-quart pot.

In a bowl, mix the harissa, chopped garlic, lemon juice, and 6 tablespoons of olive oil. Drizzle this mixture over the Swiss chard rolls in the pot. Cover the rolls with a heatproof plate to hold them in place. Pour in reserved blanching water until the rolls are submerged (top up with boiling water if needed).

Cover the pot and cook over medium heat for 40 to 45 minutes or until the chard is tender and the freekeh is fully cooked. Carefully remove the weight and, using tongs, transfer the rolls to a serving plate. Serve hot, along with the sauce from the pot.

SERVES 6

4 to 5 bunches Swiss chard (about 4 pounds)
Salt
1 tablespoon harissa, or to taste
4 garlic cloves, chopped
6 tablespoons olive oil

For the Stuffing
1 bunch parsley, chopped
1 large onion, diced
5 shallots, diced
4 plum tomatoes, diced
1 cup chopped cilantro
1 long hot or jalapeño pepper, diced (optional)
1 tablespoon cumin
1 tablespoon Tanoreen Spice (page 225) or allspice
¼ teaspoon nutmeg
1 tablespoon coriander
½ cup pomegranate molasses
Juice of 2 lemons
¼ cup olive oil
1 cup pomegranate seeds
2 cups freekeh (smoked and cracked green wheat), rinsed

FISH & SHELLFISH

Tanoreen Baked Fish

SAMAK BEL FURRON

I learned how to prepare this wonderful party dish from two men who worked for me at Tanoreen. Neither of them was a cook, but they often talked about the way their mothers baked fish. I borrowed their basic method and added some of my mother's touches—peppers, tomatoes, and potatoes. I consider myself a very picky fish eater, but this is so good that I put it on the Tanoreen menu. If using fillets, buy the fish whole and ask the fishmonger to fillet it for you. Serve with Rice and Vermicelli Pilaf, page 204.

Preheat the oven to 400°F.

In a small bowl, combine the garlic, half of the lemon juice, ½ cup oil, the parsley, cumin, salt and pepper; set aside.

Using a sharp kitchen knife, make three ⅛-inch crosswise slits along the length of each fish or on the skin side of half of the fillets. Divide the garlic mixture evenly among the fish; spread it with your fingers into the slits and cavity of the whole fish or in the slits and on the flesh side of the scored fillets.

Arrange the potatoes in a single layer in a large roasting pan. Lay the whole fish on top. If using the fillets, lay the plain halves skin side down, then top each with a seasoned fillet, skin side up. Scatter the tomatoes and peppers over the fish and pour the broth into one corner of the pan so that the vegetables don't slide off the fish. Drizzle the remaining ½ cup oil and lemon juice over the fish. Cover tightly with waxed paper then aluminum foil and bake until the fish is opaque, 15 to 20 minutes, depending on if you're using a whole fish or fillets. Remove the foil and waxed paper and cook 2 minutes more, or until the fish flakes apart easily when pricked with a fork. Arrange the fish and potatoes on a platter and spoon the pan juices over both.

SERVES 6 TO 8

9 cloves garlic, minced

Juice of 4 to 5 lemons

1 cup extra-virgin olive oil

1 cup chopped fresh parsley or cilantro

4½ teaspoons ground cumin

1 tablespoon sea salt

1 tablespoon freshly ground black pepper

4 to 6 whole striped bass or red snapper (1- to 1¼-pounds each), or 8 fillets

8 medium red potatoes, peeled and sliced into ¼-inch rounds, fried or roasted

2 plum tomatoes, diced

2 green or red bell peppers or chile peppers, seeded and minced

4 cups low-sodium chicken broth or water

Spicy Baked Fish

SAMAKA HARRA

Samaka harra literally translated, means "hot fish." The traditional preparation incorporates tahini in the sauce, but I am very fond of this version, which features crushed walnuts in the stuffing instead. This is a wonderful party dish—the whole baked fish makes for quite the conversation starter when set down in the middle of the table. Growing up, the fish was never boned—my father did it right at the table—but these days, it's more efficient to have the fishmonger debone it for you. Baking one whole fish is dramatic, but if you can't find a four- to five-pound fish, use a duo of two- to three-pound red snappers, striped bass or branzino. This makes a great meal served with my Tanoreen Green Salad, page 86, and rice.

Place the fish in front of you. Sprinkle kosher salt all over the fish and rub it down under cold water; pat it dry and place on a clean work surface.

Combine the oil and lemon juice in a measuring cup. In the bowl of a food processor, combine half of the oil and lemon juice mixture with the coriander, black pepper, salt, cumin, if using, chile pepper, cilantro, garlic and chile paste; process until smooth. Add the walnuts and process until the mixture forms a chunky paste.

Preheat the oven to 450°F. On one side of the fish, make two crosswise slits, about 2 inches apart and on the diagonal. Fill each slit with some of the walnut paste. Spread all but 1 tablespoon of the remaining walnut paste into the cavity of the fish. Rub the reserved 1 tablespoon walnut paste all over the outside of the fish.

Transfer the fish to a roasting pan and drizzle the remaining oil and lemon juice mixture over it. Cover the pan with waxed paper, then seal tightly with aluminum foil. Bake until the fish is no longer translucent and the skin is golden, 30 to 40 minutes for one large fish, depending on the desired doneness, or 20 to 25 minutes for two smaller fish. About 5 minutes before the fish is done, baste it with the pan juices.

Transfer the fish to a large serving platter and spoon the pan juices over it.

SERVES 4 TO 6

1 large or 2 small red snappers (4 to 5 pounds total)
Kosher salt for sprinkling
1 cup extra-virgin olive oil
⅔ cup fresh lemon juice
1 tablespoon ground coriander
1 tablespoon freshly ground black pepper
1 tablespoon sea salt
½ tablespoon ground cumin (optional)
1 long hot, jalapeño or poblano chile pepper, finely chopped
1 cup chopped fresh cilantro or parsley
10 cloves garlic, minced
2 tablespoons seedless Middle Eastern or Turkish chile paste
1½ cups crushed walnuts

FRESH FROM THE SEA

Sprinkling your fresh fish with salt and rubbing it down under running water takes care of any lingering fishy smell, resulting in cooking with fish as if it came fresh out of the sea.

Fisherman's Dish

SAYADIYYA

Our weekend meals always had a kind of rhythm to them: Friday was the day the freshest fish was available at the market and every family bought far more than they needed for dinner that night. We were seven, which meant that my father bought not seven fish, but seventeen! *Sayadiyya* will always symbolize Saturday dinner to me; the dish was easy for my mother to pull together when she returned home from her day of teaching because we always had fried fish leftover from Friday's late supper. She would caramelize the onions on Friday night in the same oil that was used to fry the fish, and then pull the rest of the elements together on Saturday night. It is also my daughter's favorite way to eat fish.

> **COOKING TIP** Take care not to turn the fish until it is well seared and avoid crowding the pan or the fish will steam rather than fry properly.

In a small bowl, combine the salt, pepper, allspice and cumin. Rub a third of the spice mixture into the cavities of the whole fish or all over the fillets or shrimp.

Heat the corn oil in a heavy-bottomed pot over high until hot. Working with two fish at a time or a third of the shrimp, fry them, turning once without crowding them, until golden brown on both sides, 2 to 3 minutes per side. (Do not touch the fish until the underside is golden brown or the skin will stick to the bottom of the pan.) Using a slotted spatula, transfer the fish or shrimp to a paper towel–lined platter.

Pour the corn oil through a strainer into a heatproof cup or bowl. Return it to the pot, stir in the olive oil and heat over medium-high heat. Add the onions and saute until they turn medium brown. Take care not to burn them. Transfer 1 cup of the onions to a paper-towel lined plate and reserve. Toss in the garlic and saute until soft and fragrant, about 30 seconds. Stir in the remaining two-thirds spice mixture. Add the rice and stir until thoroughly coated, about 2 minutes. Remove the pot from the heat and stir in the tomatoes. Slowly pour in the boiling water. Reduce the heat, cover, and simmer for 12 minutes, arranging the fish over the rice for the last 5 minutes of cooking. Alternatively, for a crispier fish, reheat it for 5 minutes in a 400°F oven.

To serve, spoon the rice onto the center of a large platter and surround it with the fish. Scatter the reserved onions and the toasted almonds over the top.

SERVES 6

4½ teaspoons sea salt

1 tablespoon freshly ground black pepper

1 tablespoon ground allspice

1 tablespoon ground cumin

6 whole porgies, striped bass, Chilean sea bass, or other white-fleshed fish (1 pound each), cleaned, or 3 pounds fillets, or 2 pounds (16- to 20-count) shell-on shrimp

1 cup corn oil

1 cup extra-virgin olive oil

3 Spanish onions, thinly sliced (about 4 cups)

½ tablespoon finely chopped garlic

4 cups Egyptian, Chinese, or Carolina rice

1 cup grape or cherry tomatoes

6 cups boiling water (8 cups if you are using Carolina rice)

1 cup slivered almonds, toasted

Fish Tagine

SAMAK TAGINE

My mother never used cilantro and hot sauce in the tagines she occasionally made on Saturday nights, but my version is certainly inspired by hers. Traditionally made with just tahini, caramelized onions, lemon juice and garlic, this popular fish dish is prepared when there's time available to spend in the kitchen. Serve with Rice and Vermicelli Pilaf, page 204, Arabic Bread, page 61, and a green salad.

Rub the fish all over with the salt under running water. Pat dry.

Heat the corn oil in a heavy-bottomed pot over high until hot. Slip 2 whole fish or 4 fillets into the pot, taking care not to crowd them, and fry, turning once, until they are golden brown on both sides, 2 to 3 minutes per side. Do not touch the fish until the underside is golden brown or the skin will stick to the bottom of the pan. Using a slotted spatula, transfer the fish to a paper towel–lined platter.

Pour the corn oil through a strainer into a heatproof cup or bowl. Return the oil to the pot, add the olive oil and heat over medium-high heat. Add the onions and saute until they turn golden brown. Take care not to burn them.

Preheat the oven to 450°F. Meanwhile, in a large bowl, combine the tahini sauce, stock, cilantro, garlic, shallots, if using, chile paste, pepper and cumin and whisk together.

Arrange the fried fish in a large roasting pan and scatter the onions on top. Tuck the potatoes and pepper around the fish, then pour over the tahini mixture to cover. Cover the pan tightly with foil and roast until the fish flakes easily when pricked with a fork, about 20 minutes. Remove the foil and roast 5 minutes more. Transfer to a platter and serve immediately, garnished with the parsley or cilantro, with rice and Arabic bread alongside.

SERVES 6

6 whole red snapper, striped bass or porgies (about 1 pound each), or 12 fillets
Kosher salt for sprinkling
1 cup corn oil
¾ cup extra-virgin olive oil
2 Spanish onions, thinly sliced
4 cups Thick Tahini Sauce (page 221)
2 cups stock from Seasoned Chicken with Stock (page 100) or low-sodium chicken broth
1 cup chopped cilantro
6 garlic cloves, finely chopped
2 shallots, cut into small cubes (optional)
1 tablespoon seedless Middle Eastern or Turkish chile paste
1 tablespoon freshly ground black pepper
1 tablespoon ground cumin
6 white potatoes, peeled and cut into ½-inch cubes
½ green or red bell pepper, seeded and diced
Chopped fresh parsley and cilantro for garnish
Rice and Vermicelli Pilaf (page 204) for serving
Arabic Bread (page 61) for serving

Friday Fish-Fries

Whole fried fish holds a special place in my heart, as it has been a culinary constant throughout my life. My love affair with it began in Nazareth, followed me to New York, and then zigzagged with me throughout Europe. I've had some of the best times in my life sitting around a table set with platters of crispy, succulent fish. In fact, it was during one of these meals, almost fourteen years ago, that my girlfriends convinced me to open a restaurant. We gathered at least once a month in my Brooklyn kitchen for an arak-soaked fish fry. There were platters piled high with crispy fried red snapper, hand-cut French fries, chopped tomato salad flecked with jalapeño, bowls of quartered lemons, boats of tahini-parsley sauce and lots of prodding from them, encouraging me to turn what I loved doing into a business. And here we are.

To this day, gathering around a table of fried fish conjures crystal clear memories of the Friday fish dinners we ate at home in Nazareth. These suppers were as much a series of rituals as they were a meal. To get the freshest catch, my father woke up before the sun rose to be one of the first customers at the fishmonger's counter. He usually bought *mushout*, a fish similar to porgy, from Lake Tiberias in northern Galilee, but there was also bass, and delicate barbonies.

In the evening, my mother hauled out the big pot she reserved for frying fish, filled it part way with olive oil and set it on the stove. While the oil was heating up, she salted the fish. I used to love the cackling sound the hot oil made when the fish hit it, but nothing was more exciting than watching her remove the golden, crispy fish with her big spoon to a platter. It was only a matter of seconds before my family and, more often than not, a few neighbors and friends, were picking the fish apart, scooping it up with Arabic bread and dipping it into parsley-tahini sauce. We were a noisy bunch, talking, laughing, and telling stories as the adults sipped arak. I remember my father deboning the fish for the little ones, as I did when I made this fish for my young children at home in Brooklyn.

These days most fried fish is eaten in restaurants. Nazareth is full of places that specialize in the dish. If home cooks do want to prepare whole fried fish, they do it in an outdoor fryer, which is a good option and makes for great entertaining.

> "To this day, gathering around a table of fried fish conjures crystal clear memories of the Friday fish dinners we ate at home in Nazareth. These suppers were as much a series of rituals as they were a meal."

Salmon in Pesto

Before I came to the U.S., the only way I had ever eaten salmon was smoked. My father would bring some home on very rare occasions; it simply wasn't readily available. Several months into Tanoreen's first year, I noticed that some customers would nervously scan the menu in search of a familiar dish. I created this with them in mind. Serve with Rice and Vermicelli Pilaf, page 204.

In a small bowl, combine 1½ teaspoons coriander, ½ teaspoon pepper and ½ teaspoon salt. Season the salmon on both sides with the spice mixture. Arrange the salmon in a roasting pan, skin-side down if using fillets, spacing them 2 inches apart. Set aside.

Preheat the oven to 450°F.

In a large skillet, heat ½ cup oil over medium-high heat. Add the garlic and saute until golden and fragrant, about 2 minutes. Add the artichoke hearts and saute, turning until browned all over, about 6 minutes total. Stir in the tomatoes and remaining pepper, coriander and salt and cook until the tomatoes soften slightly and release their juices, about 5 minutes. Stir in the pesto and lemon juice and return to a boil for 2 minutes.

Using a slotted spoon, transfer the artichoke mixture to the roasting pan, tucking them in between the salmon fillets. Pour the sauce over the salmon and drizzle the remaining ½ cup oil on top. Gently add the chicken stock to the pan by pouring it in at one corner so as not to wash the oil away. Cover the pan with foil and bake for 15 minutes. Remove the foil and bake 2 minutes more or until the salmon is cooked to desired doneness.

To serve, transfer the fillets to dinner plates and spoon some of the pan sauce over them. Serve with the rice pilaf and garnish with the parsley and lemon wedges.

SERVES 6

1 tablespoon ground coriander

1 teaspoon freshly ground black pepper

1 teaspoon sea salt plus more to taste

6 salmon fillets, skin on, or 2-inch-thick salmon steaks

1 cup olive oil

8 cloves garlic, finely chopped

2 bags (1 pound each) frozen artichoke hearts, thawed and cut into ½-inch thick pieces

8 plum tomatoes, diced

¾ cup Basil Pesto (page 215)

Juice of 2 to 3 lemons (about ½ cup)

1½ cups stock from Seasoned Chicken with Stock (page 100) or low-sodium chicken stock

Rice and Vermicelli Pilaf (page 204)

¼ cup chopped fresh parsley and 1 lemon, cut into wedges, for garnish

Whole Fried Fish

SAMAK MAQLEH

I remember my mother frying fish in olive oil, then using it to fry pieces of bread. She served the golden brown nuggets with a tahini parsley sauce, for dipping. These days, I fry fish in corn oil. While it is delicious prepared simply—seasoned with salt and pepper followed by a quick dredge in flour—I prefer to spice things up a bit by making slits in the flesh and stuffing them with *Tetbileh*, a sauce of garlic, chile pepper, lemon juice and olive oil. My favorite fish to fry include red snapper, striped bass, branzino, porgies and red mullet. Serve this with Thick Tahini Sauce, page 221, Tomato Salad, page 77, or Fried Tomatoes, page 196. Use any leftover fish to make Fish Tagine, page 140, or Fisherman's Dish, page 139.

Rub the fish all over with salt under cold running water. Pat dry. Make the *Tetbileh*: Mix all the ingredients in a food processor and pulse into a coarse mixture. To store, transfer to a container with a tight-fitting lid, top with olive oil and refrigerate up to 2 weeks.

Using a sharp kitchen knife, make three 1/8-inch deep crosswise slits along the length of each fish. Rub 1 tablespoon of the *Tetbileh* into the slits and cavity of each fish. Set aside.

Put the flour in a large shallow-rimmed plate. Working with one fish at a time, dredge it in the flour, using a bit of the flour to seal the cavity shut. Shake off the excess and set aside on parchment paper.

Heat the corn oil in a large, heavy-bottomed pot over high until hot. Working with one or two fish at a time fry, turning once without crowding them, until they are golden brown on both sides, 2 to 3 minutes per side. Do not touch the fish until the underside is golden brown or the skin will stick to the bottom of the pan. Using a slotted spatula, transfer the fish to a paper towel–lined platter. Serve warm with the lemon halves.

MAKES 4 SERVINGS

4 whole fish of choice (1 to 1½ pounds each), cleaned
Kosher salt for sprinkling
¼ cup *Tetbileh* (recipe follows)
1 cup all-purpose white flour
4 cups corn oil
3 lemons, halved

For the *Tetbileh* (Makes about 1¼ cups)
10 cloves garlic, chopped into a coarse paste
2 long hot or jalapeño peppers, minced
1 tablespoon paprika
1 tablespoon black pepper
1 tablespoon cumin
½ cup extra-virgin olive oil, plus extra for storing
4 tablespoons fresh lemon juice
1 tablespoon salt
½ cup chopped fresh parsley

Shrimp in Garlic Sauce

My arrival in New York was full of firsts, including tasting shrimp for the first time. Wafa was certain that I would love it, especially the way it was prepared at a seafood restaurant he had eaten at in Sheepshead Bay, Brooklyn. He was wrong. But I came to love the shellfish over the years after preparing it my way—in a flavorful garlic sauce—at home. This is a great dish to make on a busy weeknight, as it takes all of ten minutes to prepare if you ask your fishmonger to peel and devein the shrimp for you. It requires even less time if he or she butterflies them. Serve the shrimp over Rice and Vermicelli Pilaf, page 204, and with Arabic Bread, page 61, for dipping into the sauce.

In a large skillet, heat the olive oil over medium heat until hot but not smoking. Toss in the shrimp and saute until the bottom loses its pink color, about 90 seconds. Add the garlic, turn the shrimp and saute 90 seconds more. Stir in all but 2 tablespoons of the parsley, the paprika, salt and pepper and saute until fragrant, about 1 minute. Pour in the stock and lemon juice and bring to a boil. Add the ghee, if using, and the breadcrumbs and return to a boil for 2 minutes.

Arrange the shrimp over the rice pilaf and spoon some of the broth over both. Serve with the rice pilaf, Arabic bread and the lemon wedges.

SERVES 6

⅓ cup extra-virgin olive oil
2 pounds (16-to 20-count) shrimp, peeled, deveined and butterflied
10 cloves garlic, finely chopped
1 cup chopped fresh parsley
1 teaspoon paprika (optional)
1 teaspoon sea salt
1 teaspoon freshly ground black pepper
2 cups stock from Seasoned Chicken with Stock (page 100) or low-sodium chicken stock or water
Juice of 2 lemons or to taste
3 tablespoons ghee or butter (optional)
3 tablespoons dried breadcrumbs
Rice and Vermicelli Pilaf (page 204)
Arabic Bread (page 61)
Lemon wedges for garnish

Grilled Red Snapper in Grape Leaves

I decided to wrap fish in grape leaves after a visit to Jerusalem for Jumana's christening. For the celebration dinner, there was *kafta* **wrapped in the briny greens, which imparted a delightful tang to the meat (see page 179). Not only do the leaves do the same for fish, they also keep it moist. The marinade is excellent for all manner of fish and chicken.**

Using a sharp kitchen knife, make three ⅛-inch crosswise slits along the length of both sides of each fish. Set aside.

In a large baking dish, combine the oil and lemon juice with the garlic, shallots, tomatoes, sesame oil, jalapeño, oregano, cumin, coriander, and black pepper. Arrange the fish in the dish and, using your hands, rub the marinade into the slits and into the cavity of each fish. Cover the dish tightly and refrigerate overnight, turning the fish once or twice.

Prepare a charcoal grill. On a clean work surface, spread out a piece of foil several inches larger and wider than one fish. Place a piece of waxed paper of equal size on top of it. Arrange 6 to 8 grape leaves on the waxed paper, overlapping them to form a rectangular shape. Reserving the marinade, place a fish in the center of the grape leaves and fold the grape leaves onto it like an envelope. Fold up the fish in the waxed paper and then the aluminum foil, wrapping it tightly. Place the packets on the grill and grill 7 to 10 minutes per side.

In a medium pot, heat the marinade over high heat to reduce to a sauce. Using kitchen scissors, cut through the foil and waxed paper to open the packets, then transfer each wrapped fish to a dinner plate and serve with the marinade and lemon wedges.

SERVES 4 TO 6

4 to 6 whole red snapper or branzino (1 pound each), boned or bone-in
⅓ cup extra-virgin olive oil
Juice of 5 lemons
6 cloves garlic, finely chopped
3 shallots, finely chopped
2 plum tomatoes, finely chopped
2 tablespoons dark sesame oil
1 jalapeño chile pepper, seeded, if desired, and finely chopped
1 tablespoon chopped fresh oregano
1 tablespoon ground cumin
1 tablespoon ground coriander
1 tablespoon freshly ground black pepper
1 (20-ounce) jar grape leaves or, 6 to 8 grape leaves per fish, rinsed
Lemon wedges for garnish

Roasted Fish

SAMAK MHAMMAR

I was inspired by the ingredients used in the quintessential Palestinian dish, *Musakhan*, page 158, when I created this version of roasted fish. Slathered in tangy sumac and my fiery homemade chile sauce, the mellow fish comes alive with Middle Eastern flavors. Serve with the Tanoreen Green Salad, page 86.

Preheat the oven to 450°F.

Heat the oil in a large skillet over medium-high until hot. Add the onions and saute until golden, 7 to 10 minutes. Transfer the onions to a small bowl and add the lemon juice, sumac, hot sauce, allspice, pepper and cumin and mix well.

Open the porgies like a book and spread 5 tablespoons of the onion mixture into each. Transfer to a roasting pan or ovenproof skillet. Cover the pan with waxed paper, then cover tightly with foil and roast until the fish is just cooked through, 10 to 15 minutes. Transfer to a serving platter, sprinkle with the almonds and pine nuts and serve with Tanoreen green salad.

SERVES 4 TO 6

⅓ cup extra-virgin olive oil

3 red or white onions, finely chopped

Juice of 3 lemons

1 tablespoon sumac

1 tablespoon Homemade Hot Sauce (page 220) or seedless Middle Eastern or Turkish chile paste

1 tablespoon ground allspice

1 tablespoon freshly ground black pepper

1 teaspoon ground cumin

4 to 6 whole porgies (about 1 pound each)

½ cup slivered almonds

½ cup pine nuts, toasted

Tanoreen Green Salad (page 86)

CHICKEN

Whole Stuffed Chicken

DJAJ MAHSHI

This is a lavish special-occasion dish that is traditionally prepared for Easter but makes an excellent dinner-party entrée as well. The beauty of stuffed chicken is that it can be the basis for several courses. After it is stuffed and seared on the stovetop, you can add chopped fresh parsley and additional broth or water to the drippings to make a quick soup to serve while the chicken is roasting. You will have more stuffing than you need for the two chickens. Transfer the remaining stuffing alongside the chicken legs so that it appears as if it is coming out of the chicken. Serve with some yogurt.

With the rack arranged in the center, preheat the oven to 450°F.

In a small bowl, combine the allspice, salt, pepper, nutmeg and cardamom. Using your hands, rub the spice mixture all over the inside and outside of the chickens. Spoon the stuffing into the cavity of each chicken, packing in as much filling as each chicken will hold. Seal the cavities with toothpicks or short skewers. Set aside the remaining stuffing.

Fill a deep roasting pan half full with water. Set a rack in it. Rub each chicken all over with the oil and place them, side by side, on the rack. Bake until the water comes to a boil, then continue boiling for 15 minutes. Reduce the heat to 350°F. Cover the roasting pan with foil and bake until the thigh juices run clear, about 1 hour 15 minutes.

Remove the foil, turn the oven to broil and slide the roasting pan back into the oven. Broil the chickens until the skin is golden brown, turning once, about 5 minutes. Transfer to a cutting board to rest.

For a first course, spoon the cooking broth into soup bowls, add a little of the stuffing that has tumbled out of the chicken, stir in some parsley and serve with lemon wedges. Offer the stuffed chicken as a second course, served on a platter with additional stuffing and low-fat yogurt on the side.

SERVES 6 TO 8

1 tablespoon ground allspice
1 tablespoon sea salt
1 tablespoon freshly ground black pepper
1 level teaspoon freshly grated nutmeg
½ teaspoon ground cardamom
2 whole chickens (3 pounds each), rinsed and patted dry
Meat Stuffing (page 166), cooled
1 to 2 tablespoons extra-virgin olive oil
Chopped fresh parsley for garnish
Lemon wedges and low-fat plain yogurt for serving

Chicken Fetti

FETIT DJAJ

The word *fetti* is derived from the Arabic word *fetafiit*, meaning "crumbled"; in this case, crumbled squares of toasted Arabic bread covered with a tangy yogurt-tahini sauce. There are endless variations on *fetti*, including those prepared with eggplant, chickpeas or lamb. Back home in Nazareth, we ate *Kroush Fetti*, made with boiled lamb stomach. Egyptians make *fetti* without any yogurt at all; they use a mix of vinegar, garlic, and chiles. My Syrian friends in New York introduced me to this chicken version, which can be prepared in advance and assembled just before serving.

In a small bowl, combine the allspice, pepper, salt, and nutmeg in a small bowl. Rub half of the spice mixture all over the chicken pieces.

Heat ½ cup oil in a 5-quart Dutch oven over medium-high heat. Toss in the chicken pieces and saute until brown all over, leaving them untouched for at least 2 to 3 minutes to prevent sticking. Add the cinnamon stick, cardamom, cloves, bay leaves and onion. Pour 12 cups water into the pot along with the reserved neck and giblets. Raise the heat to high, bring to a boil, then reduce the heat and simmer for 1 hour. Using a strainer or slotted spoon, skim the foam that rises to the surface every 15 minutes.

Transfer the chicken to a platter and set aside to cool. Strain the broth, discard the solids and return the broth to a gentle simmer in the pot. When the chicken is cool enough to handle, discard the skin and remove the meat from the bones. Shred the chicken and sprinkle it with 1 cup broth to prevent it from drying out; cover loosely and set aside.

In a second large, heavy-bottomed pot, combine the remaining ½ cup oil and ghee and heat over medium-high heat. Add the vermicelli to the pot; if using bird's nest vermicelli, break it up with your hands first. Saute the noodles, stirring constantly, until golden brown. Add the rice and stir constantly until the grains turn pearly white. Pour in 8 cups of the simmering broth and stir in the remaining spice mixture. Cover and simmer for 12 minutes, stirring twice. Remove from the heat, cover and set aside, undisturbed, for 5 minutes.

Meanwhile, make the yogurt sauce: In the bowl of a food processor, combine the tahini sauce, yogurt, garlic and lemon juice, if needed; pulse until a smooth sauce forms. Alternatively, combine in a large bowl and mix with a hand mixer until smooth. Transfer to a saucepan and bring to a simmer over medium heat. Do not boil.

To serve, spoon the rice into the center of a large, rimmed platter, shaping it into a mound and leaving a ½ inch rim around the edge. Top with the chicken, then spoon the warm sauce over it all. Arrange the bread around the rim and garnish with the nuts and parsley.

SERVES 6 TO 8

2 tablespoons ground allspice
1 tablespoon freshly ground black pepper
5½ teaspoons sea salt
½ teaspoon grated fresh nutmeg
2 chickens (3 to 4 pounds each), each cut into 4 pieces (reserve neck, skin, and all giblets but the liver for broth)
1 cup olive oil
1 cinnamon stick
5 whole cardamom pods
5 whole cloves
3 bay leaves
1 yellow onion, peeled
4 tablespoons ghee, or 8 tablespoons (1 stick) butter
1 pound round vermicelli
4 cups short-grain Egyptian, Carolina or basmati rice

Yogurt Sauce
Thick Tahini Sauce (page 221)
2 cups plain low-fat yogurt
2 cloves garlic, minced
Juice of 1 lemon

For Serving
6 (8-inch) pieces Arabic Bread (page 61), toasted
1 cup slivered almonds, toasted
½ to 1 cup pine nuts, toasted
½ cup chopped fresh parsley

Egyptian Fetti Sauce

COOKING TIPS Leftovers can be reheated with a little water to thin the yogurt sauce. Simmer gently, being careful not to let the sauce boil, which will cause it to separate.

If you are using purchased yogurt, be sure to include the lemon juice. If you are making your own, omit it. I find if I make yogurt with room temperature milk, it tastes pleasingly sour. Cold milk produces yogurt that's on the sweeter side.

For customers who don't eat dairy, I make the *fetti* sauce the Egyptian way. It is a wonderful substitute for the tahini-based sauce and can be used not only on chicken, but with beef or lamb, too.

2 tablespoons extra-virgin olive oil, ghee or butter
6 cloves garlic, finely chopped
2 chile peppers, finely chopped
1 tablespoon ground coriander
1 teaspoon sea salt
½ teaspoon freshly ground black pepper
⅓ cup distilled white vinegar
Juice of 1 lemon

Heat the oil in a small pot over medium-high until fragrant and golden, about 1 minute. Stir in the garlic, chile peppers, coriander, salt and black pepper and saute until fragrant, about 30 seconds. Turn off the heat, stir in the vinegar and return the heat to high. Bring to a boil, add the lemon juice, return to a simmer and remove from the heat.

The Romance of *Maftool*

My father was a rather chivalrous man, particularly when it came to my mother. His gestures were not necessarily showy or grand, but they were nothing if not charming.

One of my favorite memories of my parents is tied to the ritual of making *maftool*, a pasta that is often incorrectly referred to as Israeli couscous here in America. Given how much patience and diligence is required to make the grains by hand, it is clear proof to me just how important food was and remains to our culture.

In our Nazareth home, my mother started making this pearly pasta early in the morning. The first step was roasting and grinding her own spices. The aroma of caraway, anise and cumin floated in the air. She filled a huge stockpot with either lamb bones or whole chickens, vegetables, the spices and water. While the water came to a boil, my mother shaped the pasta. She stood while rolling a bit of wheat flour with drips of water in the palms of her hands over a sieve, continuously sprinkling flour and water in her palm until the granules were the size of BB pellets. She would then coat the pasta with clarified butter to prevent the grains from sticking together while they steamed in a colander set in the pot of boiling stock. The fragrant stock perfumed the *maftool* before the two were combined in a bowl. Layering flavors this way was the key to my mother's memorable cooking. She insisted on spicing and perfuming every component of a dish.

Maftool is made with what seems like an absurd amount of pearl onions. Peeling them is one of the most time-consuming steps in making the dish. For my parents, though, it was the most charmed. Because he hated to see her cry, my father always stepped in to tackle the mountain of onions on the kitchen counter. This may not seem especially gallant these days, but back then, men simply did not carry their weight in the kitchen. Watching my dad peel all those onions made me swoon. As a little girl, it just seemed so romantic! The most endearing part of the process was not that my father saved my mom the burning eyes and endless tears, but that he'd close the kitchen door while he was preparing all of those onions because he didn't like anyone seeing *him* cry.

"Watching my dad peel all those onions made me swoon. As a little girl, it just seemed so romantic!"

Palestinian Couscous with Chicken, Chickpeas and Pearl Onions

MAFTOOL

It used to be that the whole family gathered to make homemade *Maftool*. These days, almost no one makes it by hand, which is not surprising, since the process is very involved. *Maftool* is truly a one-dish meal—there are never pickles, sauces or salads served with it because the chicken, chickpeas and onions are like side dishes themselves. I prefer fresh pearl onions, but if you need to speed things up, use the frozen variety.

In a small bowl, combine the caraway, allspice, cumin, coriander, salt, pepper, nutmeg, cardamom and cinnamon. Rub half of the spice mixture all over the chicken. Set aside the other half.

In a large, heavy-bottomed pot, heat 6 tablespoons of the oil or all of the ghee over medium heat. Slip the chicken pieces into the pan, skin-side down, and sear, leaving them untouched for 6 to 8 minutes, until golden brown. Turn over and sear the other sides, 5 minutes more. Using a slotted spoon, transfer the chicken to a plate and set aside. Add the pearl and yellow onions and saute until the onions begin to take on color, 5 to 7 minutes. Return the chicken to the pot, pour in the chickpeas and 12 cups water, raise the heat and bring to a boil. Reduce the heat and, using a spoon, skim off the foam from the top, trying not to skim off any spices along with it. Cover and simmer until the chicken is about to fall off the bone, 45 minutes to 1 hour. Stir in the lemon juice and set the pot aside.

Meanwhile, in a large skillet with a lid, heat the remaining 4 tablespoons olive oil over medium-high heat. Add the rice, stir to coat and saute until the grains are snowy white. Stir in the reserved spice mixture and until fragrant. Pour in 6 cups of the chicken broth from the pot and bring to a boil. Reduce the heat, cover, and simmer until the rice is soft, adding more broth as needed, 15 to 20 minutes.

To serve, spoon the rice onto a large, rimmed serving platter and arrange the chicken, chickpeas and onions around it.

MAKES 4 SERVINGS

6 teaspoons ground caraway seeds
1 tablespoon ground allspice
1 tablespoon ground cumin
1 tablespoon ground coriander
1 tablespoon sea salt or to taste
1 tablespoon freshly ground black pepper
½ teaspoon ground nutmeg
½ teaspoon ground cardamom
½ teaspoon ground cinnamon
1 chicken (2½ to 3 pounds), cut into 4 or 8 pieces
10 tablespoons olive oil, or 4 tablespoons ghee
2 pounds fresh pearl onions, peeled, or frozen pearl onions
4 yellow onions, chopped
1 pound dried chickpeas, soaked overnight and boiled (see page 21), or 2 (15-ounce) cans, drained and rinsed
Juice of ½ lemon
2 pounds *maftool* (see opposite) or Egyptian rice

Chicken "Pizza"

MUSAKHAN

One of the most popular Tanoreen menu items, this traditional dish was originally made by serving a whole roasted chicken, smothered with onions, on a 16-inch loaf of flatbread. Each diner would be served a big piece of the chicken, a torn piece of bread and a small mound of onions. Typically, they'd eat the dish with their hands, using the bread as a scoop. To make it easier to serve and eat (and because such a large flatbread, known as *taboun*, is difficult to find), I developed this "user-friendly," pizza-style version of *musakhan*. It makes an excellent appetizer, cut into small wedges. Pocketless Indian naan or Turkish flatbread work nicely here.

In a small bowl, combine the sumac, allspice, salt, cardamom, cumin and nutmeg and set aside.

Heat ⅓ cup oil in a large skillet over medium heat. Sprinkle in half of the spice mixture and saute, stirring, until fragrant, about 30 seconds. Add the chicken to the skillet and cook, stirring occasionally, until the chicken loses its pink color, about 7 minutes.

In another skillet, heat another ⅓ cup oil over medium heat. Stir in the remaining spice mixture until fragrant, about 10 seconds. Add the onions and saute, stirring occasionally, until soft and golden, 2 to 3 minutes. Transfer the onion mixture, scraping the pan to catch all of the spices, to the pot of chicken and stir with a wooden spoon to thoroughly combine. Add the remaining ⅓ cup oil to the chicken and simmer for 3 to 4 minutes.

Meanwhile, preheat the oven to 450°F. Arrange the flatbreads on two baking sheets. Divide the chicken and onion mixture evenly among them, spreading within a ¼ inch of the rim. Bake the pizzas until warmed through, about 5 minutes. Remove from the oven and sprinkle the top of each pizza with 1½ teaspoons each of the nuts. Sprinkle with the lemon juice, if desired, and serve.

SERVES 6

2 heaping tablespoons sumac or more to taste
1 tablespoon ground allspice
1 tablespoon sea salt
¾ teaspoon ground cardamom
¼ teaspoon ground cumin
¼ teaspoon grated fresh nutmeg
1 cup extra-virgin olive oil
2 whole boneless, skinless chicken breasts (3 pounds total), cut into 1-inch pieces
4 yellow onions, chopped
6 Arabic Breads (page 61) or Greek, Turkish or Indian flatbreads
3 tablespoons slivered almonds, toasted
3 tablespoons pine nuts, toasted
Juice of 2 lemons (optional)

Chicken with Potatoes

MHAMMAR

Every culture has a hearty chicken and potato dish. This one is in every Palestinian cook's repertoire, perhaps because it is so easy to make. I can't say this version is entirely traditional, as I tend to use spices more liberally than most because I think they give the dish a little more dimension. *Mhammar* is very forgiving, which is why no two cooks use exactly the same ingredients. If you like heat, add 2 tablespoons of red chile paste when sauteing the onions. It is also an excellent make-ahead dish; cover and refrigerate it, then when you're ready, warm in a 300°F oven until heated through. Serve with Arabic Bread, page 61, Rice and Vermicelli Pilaf, page 204, and a Tanoreen Green Salad, page 86.

In a large pot, bring the stock to a simmer.

Preheat the oven to 450°F. Arrange the potatoes in a single layer in a large roasting pan. Set aside.

In the large skillet used to fry the potatoes, reheat the reserved frying oil (if potatoes were roasted, heat the olive oil) over medium-high until hot. Toss in the onions and saute until golden and caramelized, 3 to 5 minutes. Add the chile peppers, if using, and saute until fragrant, 1 minute. Sprinkle in the sumac, allspice, lemon juice, then pour in 4 cups of the simmering chicken stock. Bring to a boil, then reduce the heat and simmer for 5 minutes. Remove from the heat.

Arrange the chicken pieces over the potatoes in the roasting pan. Pour the onion mixture over the chicken, then add the remaining 2 cups of simmering stock to the pan, pouring it slowly into the corner so as not to wash away the oil. Cover the pan with aluminum foil and bake for 20 minutes. Reduce the heat to 300°F and bake for 20 minutes more. Serve warm with Arabic bread, rice pilaf, a green salad and a squeeze of lemon.

SERVES 6 TO 8

6 cups stock and the meat, skinned and chopped, from Seasoned Chicken with Stock (page 100)

8 baking potatoes peeled, cut into ¼-inch-thick slices and fried or roasted, frying oil reserved (see page 117)

½ cup extra-virgin olive oil (if using roasted potatoes)

6 yellow onions, diced

2 chile peppers, seeded and finely diced (optional)

2 tablespoons sumac

1 tablespoon ground allspice

Juice of 2 lemons

Arabic Bread (page 61)

Rice and Vermicelli Pilaf (page 204)

Tanoreen Green Salad (page 86)

Lemon wedges for garnish

Chicken Tagine

TAGINE DJAJ

This is the Tanoreen version of the iconic Moroccan dish. I didn't grow up eating tagine, but after dining in restaurants in Morocco, and in Tunisian restaurants in Paris, Marbella and New York, I grew to love the mix of dried fruits, vegetables and chicken. Of course, Moroccans don't use basil or apricots in their tagines; their recipe features currants, cherries, raisins or plums. I happen to love the combination of dried apricots and cranberries, which make a very flavorful sauce when slow-cooked with lots of spices. The ingredient list for this is long and the cooking is slow, but for the amount of active cooking time involved, the results are worth every minute. This tastes even better reheated as leftovers.

Preheat the oven to 500°F.

In a small bowl, combine the allspice, coriander, turmeric, salt, pepper, cumin, saffron, nutmeg and cardamom. Rinse the chicken pieces and pat dry. Rub half the spice mixture all over the chicken pieces. Set aside the other half.

In a large skillet, heat ½ cup oil over medium-high until hot. Working in batches, sear the chicken on all sides, about 4 minutes total. Using a slotted spoon, remove the chicken from the pan to a plate and set aside.

In the same skillet, saute the onions until soft and fragrant, about 5 minutes. Add the garlic and saute, stirring occasionally, until fragrant, about 3 minutes. Stir in the reserved spice mixture and cook until fragrant, about 1 minute. Stir in the cilantro, basil, and parsley. Add the remaining ½ cup oil with the dried fruits, lemon juice, chile paste, olives and 4 cups water and bring to a simmer. Cook, stirring, for 2 minutes.

Meanwhile, arrange the carrots, pearl onions and potatoes on the bottom of a large roasting pan. Arrange the chicken over the vegetables. Toss in the onion mixture to thoroughly coat the chicken and vegetables. Set aside to marinate for 45 to 60 minutes. Cover the roasting pan with foil and bake until the chicken begins to sizzle, 10 to 15 minutes. Reduce the temperature to 350°F and bake 30 minutes more. Remove the foil and roast for 5 minutes more.

Spoon the rice into the middle of a large platter and arrange the chicken, vegetables, fruits and all the pan juices around it. Garnish with the nuts and serve.

SERVES 6 TO 8

1 tablespoon ground allspice
1 tablespoon ground coriander
1 tablespoon turmeric
1 tablespoon sea salt
1½ teaspoons freshly ground black pepper
1 teaspoon ground cumin
1 teaspoon saffron
¾ teaspoon ground nutmeg
½ teaspoon ground cardamom
2 chickens (2½ to 3 pounds each), each cut into quarters
1 cup extra-virgin olive oil
3 Spanish onions, chopped
8 cloves garlic, finely chopped
1 cup chopped fresh cilantro
1 cup chopped fresh basil
1 cup chopped fresh parsley
1 cup chopped dried fruits, preferably apricots and cranberries
½ cup fresh lemon juice
2 tablespoons seedless Middle Eastern or Turkish chile paste
1 cup pitted and chopped Kalamata or green olives
1 pound baby carrots or whole carrots, chopped
1 pound fresh pearl onions, peeled, or frozen pearl onions
4 white potatoes, halved lengthwise and sliced into half moons
Basmati Vegetable Rice (page 205)
Slivered almonds and pine nuts for garnish

Chicken Kebabs

SHISH TAWOOK

To serve these kebabs the traditional way, remove the skewer, wrap Arabic bread around the chicken, top with pickles and chopped lettuce and drizzle with the garlic sauce. At Tanoreen, I serve them over Rice and Vermicelli Pilaf, page 204, along with a Tanoreen Green Salad, page 86. Sometimes I punctuate every two pieces of chicken by adding a pearl onion, cherry tomato or piece of pepper to the skewer. If using wooden skewers, soak them in water first for at least 30 minutes so they won't burn on the grill.

In a large bowl, combine the lemon juice and oil with the garlic, allspice, salt, pepper, cumin, nutmeg and paprika and mix well. Add the chicken and stir to coat with the marinade. Cover and refrigerate for at least 3 hours or overnight.

Prepare a gas or charcoal grill (or preheat the broiler); the fire should be moderately hot. Divide the chicken evenly among twelve skewers, threading the chicken pieces onto them so that they are fairly tightly packed. Grill over moderate heat, turning three to four times to brown evenly, until the chicken is cooked through and browned all over, 10 to 15 minutes depending on the heat of the grill and the distance from the heat source. Serve with the garlic sauce along with the pickles, lettuce and Arabic bread.

VARIATION To make the kebabs the Indian way, add 1 cup low-fat plain yogurt to the marinade ingredients. The yogurt is a wonderful tenderizer and imparts a gorgeous color to the chicken pieces when grilled.

SERVES 6

1 cup fresh lemon juice
½ cup extra-virgin olive oil
10 cloves garlic, minced
1 tablespoon ground allspice
1 tablespoon sea salt
1 teaspoon freshly ground black pepper
½ teaspoon ground cumin
¼ teaspoon ground nutmeg
½ teaspoon ground paprika
4 pounds boneless, skinless chicken breasts, cut into 1 by 1½-inch chunks
Seasoned Garlic Sauce (page 222)
Pickles, for garnish
Lettuce, chopped, for garnish
Arabic Bread (page 61)

Grilled Quail

Quail is a special occasion food—in the same way that foie gras is. There is not a lot of meat on quail, so I tend to serve two to three per person, depending on the size of the quail. You can adjust the amount as you prefer. To grill, I flatten the bird, a method known as spatchcocking. Ask your butcher to do this for you, or learn to do it yourself following the instructions below. You can often buy your birds tunnel-boned, which means the only bones left in the bird are in the wings and legs. This makes spatchcocking much easier. Serve with Tomato Salad, page 77, or a Tanoreen Green Salad, page 86.

Place the quail in a large high-sided dish or pan.

In the bowl of a food processor, combine the lemon juice, oil and barbecue sauce with the garlic, shallots, tomato, poblano pepper, cilantro, cumin, coriander, salt and pepper. Process until the mixture forms a slightly chunky marinade. Pour the marinade over the quail, cover and refrigerate for at least 2 hours or overnight.

Prepare a gas or charcoal grill; the fire should throw off moderately high heat. Grilling in batches if necessary, place the quail, breast-side-up, on the grill, cover and cook for 5 minutes. Turn the quail over and grill the breast side with the cover off for 2 minutes more or until the juices run clear when the thickest part of the bird is pierced with a knife. Transfer to a serving platter and serve warm.

MAKES 6 TO 9 SERVINGS

18 quail, spatchcocked (see below), rinsed and patted dry
1½ cups fresh lemon juice
1 cup extra-virgin olive oil
2 tablespoons barbecue sauce
10 cloves garlic, finely chopped
4 shallots, diced
1 large Jersey tomato, chopped
1 poblano pepper, finely chopped
2 tablespoons chopped fresh cilantro
1 tablespoon ground cumin
1 tablespoon ground coriander
1 tablespoon sea salt
4¾ teaspoons freshly ground black pepper

HOW TO SPATCHCOCK A QUAIL

Place the quail, breast-side down, on a clean work surface. Using sturdy kitchen scissors, snip down the skin along each side of the backbone. Pull out the backbone and discard. Turn the quail breast-side up and press down firmly on the breastbone to flatten it.

Alternatively, place the quail, breast-side up, on a clean work surface. Insert your heaviest chopping knife into the cavity of the bird from the back end to the neck. Press down firmly alongside the backbone, one side at a time, to cut it away. Discard the backbone. Press down firmly on the breastbone to flatten the quail.

LAMB & BEEF

Stuffed Artichokes with Meat and Pine Nuts

Nobody in Nazareth prepared artichokes this way; my mother brought the idea back from a long weekend away in a nearby town. When I arrived in the States, I found that my Syrian friends had long been making stuffed artichokes with spiced meat and pine nuts—and I realized just how much my mother's cooking was influenced by neighboring nations. In Galilee, artichoke season was roughly March through May. Of course, these days every vegetable is available almost all year long, but there is something poetic about eating certain foods for a short time each year. My father would buy a box of fresh artichokes for my mother, who would spend the afternoon peeling and cleaning the large, spiky vegetables in order to stuff them. I loved to help her. Using frozen artichokes is much faster—and a perfectly acceptable way to make this dish. The heart will have a slightly different texture but it is still delicious! Serve with Rice and Vermicelli Pilaf, page 204.

Clean the fresh artichokes, if using (see opposite page). Preheat the oven to 450°F.

Heat the corn oil in a large skillet over high until hot. Slide the artichokes into the pan and saute on the stem side for 3 minutes. Using tongs, turn the artichokes over and fry on the open side for 2 minutes. Transfer to a paper towel–lined tray, open end down, to drain. Arrange the artichokes, stem end down, in a large baking dish and set aside.

In a small bowl, combine the allspice, pepper, nutmeg and cardamom, if using. Heat the olive oil in a medium skillet over medium-high heat. Add the meat and half of the spice mixture, stirring to combine, and saute for 8 to 10 minutes, stirring occasionally, until the meat loses its pink color. Toss in the pine nuts and almonds, the juice of 1 lemon and the salt. Stir to thoroughly combine and turn off the heat. Divide the meat mixture among the artichokes, filling them to almost overflowing and tucking in between the leaves. Reserve any remaining meat mixture.

Add the juice of the remaining lemon and the stock to the reserved spice mixture. Drizzle the seasoned broth over the artichokes and pour the rest into the baking pan. Distribute the reserved meat mixture in the broth in the pan. Cover the pan with foil and bake for 1 hour if using fresh artichokes, 20 minutes if using frozen.

Remove the foil from the pan, reduce the heat to 300°F and bake for an additional 3 to 5 minutes, until the broth has thickened. Arrange the artichokes on individual plates with the rice and vermicelli pilaf. Garnish with the parsley and serve.

SERVES 8

8 (8-ounce) fresh artichokes or 16 to 24 frozen, depending on the size (size 8 is the largest, 24 is the smallest)

1 cup corn oil

4½ teaspoons ground allspice

½ teaspoon freshly ground black pepper

¼ teaspoon ground nutmeg

Pinch cardamom (optional)

¼ cup extra-virgin olive oil

2 pounds ground lamb from the leg or ground beef

½ to 1 cup pine nuts, toasted

½ to 1 cup slivered almonds, toasted

2 large lemons, halved

1 teaspoon sea salt

6 cups Seasoned Chicken Stock (page 100) or low-sodium chicken stock

Rice and Vermicelli Pilaf (page 204)

Chopped fresh parsley for garnish

HOW TO CLEAN FRESH ARTICHOKES

1. Working with one artichoke at a time, hold it by the stem. Using kitchen shears, snip off the top quarter inch or so of each leaf on the artichoke (this will rid it of the barbs).

2. Lay the artichoke on its side and, using a sharp knife, slice off the top inch or so of the artichoke to reveal the choke.

3. Slice off the stem at the base of the artichoke, taking care to keep it level so that it will sit up straight in the pan.

4. Using a melon baller, dig out the center, including the feathery fronds, so that the center is clean, empty and ready to be stuffed; squeeze lemon juice all over the artichoke, inside and out, to prevent it from browning. Repeat with the remaining artichokes.

Stuffed Eggplant or Squash in Tomato Sauce

BAITINJAN OR KUSA MAHSHI

To remove the eggplant flesh—or the flesh of any soft vegetable—every Middle Eastern cook has a *manara*, a long-handled scoop designed specifically for hollowing out vegetables. An iced-tea spoon will do the trick, too. Ask your butcher to grind the meat for the stuffing just once through the machine for a coarse grind. Note: This stuffing mixture is raw, so it should be used within 24 hours of preparation. Refrigerate, covered tightly, if making in advance.

Fill a large bowl with cold water. Roll an eggplant on a clean surface until it gives a bit. Using a long-handled slim spoon or apple corer, remove the flesh and discard. Drop the vegetable in the bowl of cold water and repeat with the remaining eggplants.

Make the stuffing: In a medium skillet heat the oil. Add the allspice, pepper, cinnamon and nutmeg and stir for 5 seconds. Toss in the meat and saute until it begins to change color, 4 to 5 minutes. Remove from heat and add the rice, tomato, butter and salt, stirring to thoroughly coat.

Working with one vegetable at a time, fill an eggplant with the stuffing to within 1 inch of the top of the opening (about the length of the first third of your pinky finger). Repeat with the rest of the eggplants. Arrange the stuffed eggplants in a 5-quart, heavy-bottomed pot or Dutch oven so that they are standing vertically with the open side up. Plug each opening with a piece of diced tomato. Add the pureed or crushed tomatoes to the pot followed by 1 cup water and the salt and sugar. Place the pot, uncovered, over high heat and bring to a boil. Cover and reduce the heat to medium; cook until the eggplant skins give when pierced with a fork, about 40 minutes.

Lay two or three stuffed eggplants on a plate. Slice into them lengthwise to reveal the stuffing without cutting the eggplants in half, then spoon the tomato sauce on top.

VARIATION *Add 3 chopped plum tomatoes to create a colorful stuffing for eggplant, squash or grape leaves. To make stuffed cabbage, add 3 finely chopped garlic cloves.*

SERVES 6 TO 8

16 medium Italian eggplants or 10 small eggplants, zucchini or Arabic squash (about 6 pounds, total) or a combination, stem ends trimmed and tops reserved

Meat Stuffing (see below)

1 Jersey tomato, diced into 12 pieces

4 pounds fresh tomatoes, pureed, or 1 (28-ounce) can crushed tomatoes

1 teaspoon sea salt

½ teaspoon sugar

For the Meat Stuffing

½ cup corn or extra-virgin olive oil

2 tablespoons allspice

1 teaspoon freshly ground black pepper

¼ teaspoon cinnamon

¼ teaspoon nutmeg

2½ pounds coarsely chopped lamb from the leg or shoulder or beef sirloin

1½ cups short grain rice, rinsed

2 plum or 1 beefsteak tomato, diced

6 tablespoons butter or ghee

1 tablespoon sea salt, or to taste

Stuffed Eggplant with Lamb in Lemon Sauce

BAITINJAN SHEIKH IL MAHSHI

This dish is typically served for big family celebrations but I've adjusted the recipe to serve four to six people. It takes time to prepare, but is worth every minute of effort even for a small group. My mother used to peel the skin from the eggplant every one-fourth inch or so that it appeared to be vertically striped. It's a nice touch. Add a chopped jalapeño when sauteing the onions if you want to give the dish a kick.

Using a knife or your hands, open each eggplant along its length to prepare it for stuffing. Arrange in a roasting pan and set aside.

Heat the oil in a large skillet over high heat. Add the onion and saute until golden, about 5 minutes. Add the garlic and saute until it takes on color, about 1 minute. Sprinkle in the allspice, salt, pepper, cinnamon and nutmeg and cook until fragrant, about 30 seconds. Add the meat and saute, turning occasionally, until it loses its color, 5 to 10 minutes. Stir in the pine nuts, almonds and 2 tablespoons lemon juice until thoroughly incorporated for 1 minute. Turn off the heat.

Preheat the oven to 400°F.

Divide the meat stuffing evenly among the eggplants, spooning it into the opening in each. Spoon any excess stuffing into the bottom of the pan and arrange the eggplants over it. In the same skillet, combine the remaining 6 tablespoons lemon juice with the stock, tomatoes and pomegranate molasses or tamarind paste, if using, and bring to a boil. Pour the stock into the pan with the eggplants, cover with foil and bake until a fork slides easily into the eggplants, 20 to 30 minutes. Remove the foil and roast until the eggplants brown, 3 to 5 minutes more.

Serve warm with the pilaf on the side.

VARIATION *Stuffed Eggplant in Yogurt Sauce* (*Makdous Fetti*)
Prepare the Yogurt Sauce on page 154. Place a scoop of rice on a deep platter and surround it with toasted Arabic Bread, page 61. Place the stuffed eggplant over the rice and top with the yogurt sauce.

SERVES 4 TO 6

12 medium Italian or Holland eggplants (about 6 pounds total), fried and peeled (see page 43)
¼ cup extra-virgin olive oil
1 medium yellow onion, diced
1 tablespoon finely chopped garlic
1 tablespoon ground allspice
1 teaspoon sea salt or to taste
1 teaspoon freshly ground black pepper
½ teaspoon ground cinnamon
⅓ teaspoon ground nutmeg
3 pounds chopped lamb meat from the leg or chopped beef tenderloin
½ cup pine nuts, toasted
½ cup slivered almonds
½ cup fresh lemon juice
6 cups chicken, lamb or beef stock
2 plum tomatoes, chopped
3 tablespoons pomegranate molasses, or 2 tablespoons tamarind paste (optional)
Rice and Vermicelli Pilaf (page 204)

Stuffed Grape Leaves

WARAK ANAB

I have seen friends and family eat 40 to 50 of these in one sitting! But that's because true stuffed grape leaves should be no bigger than a pinkie finger. I only recently found fresh grape leaves in a produce store near the restaurant—they're at their best when they are fresh (and always delicious with Tabouleh, page 81) but their availability is a bit random. If you do happen to find them, look for the smallest ones and be sure the surface is smooth and free of discernible fuzz. And buy extra so that you can freeze them! Of course, brined grape leaves are far easier to procure; use them if you can't find fresh.

Arrange the grape leaves in a stack, shiny side down, with the stem end facing you. If the indentations in any particular leaf are deep, close them up by overlapping the two segments or by patching them together with pieces of another leaf. Place the reserved stems in a 5-quart pot or Dutch oven.

Working with one grape leaf at a time, spoon 1 tablespoon of the stuffing onto the base of the leaf, just above the stem. Fold either side of the leaf over the stuffing and roll the leaf around itself to the tip, rolling tightly to keep the filling in. Place in the pot, arranging the rolls in concentric circles and layering them one on top of the other. Continue with the remaining leaves and filling.

Set a small, heatproof plate directly on top of the grape leaves. Pour the stock into the pot. Combine 2 cups water with the salt and add to the pot. Cover the pot and bring the liquid to a boil over high heat, then reduce the heat to medium and cook until the rice is tender and the grape leaves are soft, 1 to 1½ hours.

Remove the lid from the pot. Using an oven mitt, hold the rolls in place with the plate while draining the liquid from the pot. Remove the plate, invert a serving platter over the pot and flip it over. Discard the grape stems. Serve the grape leaves garnished with the lemon wedges.

MAKES 100 GRAPE LEAVES

2 (16-ounce) jars grape leaves, rinsed or 100 fresh, stems trimmed and reserved

Meat Stuffing (page 166)

5 cups stock from Seasoned Chicken with Stock or Seasoned Lamb with Stock (page 100 or 112) or low-sodium chicken stock or water

½ teaspoon sea salt

Lemon wedges for garnish

Stuffed Grape Leaves and Squash

KUSA WA WARAK

Kusa is summer squash and *warak*, literally translated, is "paper," or in this case, the grape leaves. My mother made this special combination of stuffed vegetables often for Sunday supper, her only day off. We always had relatives staying at my parents' home in Nazareth and the women loved to roll the grape leaves while they caught up on the latest neighborhood news. It is customary, in fact, for guests to do this task. It may seem like an enormous amount of food for six people, but I can say first hand that whenever a customer orders this at the restaurant, the plate always comes back licked clean!

> **COOKING TIP** Be sure to turn this out on a rimmed tray that is 4 inches wider than the pot you're cooking it in.

In a small bowl, combine the allspice, salt, pepper, nutmeg and cardamom, if using. Sprinkle the spice mixture all over the lamb chops and set aside.

Arrange the tomato slices in the bottom of a heavy-bottomed 5-quart pot or a Dutch oven. Lay the lamb chops over the tomatoes, with the bones pointing to the center and the meat around the rim. Arrange the squash on top, laying them on their sides, then arrange the grape leaves, in layers, on top of the squash. Add 5 cups water and salt to the pot. Set a heatproof plate on top of the grape leaves, pressing down firmly. Cover and bring to a boil over high heat. Reduce the heat to low and cook until the grape leaves are tender, 40 to 60 minutes. Add the lemon juice to the pot and return to a boil; boil for 2 minutes. Turn off the heat and let rest for 5 minutes.

Remove the lid and plate and invert a rimmed serving platter over the pot. Flip it over and serve immediately, garnished with the lemon wedges.

SERVES 6

1 teaspoon ground allspice

1 teaspoon sea salt, plus more for the pot

½ teaspoon freshly ground black pepper

½ teaspoon ground nutmeg

Pinch ground cardamom (optional)

8 lamb chops (about 3½ pounds total), trimmed

2 Jersey tomatoes, sliced ¼ inch thick

Stuffed Squash (page 166), uncooked

Stuffed Grape Leaves (page 169), uncooked

Juice of 2 lemons

Lemon wedges for garnish

Stuffed Cabbage

MALFOOF

I know how strange this may sound, but the cabbage at home is more, well, more cabbagey than the heads I find in the States. It is partly, I suppose, because it is never watered except by the rain. Whenever I make this dish, I am reminded of the huge cabbage I once spotted in a market in Jersusalem. This cabbage was 2½ feet across—enough to feed more than a village! I carried it from Jerusalem to Tarshiha. When I arrived, I invited every friend and family member to come for a dinner with a menu based on that one vegetable alone! Here in the States, I have had success stuffing white cabbage leaves. You can make the rolls a day in advance and cook them the next day and serve with a bowl of yogurt for sharing. I often pair the rolls with a favorite salad of shredded cabbage dressed in lemon juice, olive oil and garlic. Note: This stuffing mixture is raw, so it should be used within 24 hours of preparation. Refrigerate, covered tightly, if making the stuffing in advance.

Using a sharp knife, cut away the tough ribs from each boiled cabbage leaf and reserve them, stacking the leaves as you go. Place the ribs in a 5-quart, heavy-bottomed pot. Arrange the lamb chops on top, then add the halved garlic heads to the pot.

Make the stuffing: In a medium skillet, heat the oil. Add the allspice, pepper, cinnamon and nutmeg and stir for 5 seconds. Toss in the meat and saute for 4 to 5 minutes, until it begins to change color. Remove from the heat and add the rice, ghee, garlic and salt.

Working with one cabbage leaf at a time, place it on a clean work surface with the stem end facing you. Place 1 tablespoon of the stuffing in the center of the leaf. Fold either side of the leaf over the stuffing and roll the leaf up to the tip, rolling tightly to keep the filling in. Arrange the rolls in concentric circles over the lamb chops, then stack in layers on top of each other. Place a heatproof plate directly on top of the rolls and press down firmly. Pour 3 cups water into the pot, turn the heat to high and bring to a boil. Reduce the heat to low and simmer until a fork inserted into the cabbage leaf doesn't resist, 40 to 60 minutes.

In a small bowl, combine the chopped garlic with the lemon juice. Pour the mixture into the pot, cover, and return to a boil; boil for 1 minute. Remove the pot from the heat, then remove the lid. Wearing an oven mitt and holding the rolls in place with the plate, pour the liquid from the pot. Invert a serving platter over the pot and flip it over. Leave the pot on the rolls for a few minutes to allow them to settle. Remove the pot and the ribs from the top of the layers. Serve the lamb chops and cabbage rolls with lemon wedges.

BOILED CABBAGE

Fill a stockpot large enough to hold a single cabbage with enough water to cover and bring to a boil over high heat. Drop the cabbage into the pot, core side up. As the cabbage boils, the core will soften. Plunge a long fork into the core; when the core is soft enough for the fork to just reach the middle of the cabbage, boil for 3 minutes more. The cabbage should be *al dente* and the leaves should be separating but not mushy. Transfer to a colander to cool.

SERVES 4

2 large white cabbages (about 4½ pounds each), boiled (see above)
4 to 6 lamb chops or pieces of lamb shoulder on the bone (2½ to 3 pounds total)
2 heads garlic, halved
5 cloves garlic, finely chopped
½ cup fresh lemon juice
Lemon wedges for garnish

For the *Hashwi* Stuffing
½ cup corn oil
3 tablespoons allspice
1 tablespoon freshly ground black pepper
⅓ teaspoon cinnamon
⅓ teaspoon nutmeg
2½ pounds coarsely chopped lamb from the leg or shoulder
2½ cups short-grain rice, washed
⅓ cup ghee or butter
1 tablespoon garlic (or a bit more if you love it!)
1 tablespoon sea salt

Rice with Lamb and Pine Nuts

MANSAAF

Every region in the Middle East has its own version of this dish, which is invariably a part of every wedding feast. In Jordan, the Bedouin version is cooked with dry yogurt (which is made by boiling yogurt and removing the liquid that floats to the top; it is then strained, shaped into balls and left outside in the sun to dry completely) and rice with few, if any, spices. In Galilee, cooks make it with various spices and always nuts. It is always served on a *sidir*, which, literally translated, is Arabic for a large round tray—a symbol that there's a party going on. *Mansaaf* is the traditional stuffing for a whole roasted lamb, but that's a recipe for another cookbook! I've come to change my mind about stuffing the mixture inside the lamb—it takes away the juiciness of the meat. So I cook them separately and use the fat from the lamb in the stuffing.

In a small bowl, combine the allspice, cardamom, black pepper, nutmeg, and cinnamon; set aside.

In a large skillet, heat the corn oil over medium-high heat. Add the lamb and half the spice mixture and saute, stirring to coat the meat all over with the spices. Remove from the heat and set aside.

In a 5-quart Dutch oven, heat the ghee over high until hot. Stir in the rice to coat the grains all over, and saute until the grains begin to turn pearly white, 3 to 5 minutes. Add the remaining spice mixture, lamb, pine nuts, almonds and boiling water to the pot. Bring to a boil, reduce the heat and simmer, covered, until the rice is cooked, 11 to 12 minutes. Serve warm.

VARIATION To make an express mansaaf, *saute 2 pounds of chopped boneless, skinless chicken breast in ¼ cup extra-virgin olive oil until it loses its pink color. Use 6 cups water or low-sodium chicken broth in place of the stock. Proceed with the recipe as above.*

SERVES 8 TO 10

4¾ teaspoons ground allspice

⅓ teaspoon ground cardamom or 3 cardamom pods, finely ground

1 teaspoon freshly ground black pepper

⅓ teaspoon ground nutmeg

⅓ teaspoon ground cinnamon

3 tablespoons corn oil

Seasoned Lamb with Stock (page 112), lamb cooled and pulled from the bones

¼ cup ghee, butter or corn oil

4 cups Egyptian rice

1 cup pine nuts

1 cup slivered almonds

6 cups boiling water

Kafta

Kafta is common and popular across North Africa, throughout the Middle East (*kefte* or *kufta*) and in Greece (*keftedes*), Turkey, Iran, and all the way to India (*kofta*). The name, in all its variations, is derived from *kuftan*, which means "to grind" in Farsi. Every country, town, village, indeed, every cook, has a version of *kafta*. It is prepared in myriad ways—it can be baked, broiled, boiled, grilled, fried, steamed, poached or simply spread on a sheet pan, rolled into balls or folded into thirds over a filling like a crepe. Many believe *kafta* is Turkish in origin, but Syrians from Aleppo believe they are the best at making it. If using lamb, select meat from the leg only; the shoulder is too fatty.

In a large bowl, combine the meat with the onion, tomato, parsley, pepper, salt, allspice, nutmeg, and cumin, if using, and mix together with your hands. Transfer to a clean work surface and knead the mixture with your hands until smooth. Shape according to recipe instructions.

SERVES 6 TO 8

1½ pounds each beef and lamb, coarsely ground, or 3 pounds total of either
1 large yellow onion, finely chopped
1 plum tomato, finely diced
1 cup chopped fresh parsley
1 tablespoon freshly ground black pepper
1 tablespoon sea salt or to taste
4½ teaspoons ground allspice
¼ teaspoon ground nutmeg
¼ teaspoon ground cumin (optional)

Tomato Sauce

I created the very versatile tomato sauce for several dishes on the Tanoreen menu. It is wonderful for stewing okra and on the occasion when my daughter is craving pasta, I add a tablespoon of chopped basil to the sauce and ladle it over the spaghetti. It's also great for ladling over roasted chicken, meat or fish. The sauce freezes beautifully. Pour any leftover sauce into a resealable plastic bag and freeze up to four months. Add a pinch of cumin and allspice when you reheat it; freezing can sometimes diminish the potency of spices. For a milder version, eliminate the poblano or jalapeño. You'll notice derivations of this tomato sauce are part of my String Bean and Tomato Stew, page 111, and White Bean and Beef Stew, page 116.

In a large skillet, heat the oil over medium-high heat. Toss in the shallots and saute 3 to 4 minutes. Add the poblano and saute 2 minutes. Add the garlic and saute until soft, about 1 minute. Stir in the cumin, allspice, black pepper and salt and saute until fragrant, 30 seconds. Toss in the fresh tomatoes and cook, stirring occasionally, until the tomatoes soften and release their juices, 4 to 5 minutes. Stir in the tomato paste, crushed tomatoes, sugar or lemon juice, and 2 cups water. Bring to a boil, stirring occasionally. Reduce the heat and simmer until the sauce has thickened slightly, about 10 minutes.

MAKES 1½ QUARTS (ENOUGH TO SERVE 10)

½ cup extra-virgin olive oil
2 shallots, or 1 small yellow onion, finely chopped
1 poblano, or 2 jalapeños chile peppers, finely chopped
6 cloves garlic, finely chopped
1 teaspoon ground cumin
1 teaspoon ground allspice
1 teaspoon freshly ground black pepper
Sea salt to taste
4 beefsteak tomatoes, or 8 plum tomatoes (about 3 pounds total), chopped
1 tablespoon tomato paste
1 (16-ounce) can crushed tomatoes
1 teaspoon sugar, or ¼ cup fresh lemon juice

Kafta with Tahini Sauce or Tomato Sauce

KAFTA BIL TAHINA OR KAFTA BIL BANDOORA

My mother always divided the *kafta* and prepared half with tahini sauce and half with tomato sauce. It's a great way to enjoy both—and the extra sauce will keep in the refrigerator for another use. Tahini sauce is a classic topping for a tray of baked *kafta*; this recipe is the most common preparation all over the Middle East.

Preheat the oven to 450°F. Grease a 12 by 20-inch baking sheet with olive oil and set aside.

Spread the *kafta* meat evenly into the bottom of the baking sheet, pushing it out to the edges. Using the side of your hand, make slight indentations in the meat in a grid pattern to outline eight servings. Spread 3 tablespoons olive oil all over the meat with your hands. Bake until the meat has lost its pink color, about 20 minutes. Remove the pan from the oven and reduce the heat to 300°F if roasting the potatoes.

If frying the potatoes, heat the corn oil in a large, high-sided skillet over high until hot. Working in batches, if necessary, carefully slip the potatoes into the skillet and fry, turning once, until golden brown, about 4 minutes total. Using a slotted spoon, transfer the potatoes to paper towels or brown paper bags to drain. Alternatively, brush them all over with the oil, arrange in a single layer on a baking sheet and roast in the oven until golden, about 20 minutes.

Cut the *kafta* along the scored markings but leave in the pan. Top with the potato slices and drizzle the tahini or tomato sauce all over. Return the pan to the oven and bake for 5 minutes more. Serve warm.

SERVES 6 TO 8

3 tablespoons extra-virgin olive oil, plus more for the pan

Kafta (see opposite page)

2 cups corn oil for frying

3 baking potatoes, peeled, halved lengthwise and sliced crosswise into ¼-inch half moons

Thick Tahini Sauce (page 221) or Tomato Sauce (see opposite)

Tanoreen *Kafta* Roll

Most Middle Eastern cooks make this the traditional way, with traditional tahini sauce, but I thought it could use the sweet-sour tang that comes from pomegranate molasses and a spicy kick from chile paste. The sauce is delicious on any grilled meats, roasts and even drizzled over baked potatoes. Serve this alongside Rice and Vermicelli Pilaf (page 204) or roasted carrots and potatoes.

Heat 2 tablespoons oil in a large skillet. Add the onions and saute until soft and golden, 8 to 10 minutes. Remove 2 tablespoons of the onions to set aside. To the skillet, add the tomatoes and all but 2 tablespoons of the parsley, the sumac, pepper, garlic and lemon juice. Stir to thoroughly combine, then remove from the heat.

Preheat the oven to 450°F. Place a 9-inch square of waxed paper on a clean work surface. Working with 1 cup of *kafta* at a time, roll into a ball. Put the ball in one hand and, with the open palm of your other hand, flatten the ball by exerting pressure on it. Place on the waxed paper and shape into a 7-inch round. Spoon 3 tablespoons of the stuffing down the center. Slide your hand under the waxed paper to fold one third of the patty over the stuffing, then fold the opposite third over to completely enclose the stuffing.

Transfer to a baking sheet and repeat with the remaining meat mixture and filling, making a total of 6 to 8 pieces (use ⅔ to ¾ cup meat to make smaller patties, if desired). Bake until cooked through and no longer pink, 10 to 15 minutes. Drizzle the spicy tahini sauce all over the patties and return to the oven for 3 to 5 minutes more. Sprinkle with the toasted nuts and reserved onions and serve warm.

SERVES 8 TO 10

5 tablespoons extra-virgin olive oil
4 medium yellow onions, finely chopped
3 plum tomatoes, chopped
½ cup chopped fresh parsley
1 tablespoon sumac
1 teaspoon freshly ground black pepper
1 teaspoon finely chopped garlic
Juice of 1 lemon
Kafta (page 174)
Spicy Tahini Sauce (page 221)
1 cup slivered almonds or pine nuts, toasted

Kibbeh in the Tray

KIBBEH BIL SINIYAH

Named for the round pan that it is traditionally baked in, this dish is very popular throughout the Middle East, and is the way that Lebanese and Syrians typically eat kibbeh. It is lovely served with yogurt, Tomato Salad, page 77, and some olives.

Preheat the oven to 450°F. Brush a 15-inch-wide round rimmed baking tray or a 4-quart baking dish with some of the oil from the *hossi*.

Press half the kibbeh into the tray, spreading it all the way to the edge and smoothing with your hand so that the surface is level. Spread the strained *hossi* mixture all over the kibbeh, making sure to cover the outer edges. Spread the remaining kibbeh over the *hossi* out to the edges by dipping your hands in cold water and smoothing it out. Using a knife, slice through only the top layer of the kibbeh on a diagonal, scoring it in 2½-inch-wide sections. Bake until the meat takes on color and is cooked through, 20 to 30 minutes.

Hossi (page 54), oil strained and reserved
Kibbeh (page 37)

Kafta-Stuffed Grape Leaves

This dish is often celebrated as a Jerusalem specialty, but it actually traces back to Aleppo, Syria. I first discovered it when I visited a friend in Jerusalem. She made it for us, and being a fan of grape leaves, I was immediately hooked. I couldn't wait to share the recipe with my mom, and fortunately, grape leaves were in season, so we had the freshest ones to use.

This dish is a beautiful example of how regional dishes evolve and travel. Back in the day, people cooked with what was in season. There were no imported ingredients—just local, fresh produce that defined the flavors of our food.

In a large bowl, combine the ground meat, onion, shallots, chopped tomato, parsley, cilantro, and poblano pepper. Add ½ teaspoon of the Tanoreen Spice. Season with 1 teaspoon of salt (or to taste). Mix thoroughly, using your hands or a spatula, until the ingredients are well blended, then knead the mixture with your hands to ensure its evenly mixed.

Line the base of a Dutch oven or deep, round baking dish with a single layer of sliced potatoes. Sprinkle them with salt. Add a layer of sliced tomatoes on top of the potatoes. Repeat until you have used all of the potatoes and tomatoes, and the base of the pan is covered. Sprinkle the remaining ½ teaspoon of Tanoreen Spice over the layers and drizzle with 2 tablespoons of the lemon juice.

Drain and rinse the jarred grape leaves. Boil the jarred or fresh leaves in water for 2 minutes to soften, then drain and let them cool before using.

Divide the meat mixture into teaspoon-sized balls. Place a ball in the center of a grape leaf, then flatten it with your palm or a spatula to form a 2-inch circle. Wrap the grape leaf around the meat, folding the sides over first, then the top and bottom, creating a flat, round parcel. Arrange the filled grape leaves seam-side down in the pot or dish, layering them on top of the tomato slices. Repeat with the remaining filling and grape leaves.

Preheat the oven to 350°F.

In a jug, combine the remaining 2 tablespoons of lemon juice with the water or stock, minced garlic, and olive oil. Pour this mixture evenly over the layered grape leaves. Set a small, heatproof plate directly on top of the grape leaves to hold them in place, then cover the pot or dish.

Bake for 20 minutes, then lower the temperature to 200°F and bake for an additional 10 minutes, until the meat filling is cooked. To serve, remove the lid from the pot. Using an oven mitt, hold the vine leaves in place with the plate and drain the liquid from the pot. Remove the plate, invert a serving platter over the pot and flip it over, to serve with the potatoes and tomatoes on top.

Serve warm, with fresh bread, a tomato salad, or plain yogurt with mint.

SERVES 4

- 1 pound ground lamb, beef, or a mixture (I use lamb)
- 1 onion, finely chopped
- 2 shallots, finely chopped
- 1 tomato, chopped
- ¼ cup chopped parsley
- ¼ cup chopped cilantro
- 1 poblano pepper, finely chopped
- 1 teaspoon Tanoreen Spice (page 225) or allspice
- 4 large potatoes, sliced
- 2 tomatoes, sliced
- 4 tablespoons lemon juice
- One 1-pound jar grape leaves, drained (or 60 to 70 fresh leaves)
- 2 cups water or stock
- 4 garlic cloves, minced
- ¼ cup olive oil
- Salt

Upside-Down Lamb and Vegetables

MAKLOOBEH

When Jumana was a graduate student in Cairo, she and her roommates would often cook the national dishes from their respective countries for each other. Her Egyptian friends prepared *koshari*, a dish of lentils, rice, pasta, tomatoes and onion. Her Jordanian roommate made *mansaaf*, page 173, that country's national dish. Jumana prepared *makloobeh*, the impressive Palestinian lamb dish meant to feed a crowd. The exact translation of *makloobeh* in Arabic is "upside down," because the pot, filled with layers of rice, meat and vegetables, is flipped over onto a rimmed platter. Serve with plain yogurt or Tomato Salad, page 77. Leftovers keep, tightly covered, in the refrigerator for up to one week.

In a large skillet, heat the ghee and the oil over high heat. Toss in the onions and saute until they are soft and golden, 7 to 10 minutes. Add the garlic cloves and stir until they begin to take on color. Stir in the rice until the kernels are no longer translucent, 3 to 5 minutes. Add the allspice, salt, pepper, nutmeg, cumin, and cardomom, if using, and stir until fragrant, about 30 seconds. Turn off the heat.

In a medium pot, bring the lamb stock to a boil.

Meanwhile, in a low, wide, heavy-bottomed 5-quart pot with a tight-fitting lid, arrange the carrot slices in concentric circles, beginning in the center and working your way out. Arrange the tomato slices on top of the carrots. Spoon the lamb over the tomatoes and top with the eggplant. Cover with the rice mixture. Pour in 6 cups lamb stock, the pomegranate molasses and the soy sauce, if using, to the pot. Cover and bring to a boil over high heat. Reduce the heat to low and simmer until the rice has absorbed all of the liquid and is cooked through, about 30 minutes. If the rice remains undercooked, drizzle additional broth over it, ½ cup at a time, until the rice is cooked to desired texture. Turn off the heat and let stand, covered, for 5 to 10 minutes.

Remove the lid and place a serving platter 4 inches wider than the pot over it. Flip the pot and gently remove it. Scatter the pine nuts and almonds over the top. Serve warm.

VARIATION *From the outside, all* makloobeh *looks the same, but the vegetable layer leaves room for surprises—and lots of opportunity for interpretation. Some of my favorite combinations are:*

Use Seasoned Chicken with Stock, page 100 or Seasoned Beef with Stock, page 112, with 4 to 5 pounds roasted or fried cauliflower florets, in place of the eggplant.

Use Seasoned Lamb with Stock, page 112, with 4 pounds sauteed fresh fava beans or 4 pounds sweet peas (add 1 teaspoon turmeric to the spice mixture when making the rice) in place of the eggplant.

SERVES 6 TO 8

¼ cup ghee

⅓ cup extra-virgin olive oil

3 yellow onions, halved and sliced into half moons

10 cloves garlic, peeled

4 cups Egyptian rice

1 tablespoon ground allspice

1 tablespoon sea salt

1 teaspoon freshly ground black pepper

⅓ teaspoon ground nutmeg

½ teaspoon ground cumin

Pinch ground cardamom (optional)

8 cups stock and the meat from Seasoned Lamb with Stock (page 112), meat cut into cubes

2 carrots, sliced crosswise on the diagonal into ¼-inch-thick slices

2 beefsteak tomatoes, thinly sliced crosswise into ¼-inch-thick slices

4 medium eggplants, sliced crosswise into ½-inch-thick rounds, fried or roasted (see page 43)

¼ cup pomegranate molasses

3 tablespoons dark soy sauce (optional)

½ cup pine nuts, fried (see page 26)

½ cup slivered almonds, fried (see page 29)

Layered Rice with Lamb and Vegetables

KABSAH

Kabsah, literally translated, means "pressed." In this dish, rice, vegetables, meat, and spices pressed together in one pot to cook. Methods for cooking this dish vary in different regions of the Arab world. In the Arabian Gulf, it is loved for its simplicity and was traditionally cooked in earthenware pots underground. I first tried it in the desert of Qatar and was determined to recreate it at home. After experimenting with my own spice blend, I finally achieved the flavors and aromas I remembered. Don't be deterred by the number of ingredients in the recipe! Adding many herbs and spices is definitely a defining feature of my cooking style. If you find a dish you like, try to recreate it at home and adjust the spices and herbs to add your own twist. I do this often and you should too. It makes cooking fun and personal.

At Tanoreen, we serve this dish with lamb, but you can also use beef or chicken. I have even made it with shrimp. Look for dried lemons/limes in Middle Eastern and Persian grocery stores.

In a small bowl, steep the saffron in ½ cup warm water for 10 minutes.

Meanwhile, in another small bowl, combine the turmeric, cardamom, cloves, coriander, cumin, nutmeg, fennel, ginger, black pepper, cinnamon and 1 tablespoon of salt. Massage one third of the spice blend into the lamb cubes, ensuring all sides are coated.

In an extra-large pot, heat the olive oil over high heat. Sear the lamb on all sides until browned, to lock in the juices. Add 12 cups of water to the pot and bring to a boil. Season with 1 teaspoon of salt (or to your liking). Reduce the heat, and simmer the lamb until cooked through and tender, about 60 minutes (50 minutes if using beef, 45 minutes for chicken). Drain the lamb, reserving the broth (you should have about 10 cups). Wipe the pot clean and set aside.

In a large sauté pan, heat the vegetable oil over medium heat. Add the onions, shallots and jalapeños, and sauté until the onions are translucent, about 10 minutes. Add the garlic and sauté for a minute until fragrant, then add the celery, carrots, scallions, and cilantro. Cover the pot and cook on low heat for about 5 minutes, or until the carrots start to soften. Add the tomatoes, artichoke hearts, mushrooms, and tomato paste. Cover again and cook for 10 more minutes, until the tomatoes break down. Remove from the heat.

Meanwhile, place 8 cups of the reserved broth in a pot and bring to a boil. Add the basmati rice, return to a boil, and then reduce the heat to low. Stir the rice once, cover and cook for 10 minutes, or until the rice is partially cooked, but still retains some bite. Drain the rice and set aside.

Spread 1 tablespoon of the ghee evenly on the bottom of your extra-large pot. Line the bottom and sides of the pot (about 4 inches high) with pita bread or filo sheets. Brush the remaining ghee over the bread or filo sheets.

SERVES 6 TO 8

1 teaspoon saffron

1 teaspoon turmeric

½ teaspoon cardamom

5 cloves

1 tablespoon coriander

1 tablespoon cumin

¼ teaspoon nutmeg

½ teaspoon fennel

1 teaspoon ginger

1 teaspoon black pepper

½ teaspoon cinnamon

4 pounds lamb from the leg or shoulder, cut into 2-inch cubes

2 tablespoons olive oil

4 tablespoons vegetable oil

2 onions, chopped

5 shallots, chopped

2 jalapeños, chopped (leave whole if you prefer a milder dish)

6 cloves garlic, chopped

4 stalks celery, peeled and chopped

2 carrots, peeled and sliced into half moons

1 bunch scallions, chopped (1½ packed cups)

1 bunch cilantro, chopped (1½ packed cups)

4 plum tomatoes, or 2 beefsteak tomatoes, diced

10 artichoke hearts, sliced (frozen or canned will work)

2 cups baby portobella mushrooms, cleaned and sliced

1 tablespoon tomato paste

4 cups basmati rice

2 tablespoons ghee or butter, melted

6 pieces Arabic Bread (page 61), or 1 (16-ounce) package filo pastry, thawed

6 dried lemons/limes (*lumi* or *limu*)

Salt

Begin layering your *kabsah*: Spread about one-quarter of the par-cooked rice on top of the bread or filo at the bottom. Add about one-third of the sautéed vegetables, followed by 2 dried lemons/limes and about 7 pieces of lamb. Sprinkle a bit of the remaining spice mix over the layer. Repeat the layering process (rice, vegetables, dried lemons/limes, meat and spices) until you have at least three layers, ending with a layer of rice. Sprinkle the saffron water over the top layer of rice.

Pour the remaining 2 cups of lamb broth over the layers in the pot. Bring to a boil, then reduce the heat to low, cover the pot and simmer for 25 minutes, or until the rice is tender.

When you are ready to serve, remove the lid and place a large, flat serving tray over the pot. Carefully flip the pot to invert the dish onto the tray, with the crispy bread or filo on top. Serve hot, accompanied by a fresh salad and plain yogurt.

Spiced Lamb Shank

MOZZAT MHAMMARA

This is most certainly a Tanoreen dish. We rarely, if ever, prepared lamb shanks in Nazareth, because when we purchased lamb, we got the whole animal, which meant there were only four shanks for a family of seven. The meat on this part of the lamb is particularly tough—it is full of connective tissue that, when cooked over low heat for a long time, tenderizes the meat. Though the meat braises for three hours, very little of this time is active cooking time—and the meat falls right off the bone. Serve with Rice and Vermicelli Pilaf, page 204, or Basmati Vegetable Rice, page 205.

Preheat the oven to 500°F. In a small bowl, combine the allspice, black pepper, cardamom, cinnamon, nutmeg and cumin. Rub half the spice mixture all over the lamb shanks.

In a large skillet, heat ½ cup oil over medium-high heat. Working in batches, sear the shanks all over, about 3 to 5 minutes per side. Remove the shanks to a plate. Toss in the onions to the skillet and saute until soft and golden, 3 minutes. Add the remaining spice mixture and garlic and saute, stirring, until fragrant, about 1 minute. Stir in the basil, parsley and cilantro and cook until the herbs begin to turn color, 2 to 3 minutes. Add the tomatoes and saute, stirring occasionally, until they become soft, 5 to 7 minutes. Stir in the lemon juice and salt and turn off the heat.

Place the potatoes, carrots and chile peppers, if using, in a large deep roasting pan, and brush them with the remaining ½ cup oil. Roast the vegetables for 10 minutes, tossing once halfway through. Remove the pan from the oven and arrange the shanks on top of the vegetables. Using a large spoon, place a scoop of the remaining onion and spice mixture on top of each shank. Fill the pan halfway with hot water, cover the shanks with waxed paper and cover the pan tightly with foil. Bake for 1 hour, check the water level and fill to halfway again if some of the water has evaporated. Reduce the oven temperature to 400°F and bake for 1 hour more. Check the water level and add enough water to return it to its original level; bake for a final hour or until the meat falls easily off the bone.

To serve, place each lamb shank on a plate and spoon the vegetables next to it.

SERVES 6 TO 8

2 tablespoons ground allspice

1 tablespoon freshly ground black pepper

½ teaspoon ground cardamom

½ teaspoon ground cinnamon

½ teaspoon ground nutmeg

1 teaspoon ground cumin

6 large lamb shanks, fat trimmed and discarded

1 cup olive or corn oil

2 yellow onions, chopped

6 cloves garlic, finely chopped

1 cup chopped fresh basil

½ cup chopped fresh parsley

1 cup chopped fresh cilantro

6 plum tomatoes, or 3 beefsteak tomatoes, chopped

½ cup fresh lemon juice

1 tablespoon sea salt

6 baking potatoes, peeled, halved lengthwise, and sliced into ¼-inch-thick half moons

2 carrots, halved lengthwise and sliced into ¼-inch-thick half moons

2 chile peppers, seeded and finely chopped (optional)

Freekeh with Lamb

FREEKEH BEL LAHMEH

Long considered peasant food in the Middle East, freekeh, or smoked green wheat berries, has become quite fashionable on menus not only in that region but also here in the States. Its smoky, toasted flavor is wonderfully compatible with lamb and nuts, a combination my mother used to amp up by using not just the standard almonds and pine nuts as I do here, but by scattering walnuts on top, as well. She always served freekeh with plain yogurt and Tomato Salad, page 77. Fattoush, page 78, makes a nice accompaniment, too.

> **COOKING TIP** I like the wheat to be *al dente*, like risotto, but if you prefer it slightly softer, add more stock to the pot once the initial 6 cups is absorbed and cook until the grains have soaked it all in.

Heat the olive oil in a large pot over medium heat until hot but not smoking. Toss in the onion and saute until softened and fragrant, 3 to 4 minutes. Add the garlic and saute 1 minute more. Add the allspice, pepper, cardamom, if using, and nutmeg and cook, stirring, until fragrant, about 30 seconds. Stir in the freekeh to thoroughly coat with the spice mixture, about 2 minutes. Add the seasoned meat and 6 cups of the stock, raise the heat to high and bring to a boil. Reduce the heat to medium and simmer for 15 minutes or until the freekeh absorbs all of the liquid. If the grains are not cooked enough to your liking, add stock by the ½ cup and cook, covered, until it is absorbed.

Spoon the freekeh and lamb mixture onto a large platter, scatter the almonds and pine nuts on top and serve.

SERVES 8

⅔ cup extra-virgin olive oil
1 yellow onion, diced
3 to 4 cloves garlic, finely chopped
1 tablespoon ground allspice
1 teaspoon freshly ground black pepper
⅓ teaspoon ground cardamom (optional)
¼ teaspoon ground nutmeg
3 cups freekeh (smoked and cracked green wheat)
Seasoned Lamb or Beef with Stock (page 112)
½ cup slivered almonds, fried (see page 29)
¼ cup pine nuts, fried (see page 26)

Baked Eggplant with Lamb

SINNIYAT BAITINJAN

The Greeks have their moussaka, the Italians have their lasagna—in the Middle East we have *sinniyat baitinjan*. This casserole is comfort food at its best, a great family dish and one of the most popular at Tanoreen. I have customers who have been ordering it faithfully for the last fourteen years. The key to a succulent *sinniyat baitinjan* is to season it properly with the cumin and cover the meat entirely with the eggplant to prevent it from drying out. Serve with Rice and Vermicelli Pilaf, page 204.

Heat the oil in a large pot over high heat until hot. Toss in the onions and cook until golden, about 3 minutes. Add the garlic and cook until fragrant, about 2 minutes. Stir in the allspice, coriander, cumin, if using, pepper, nutmeg, and cinnamon and saute until fragrant, about 30 seconds. Add the meat and saute, turning occasionally, until it loses its color, 7 to 10 minutes. Pour in the chopped tomatoes and lemon juice and cook until the tomatoes soften and release their juices, 3 to 5 minutes. Sprinkle in the salt and turn off the heat. Stir in the pine nuts and almonds until thoroughly incorporated. Set aside 1 heaping tablespoon of the meat mixture in a small bowl.

Preheat the oven to 450°F. Arrange the potato slices in a single layer in a 4-quart baking dish. Spread a third of the meat mixture over the potatoes and top with a single layer of the eggplant slices, followed by half of the remaining meat mixture. Top with a second layer of eggplant followed by the remaining meat. Top with a final layer of eggplant.

In a medium bowl, combine the reserved meat mixture with the stock and the bouillon and stir until the bouillon dissolves. Drizzle the mixture all over the top of eggplant. Arrange the plum tomato slices in a single layer on top and drizzle all over with oil. Cover with foil and bake for 30 minutes. Uncover, reduce the heat to 300°F and bake until the tomatoes darken, about 20 minutes more. Serve warm with rice and vermicelli pilaf.

VARIATION *This is a great way to transform any leftover* sinniyat *into a new dish altogether. Arrange whole toasted Arabic breads, page 61, on top of the tomatoes to cover. Combine 2 cups yogurt with 3 chopped cloves of garlic, the juice of 1 lemon, 2 tablespoons tahini, 2 tablespoons chopped fresh mint or 1 tablespoon dried (optional), and salt to taste. Thoroughly mix together. Spread on top of the bread and bake at 450°F until heated through, about 20 minutes.*

SERVES 6 TO 8

⅓ cup extra-virgin olive oil, plus more for drizzling

2 yellow onions, chopped

3 cloves garlic, finely chopped

4½ teaspoons ground allspice

1 teaspoon ground coriander

½ teaspoon ground cumin (optional)

½ teaspoon black pepper

⅓ teaspoon ground nutmeg

¼ teaspoon ground cinnamon

2½ to 3 pounds lean beef or lamb from the leg, chopped

2 ripe beefsteak tomatoes, chopped

Juice of 2 lemons

1 tablespoon sea salt

½ cup pine nuts, toasted

½ slivered almonds, toasted

4 baking potatoes, peeled and sliced crosswise into ¼-inch-thick slices, fried or roasted (see page 117)

4 Italian eggplants (3½ to 4 pounds total), peeled and slice lengthwise into ½-inch-thick slices and fried or roasted (see page 43)

2 cups low-sodium chicken, beef or lamb stock or water

1 tablespoon powdered chicken bouillon

5 plum tomatoes, thinly sliced

Rice and Vermicelli Pilaf (page 204) for serving

Beef-Baked Spaghetti

SINNIYAT MACARONA

My mother rarely made pasta, but when she did, this was one of her go-to dishes. Back then, I much preferred the noodles with plain tomato sauce, but through the years, I have embellished her version to my own taste and love it as much as my husband always has. Unlike my mother, his mother made pasta quite often.

> **COOKING TIP** If using *akawi*, a soft, white salty cheese, taste it to test its saltiness. If it is too salty for your taste, boil it for 10 to 15 minutes and rinse under cold water. *Akawi* is available in Middle Eastern grocery stores and some specialty markets. You can use any cheese you like, so long as it is a good melting variety.

Fill a large pot with water and add the salt and a drop of olive oil. Bring to a boil over high heat. Add the spaghetti and cook for 7 to 10 minutes, until *al dente*. Drain and transfer the spaghetti to a 9 by 14-inch baking dish. Preheat the oven to 500°F.

In a large pot, heat ½ cup olive oil over medium-high heat. Toss in the shallots and saute until they are soft and golden, about 3 minutes. Add the garlic and saute until fragrant and soft, 30 seconds. Stir in the allspice and pepper, then add the bay leaves. Add the crushed tomatoes, tomato paste and stock. Bring to a simmer and continue to simmer for 5 minutes. Pour in the meat, bring to a boil and continue to boil for 3 to 5 minutes; the sauce will thicken slightly. Remove from the heat.

Drizzle the remaining ½ cup oil over the spaghetti in the baking dish. Slide the spaghetti into the oven and at the same time, toast the Arabic bread for 5 minutes, tossing twice during toasting to evenly brown. Remove the spaghetti and reduce the heat to 350°F. Spoon the sauce and meat over the spaghetti and stir until thoroughly incorporated. Cover with aluminum foil and bake for 20 to 30 minutes. Remove the foil and scatter the cheese on top of the spaghetti. Return to the oven and bake until the cheese is melted and golden brown, about 5 minutes. Let rest for at least 5 minutes to allow the casserole to firm up before cutting.

SERVES 6 TO 8

½ teaspoon sea salt

1 cup extra-virgin olive oil plus a drop for the pasta pot

2 pounds thick spaghetti (#8 or #9)

3 shallots, finely chopped

8 cloves garlic, finely chopped

1 tablespoon ground allspice

1 teaspoon freshly ground black pepper

5 bay leaves

1 (28-ounce) can crushed tomatoes

1 (16-ounce) can tomato paste

3 cups stock and the meat from Seasoned Beef with Stock, page 112, meat cut into 1-inch cubes

Arabic Bread (page 61)

1½ pounds *akawi* (not in brine), mozzarella or halloumi, grated

SIDES

Straight from the Earth

Long before I opened Tanoreen, I understood the importance—and beauty—of cooking with pure ingredients that came straight from the earth. Growing up in Nazareth, my family—in fact most families—cooked food gathered from their own backyards. Depending on the time of year, every garden behind every home in our neighborhood was dotted with pomegranate, lemon and tangerine trees. Almost everyone had an ample grapevine, too. My parents' garden bore enormous red tomatoes, fava beans, grassy dandelion greens, squash and cucumbers along with a tiny grove of apricot, walnut and fig trees. My mother planted her own fragrant basil, refreshing peppermint and tangy scallions. Some of our neighbors raised goats and generously shared the fresh yogurt and cheese that they made with the milk.

If we didn't grow it and a neighbor or family member didn't either, we journeyed to the local grocer or farmers' market, where there was no such thing as processed food. Everything on offer was organic. But there were two items that we never bought: olives and olive oil. We picked, cured and pressed the olives ourselves. While my mother used these fresh ingredients in every part of the meal, she reserved the simplest preparations for the vegetable and grain side dishes that accompanied every meal.

When I moved to the States, I was determined to cook the way my mother did, with the freshest ingredients I could find. And while my backyard garden in Brooklyn is only a shadow of the one I grew up with (and without olive trees!), and the wheat harvest is a faint memory, I am lucky to live in an area in which I have easy access to farmers' markets, organic produce stores and artisanal food purveyors. Nothing takes me back home quite like a visit to the farmers' market, where the string beans, dandelion greens, kale, okra, and tomatoes—to name a few of the vegetables I cook so very often—conjure memories of the pride my mother took in making delicious dishes from such humble vegetables. I have found top quality grains—bulgur, jasmine and basmati rices—that make preparing classic Middle Eastern side dishes such as *Mujadara* (Lentil Pilaf), page 198, *Shulbato* (Bulgur in Tomato Sauce), page 202, and Jasmine Rice with Pine Nuts and Raisins, page 204, as much a pleasure as I know my mother took in doing the same.

"My parents' garden bore enormous red tomatoes, fava beans, grassy dandelion greens, squash and cucumbers along with a tiny grove of apricot, walnut and fig trees."

Sauteed String Beans

FASOOLIYA BI ZEIT

When I was growing up, string beans and tomatoes were ubiquitous in the Palestinian cook's garden. I could always count on this dish on our Friday night dinner table; sometimes we ate it with rice as a main course and other times it was a side dish accompanied by Arabic bread. These days, I serve it as part of a mezze spread, too.

> **COOKING TIP** The sauteed beans will keep, tightly covered, in the refrigerator up to 5 days. This recipe can also be halved directly.

In a large pot, heat the oil over high until hot but not smoking, about 30 seconds. Toss in the shallots and saute until soft and fragrant, about 3 minutes. Add the garlic and cook until golden, 3 minutes more.

In a small dish, combine the coriander, pepper and allspice. Stir the spice mixture into the pot and cook until fragrant, about 30 seconds. Add the string beans and salt and stir to combine. Reduce the heat to medium, cover and cook until the string beans are tender, about 10 minutes. Stir in the plum tomatoes, cover and cook until the tomatoes begin to soften, 4 to 5 minutes. Add the crushed tomatoes and lemon juice and cook for 3 to 5 minutes more. Stir in the *teklai* and serve hot.

SERVES 8 TO 10

1 cup extra-virgin olive oil
2 shallots, diced
10 cloves garlic, finely chopped
2 heaping tablespoons ground coriander
1½ teaspoons freshly ground black pepper
1 to 1½ teaspoons ground allspice
5 pounds string beans, both ends trimmed, cut into 1½-inch pieces
1 tablespoon sea salt or to taste
6 plum tomatoes, chopped, with their juices
1 (16-ounce) can crushed tomatoes
Juice of ½ lemon
1 tablespoon *Teklai* (page 222)

> **MAKE IT A MAIN**
>
> To make a beef or lamb stew, prepare the Seasoned Lamb or Beef with Stock on page 112. After adding and cooking the crushed tomatoes and lemon juice, add 2 cups of the beef or lamb stock plus the meat to the pot, raise the heat to high, cover and bring to a boil. Cook for 3 minutes. Uncover and cook 10 minutes more to allow the stew to thicken slightly. Stir in the *teklai* and remove from the heat. Serve hot.

Sauteed Dandelion Greens with Caramelized Onions

HENDBEH

Back home, dandelion greens were considered weeds by most—too bitter and tough to be edible—unless you were among the older peasant women who went up to the mountains in June and July to collect them by the bagful. When they got the greens home, these women always prepared them simply, with sauteed onions and olive oil, and ate them with Arabic bread. Personally, I feel great when I eat dandelion greens—they just *taste* healthy, especially with a squeeze of lemon juice. Delicious. When I began making this dish at Tanoreen, my older Italian customers were in awe; they routinely ate the greens in the old country but had a hard time finding them in the States. Now they're available at farmers' markets and specialty produce stores.

In a large pot, bring 12 cups water to a boil over high heat. Add the dandelion greens and return to a boil; cook until tender, 5 to 10 minutes. Transfer to a strainer to drain. When cool enough to handle, squeeze the excess water from the greens with your hands.

In a large skillet, heat the oil over medium-high heat until hot. Add the onions and saute until golden brown, about 2 minutes. Using a slotted spoon, transfer the onions to a plate and set aside. To the same skillet, add the dandelion greens in batches, stirring after each addition, and saute for 7 to 10 minutes. Season with the salt and pepper.

Transfer the greens to a serving platter. Drizzle with olive oil and spoon the onions on top. Garnish with the lemon wedges and serve with Arabic bread and either black or green olives.

SERVES 4 TO 6

8 packed cups chopped dandelion greens
½ cup extra-virgin olive oil, plus more for drizzling
2 cups thinly sliced white onions
1 teaspoon sea salt
½ teaspoon freshly ground black pepper
Lemon wedges for garnish
Arabic Bread (page 61) and black or green olives for serving

Fried Tomatoes

KALAYET BANDOORA

It may surprise you to hear that I was a very picky eater throughout my childhood. When my mother cooked a dish I didn't like, I ate fried tomatoes and French fries! This was among my favorite ways to eat tomatoes then and my fondness has never waned. Serve these as an accompaniment to Whole Fried Fish, page 145, or Falafel, page 56. And, of course, I'd eat them as a vegetarian main course with a nice chunk of Arabic bread for dipping into the sauce.

In a small bowl, combine the cumin, pepper and salt. Sprinkle half of the spice mixture over the tomato slices.

Heat the oil in a large skillet or sauté pan over medium-high heat. Working in batches, gently slip the tomato slices into the pan and fry until golden, about 2 minutes per side. Using a slotted spoon, transfer to a platter. Reduce the heat to low, add the jalapeños, if using, and saute for 1 minute. Add the garlic and saute until soft and golden, about 1 minute. Stir in the remaining spice mixture and cook until fragrant, about 10 seconds. Return the tomatoes with their juices to the pan. Add the lemon juice and cook for 3 to 5 minutes.. Transfer to a platter and serve immediately.

SERVES 4 TO 6

1½ teaspoons ground cumin
1½ teaspoons freshly ground black pepper
1 tablespoon sea salt
6 large ripe Jersey or beefsteak tomatoes, sliced into ½-inch-thick rounds
1 cup olive oil
1 to 2 jalapeño chile peppers, seeded and thinly sliced (optional)
6 cloves garlic, finely chopped
Juice of 1 lemon

Kale with Shallots and Olive Oil

KHUBEZEH

Kale is an excellent alternative to *khubezeh*, the ubiquitous Middle Eastern green that grows wild throughout the region but is unavailable in the U.S. I love it and often implore friends and family traveling back from the Middle East to bring it back for me. Here, I adapt one of the popular *khubezeh* recipes to kale. Best eaten with a squeeze of fresh lemon juice, black Kalamata olives and fresh Arabic Bread, page 61, offer a dash of Harissa, page 220, and Olive Spread, page 220, too.

Heat ¾ cup of the oil in a heavy-bottomed pot over medium heat until hot. Add the coriander, cumin, black pepper and salt and saute until fragrant, about 1 minute. Toss in the onions and saute until golden, 7 to 8 minutes. Remove 2 tablespoons of the mixture and set aside for garnish. Stir in the garlic and cook until fragrant, about 1 minute. Stir in the chile pepper, if using. Add the kale, stirring, until halved in bulk, 3 to 5 minutes. Reduce the heat, cover and cook, stirring occasionally, until tender, 15 minutes or so.

Remove from the heat, drizzle the remaining ¼ cup oil over the kale, cover and let sit until the olive oil is absorbed, 1 to 2 minutes. Transfer to a serving dish, drizzle with the lemon juice and garnish with the reserved onion mixture. Serve warm.

SERVES 6 TO 8

1 cup extra-virgin olive oil
1 tablespoon ground coriander
1 scant tablespoon ground cumin
½ tablespoon freshly ground black pepper
1 tablespoon sea salt
2 cups chopped yellow onions
½ tablespoon finely chopped garlic
1 jalapeño chile pepper, finely chopped (optional)
8 heaping cups chopped kale (3½ to 4 pounds), hard stems removed
Juice of 1 lemon

Lentil Pilaf

MUJADARA

You would be hard pressed to find a Palestinian pantry that does not include lentils and bulgur, the primary ingredients in this classic dish beloved all over the Arab world. Some cooks make it with rice, others vary the spices, but all caramelize the onions that crown this dish. I use the coarsest bulgur available—#4—though not whole bulgur. I love the subtle flavor that the sauteed fennel lends to this dish, an addition I began making when I opened Tanoreen. Serve with olives and Pickled Turnips and Beets, page 210, along with a bowl of cooling yogurt.

Place the lentils in a deep saucepan with enough cold water to cover. Bring to a boil, reduce the heat and simmer until the lentils are barely tender, 20 to 25 minutes. Drain and set aside.

In a medium pot, heat the oil over medium-high heat. Add the onions and saute until golden brown, about 2 minutes. Do not let them burn as the color and flavor of the sauteed onions determines the final quality of the dish. Remove a scoopful of the golden brown onions and set aside for the garnish.

Sprinkle the allspice, pepper, cumin, cinnamon and nutmeg into the pot and cook, stirring until lightly toasted, about 10 seconds. Add the fennel and cook, stirring, for 2 minutes. Stir in the bulgur to coat all over with the spices and cook for 2 minutes. Add the lentils and cook 2 minutes more, stirring to thoroughly combine. Pour the boiling water and salt into the pot, cover and cook on low heat for 15 to 20 minutes, stirring occasionally.

Transfer to a serving platter and garnish with the reserved onions. Drizzle with olive oil and serve.

VARIATION *For those with gluten sensitivities, substitute Egyptian rice, or any other short-grain rice, for the bulgur.*

SERVES 8

3 cups small brown lentils

1 cup extra-virgin olive oil, plus more for drizzling

2 large Spanish onions, thinly sliced

1 tablespoon ground allspice

1 tablespoon freshly ground black pepper

4½ teaspoons ground cumin

¼ teaspoon ground cinnamon

¼ teaspoon grated fresh nutmeg

1 large fennel bulb (about ¾ pound), fronds trimmed and bulb diced

2 cups coarse bulgur (#4)

6 cups boiling water

1 tablespoon sea salt

Lunch Under the Olive Trees

At the start of the annual fall olive harvest, my family—cousins, uncles and aunts included—would venture to my mother's inherited hillside olive groves in her hometown of Rama, a village quite famous for its bountiful, plump olives and lush olive trees. As soon as the sun was up, we set out to do the picking, timing it so that lunch coincided perfectly with the hour when the sun was at its most intense. We gathered under a clutch of olive trees, where my mother laid out a delicious picnic. Lunch was always the same—a huge pot of *mujadara*. Stretched out on a lush hillside, blissfully exhausted, surrounded by the people I loved the most and eating that delicious lentil pilaf with the shaved fennel and frizzled onions—this image is forever etched in my memory.

It may seem odd to serve such a dish for a picnic. But *mujadara* was a strategic choice. It's vegetarian—vegan even—and cooked in olive oil from the prior year's press, so it didn't need to be chilled or reheated. It tastes delicious at room temperature. But, more important, it was hearty enough to fuel us for the next twelve hours of climbing trees, picking olives and carrying baskets overflowing with them. *Mujadara* was also quite affordable to make for a large group.

To this day, sometimes for lunch, I'll snack on a few olives with my *mujadara* and recall those picnics on that hillside in Rameh so many years ago. It fills me with nostalgia.

Spicy Mashed Potatoes

When I was a teenager, I was a picky eater. My father tried to enforce the rule: "You either eat what's on the table, or you don't eat." Little did he know, my sister and I would sneak into the kitchen late at night to make this dish. It's still a favorite today.

Cook the potatoes: Peel and boil the potatoes in salted water until cooked, about 30 minutes, then drain. Or, preheat the oven to 425°F, keep the skin on, and bake them for 40 to 60 minutes until tender, then remove the skin. Baking gives them the best flavor, though it takes longer.

In a small cup or jar, combine the lemon juice, garlic, olive oil, harissa, salt, and black pepper. Shake or stir well until the mixture emulsifies.

Once cooked, place the potatoes in a large bowl and coarsely mash them, leaving some texture if you like. Drizzle the lemon-garlic dressing over the potatoes. Add the parsley or cilantro and chile pepper, if using. Mix everything together until the potatoes are well-coated.

Enjoy as a side dish or a simple dinner, with extra olive oil drizzled on top, if desired.

SERVES 4 TO 6

6 large all-purpose potatoes like Yukon Gold
Juice of 1 lemon, or more to taste
4 cloves garlic, chopped
6 tablespoons olive oil, plus extra for drizzling
1 teaspoon harissa
1 teaspoon salt, or to taste
1 teaspoon black pepper
½ cup chopped parsley or cilantro
1 long hot pepper or jalapeño, diced (optional)

Okra with Tomatoes

BAMYA BELZAIT

When small fresh okra is available, I invariably make this dish, the vegetarian version of a traditional okra recipe prepared with lamb.

If using fried okra, leave the frying oil in the pan. If using roasted okra, heat the 2 tablespoons oil in a skillet over medium-high heat. Add the shallots and saute until golden, 4 to 5 minutes. Using a slotted spoon, transfer to a plate and set aside.

Dump the oil out of the skillet and discard. Return the skillet to high heat and add the remaining ½ cup oil. Add the garlic and cook until fragrant and golden, about 1 minute. Stir in the coriander until fragrant, 10 to 15 seconds. Sprinkle in the salt, pepper and cumin and cook for just 2 seconds. Add the cilantro and stir for 1 minute.

Add the chopped tomatoes to the skillet, reduce the heat to low and cook until they break up and release their juices to form a sauce, 8 to 10 minutes. Add the crushed tomatoes and lemon juice and bring to a boil, stirring, 2 to 3 minutes. Add the okra to the skillet, reduce the heat to low and simmer until the okra is tender, about 20 minutes, taking care not to let the tomatoes stick to the bottom of the skillet.

Transfer to a large platter and garnish with the fried shallots. Serve with the bread.

SERVES 4 TO 6

2 pounds fresh baby okra, fried or roasted (see page 119)
½ cup extra-virgin olive oil, plus 2 tablespoons if using roasted okra
2 shallots, thinly sliced
2 tablespoons finely chopped garlic
1½ tablespoons ground coriander
1 teaspoon sea salt
1 teaspoon freshly ground black pepper
½ teaspoons ground cumin
3 tablespoons chopped fresh cilantro
4 cups chopped Jersey or plum tomatoes
4 tablespoons canned crushed tomatoes
¼ cup fresh lemon juice
Arabic Bread (page 61) for serving

Bulgur in Tomato Sauce

SHULBATO

My childhood summers in my father's native village of Tarshiha are synonymous with *shulbato*, a delicious, healthy bulgur pilaf that was made with the first wheat harvest. Whatever vegetables were ripe in the garden went into this. It is, perhaps, my favorite simple meal. Serve with black or green olives.

Heat ¾ cup of the oil in a large skillet over medium-high until hot. Toss in the onions and saute until golden brown, about 5 minutes. Stir in the cumin, salt and pepper. Add the bulgur and stir until coated all over. Add the tomatoes and cook until they release their juices, about 3 minutes. Stir in the tomato paste and cook for 1 minute. Pour in 6 cups water, the chickpeas and half of the roasted vegetables and bring to a boil. Reduce the heat, cover and simmer, stirring occasionally, for 15 minutes.

Transfer to a platter, top with the remaining roasted vegetables, drizzle with the remaining ¼ cup olive oil and serve hot, cold or at room temperature.

VARIATION At Tanoreen, I offer a vegetarian sandwich that uses *shulbato*. Spread some Olive Spread, page 220, or a good-quality store-bought version into Arabic bread and fill it with shulbato.

SERVES 4 TO 6

1 cup extra-virgin olive oil
2 yellow onions, diced
1 tablespoon ground cumin
1 tablespoon sea salt
1 tablespoon freshly ground black pepper
3 cups bulgur (#4)
4 plum tomatoes, diced
12 ounces tomato paste
1 (15-ounce) can chickpeas, drained and rinsed
3 Arabic squash or zucchini, diced and roasted
2 long hot chile peppers, chopped and roasted
1 eggplant, diced and roasted

Rice and Vermicelli Pilaf

When in doubt, serve any entree with this mix of rice and broken pasta strands. When my daughter, Jumana, was a young girl, she made it her main course whenever she didn't want what I was serving. Centuries ago, this pilaf was made exclusively with bulgur or smoked wheat, but when rice was introduced to the Arab world, it became a popular substitute. Egyptian rice kernels are small, round and broken; this is the only rice to use to make the authentic version of this dish. Chinese or Carolina white rice are the next best things. If you are have gluten sensitivities, eliminate the vermicelli altogether along with 1 cup of the water, then add another ½ cup of rice.

SERVES 8 TO 10

⅔ cup extra-virgin olive oil
¼ cup ghee or butter
1 pound vermicelli
4 cups Egyptian or Chinese or Carolina rice
8 to 9 cups boiling water
1 tablespoon sea salt or to taste

Combine the oil and ghee in a large pot and heat over high until hot. Add the vermicelli and stir until golden brown, 7 to 10 minutes. Add the rice and stir until opaque, 3 to 5 minutes. Pour in the boiling water and salt, reduce the heat to low, cover and simmer until the rice is fluffy, about 12 minutes, stirring once halfway through. Off the heat, stir once more, cover and let stand for 5 minutes. Serve warm.

Jasmine Rice with Pine Nuts and Raisins

ROZ BEL MAZAHER

This earthy, sweet and fragrant rice is a wonderful side dish with grilled meats or Chicken Tagine, page 161. Strain the oil from the fried nuts and use it, along with the ghee or butter, to coat the rice. Sometimes I sprinkle a little cinnamon on top to add another layer of flavor.

SERVES 6

¼ cup corn oil
½ cup pine nuts
½ cup slivered almonds
¼ cup ghee
3 cups jasmine rice
1 tablespoon sea salt
6 cups Seasoned Chicken Stock (page 100)
   or low-sodium chicken stock or water
1 cup golden raisins
4 tablespoons orange blossom water

> **INGREDIENT NOTE** The distilled essence of fresh bitter orange blossoms, orange blossom water is an intensely floral flavoring that lends a fragrant note to all manner of Middle Eastern dishes. It is most commonly used in desserts, but I am not afraid to add a little to savory dishes to give them another, very subtle layer of flavor. A little goes a long way; it should be used with a light touch unless otherwise noted. It can be found in specialty grocery stores, in Middle Eastern markets, and online.

In a medium pot, combine the oil with the pine nuts and slivered almonds and fry until golden over medium heat; transfer to a plate. Mix the ghee with the oil in the pot and heat over medium-high until hot. Add the rice and saute for 3 to 5 minutes or until it begins to take on color. Add the salt, stock and raisins and bring to a boil. Reduce the heat, cover and simmer for 15 minutes.

Off the heat, uncover the pot, drizzle the orange water over the rice, cover again, and let stand for 3 minutes. Transfer to a serving dish and top with the pine nuts and almonds.

Basmati Vegetable Rice

Basmati is one of my favorite grains and is perfectly delicious eaten plain but here I've made it a bit more special by adding whatever vegetables I could find and playing with some spices. The perfect side for Chicken Tagine, page 161, or any grilled meat, chicken or fish, this also makes a lovely vegetarian meal with a Tanoreen Green Salad, page 86.

SERVES 4 TO 6

½ cup extra-virgin olive oil
3 cups basmati rice
2 shallots, finely chopped
3 cloves garlic, finely chopped
1 tablespoon turmeric
1 tablespoon ground allspice
1 tablespoon ground coriander
1 tablespoon sea salt
½ teaspoon ground cardamom
½ tablespoon ground cumin
½ cup chopped fresh parsley
½ cup chopped fresh cilantro
1 tablespoon finely chopped fresh sage
2 cups fresh or frozen baby peas
2 medium carrots, peeled and diced
3 plum tomatoes, diced
1 stalk celery, chopped
1 chile pepper, finely chopped (optional)
4 cups Seasoned Chicken Stock (page 100) or low-sodium chicken or vegetable stock or water

Heat ¼ cup olive oil in a large pot over medium-high heat. Stir in the rice to coat. Saute, stirring constantly, until it begins to take on color, 3 to 5 minutes. Remove from the heat and stir in the remaining ¼ cup oil.

Return the pot to medium-high heat, toss in the shallots and saute for 3 minutes, stirring every 30 seconds. Add the garlic and saute for 1 minute. Stir in the spices and cook until fragrant, 30 seconds. Stir in the herbs, and saute for 1 minute more. Add the vegetables, and saute, stirring occasionally, until softened, 3 to 5 minutes. Carefully pour in ½ cup stock; the liquid may spatter. Pour in the remaining 3½ cups stock, bring to a boil, reduce the heat, cover and simmer until the liquid is absorbed, 12 to 15 minutes, stirring once. Transfer to a platter and serve warm.

Spicy Rice

I prefer using short-grain rice such as Egyptian or basmati for this dish, but any rice works. Spicy rice is a delicious companion to fish or shrimp or any grilled meat. It can also stand alone as a vegetarian meal. I always make more than I need, as it tastes great reheated the day after it's made.

SERVES 8 TO 10

12 plum tomatoes, chopped
2 to 3 medium shallots, chopped
6 cloves garlic, chopped
4 scallions, green and white parts, chopped
2 jalapeño peppers, chopped
1 cup chopped fresh cilantro
3 tablespoons fresh lemon juice
Sea salt
9 to 10 cups Seasoned Chicken Stock (page 100) or low-sodium chicken or vegetable stock or water
1 cup extra-virgin olive oil
6 cups rice
1 tablespoon ground cumin
1 tablespoon ground coriander
1 tablespoon freshly ground black pepper
1 pound sweet peas (optional)

In the bowl of a food processor, combine the tomatoes with half the shallots, half the garlic, the scallions, jalapeños, cilantro, lemon juice and salt to taste; process until pureed. Measure and add enough stock or water to total 9 cups (10 cups if using basmati). Transfer to a medium pot and bring to a boil over high heat.

Meanwhile, heat the oil in a large pot over medium-high. Toss in the remaining shallots and saute until softened, 3 minutes. Add the remaining garlic and saute for 1 minute. Sprinkle in the rice, cumin, coriander and pepper, stir to coat the rice with the oil and saute, stirring occasionally, until the rice begins to turn white, about 3 minutes. Add the sweet peas, if using, then gradually add the hot tomato puree, stirring to incorporate. Reduce the heat, cover and simmer for 12 to 15 minutes. Transfer to a platter and serve warm.

PICKLES, SAUCES & SEASONINGS

Snacks with Bite and Sauces with Spice

A Middle Eastern meal is not a meal without a small dish of mouth-puckering pickled vegetables and a sauce served somewhere along the way.

Pickles are as essential to breakfast, lunch and dinner as Arabic bread. Briny chunks of cauliflower, carrots, hot peppers and turnips, to name a few, provide a wonderful, tangy counterpoint to fried falafel sandwiches, hearty stews, hummus or *foul*.

Growing up, pickle making was a yearly end-of-summer ritual for us. It would take an entire day and the preparations engaged the entire family. My father seemed to have a supernatural ability to pick the freshest, smallest, least expensive vegetables in the market, so that job fell to him. He came home with boxes piled high with cucumbers, baby eggplants, cauliflower, bell peppers, turnips, beets, carrots and huge bunches of dill. My mother set to work chopping on the big, worn wooden board that came to symbolize the pickling season. She chopped for hours, the knife blade hitting the wood over and over sounding a curiously soothing beat.

Before we knew it, my mother had chopped turnips into half moons, beets into slivers, jalapeños into thin rings and garlic into slices. She used her hands to break up the cauliflower into florets and tossed them with chunks of carrots, then doused the mix with spicy, salty *amba*, a curry-like mango paste. I especially loved the baby cucumbers packed in vinegar and fresh dill. There were also black olives cured in olive oil and purslane and green olives spiced with chile paste. When it was time to package them, we all got into the act, sweeping the vegetables from the counter into metal tins, then adding the white vinegar, salt and herbs. After all the tins were filled to the brim, my father fitted the lids on, welding them shut for winter storage, and lugged them onto the roof. We opened the tins throughout the year as needed. And need we did. We ate them at every meal.

My passion for pickles was fostered in Nazareth and only became more intense when I moved to New York. I love anything with a bite. In fact, these days, my idea of the perfect snack is a peeled lemon, cut into wedges, and liberally sprinkled with sea salt. I make all of the pickles we serve at Tanoreen, and while we don't store them on the restaurant's roof, the method is exactly the same as the one my mother used. For most of the recipes in this chapter, there is a week's wait before the pickles are ready. To reduce it to three days, simply boil the vinegar before adding it to the jars.

Almost every Middle Eastern dish benefits from the addition of a sauce. Indeed, there is almost no stew that can't be enhanced by a

"My father seemed to have a supernatural ability to pick the freshest, smallest, least expensive vegetables in the market, so that job fell to him."

spoonful of the garlicky spice mixture known as *Teklai*, page 222. When it is stirred into boiling hot broth, it makes a very satisfying swooshing sound, a signal that the intense flavors of coriander and garlic have been released into the broth. A few dashes of *Harissa*, page 220, the homemade hot sauce found in every Middle Eastern pantry, can transform a dish; it is a wonderful way to amp up a vegetable dish or impart a bit of heat to a mellow stew. Some of the sauces on the following pages might be better described as spreads, among them Olive Spread, page 220, and Tomato and Dill Spread, page 222, both of which are terrific brushed on bread before adding the fillings to a sandwich.

Of course, no proper Middle Eastern pantry is complete without Thick Tahini Sauce, page 221, a tangy blend of sesame paste, garlic and lemon juice. It is drizzled on Cauliflower Salad, page 85, and Brussels Sprouts with Panko, page 49, and used in all manner of meat and chicken dishes. But its most important role is as a primary ingredient in Hummus, page 38, and Baba Ghanouj, page 44, the two most popular dips in the Middle Eastern repertoire.

You'll find a pesto here, too, because I was hooked on it the minute I first tasted it upon arriving in New York. In fact, Basil Pesto, page 215, is the recipe in this chapter that best describes the journey I've taken: I serve it as a dip with *Sambosek*, page 66, stir it into tagines and use it as a marinade for chicken.

PICKLES, SAUCES & SEASONINGS

Pickled Turnips and Beets

LEFET MAKBOUS

For me, no pickled combination is more appealing than turnips and beets, a marriage of sweet and hot flavors. I consider these pickles a snack, as my palate has always veered more toward pungent, salty foods than any other. I suppose I believe others love them as much as I do, as I serve them at every table at Tanoreen. The original recipe for these is quite basic, so I've given mine the Tanoreen "touch" by adding jalapeños to the mix.

In a 1-gallon sterilized jar with a tight-fitting lid, combine the turnips, beets, jalapeños, garlic and citric acid. Fill a third of the jar with vinegar and 2 tablespoons of salt. Fill the jar with water to the top in 1-cup portions. For each cup water added, add 1 tablespoon salt. Cover tightly and set aside at room temperature, not to exceed 75°F, for at least 5 days. Refrigerate after opening for up to 3 months.

MAKES ½ GALLON

10 turnips, cut into ¼- to ½-inch-thick matchsticks

2 beets, cut into ¼- to ½-inch thick matchsticks

2 jalapeños, seeded (optional) and thinly sliced

2 cloves garlic, thinly sliced

1 teaspoon citric acid

Distilled white vinegar and sea salt for pickling

Pickled Jalapeños and Carrots

Recently I pickled this spicy combination in the morning and they were ready to serve for a party at the restaurant three hours later. They were a big hit; no one could believe that they had been made in a few hours!

In a medium saucepan, combine the vinegar and 1 cup water with the salt, dill and oregano and bring to a boil. Drop the jalapeño, carrots and garlic into the pot and return to a boil. Remove the pan from the heat and set aside to cool.

Transfer to a sterilized jar with a tight-fitting lid. Pour the oil into the jar and seal tightly. The pickles will keep up to 3 months in the refrigerator.

MAKES 1 QUART

1 cup distilled white vinegar

2 tablespoons sea salt

2 stems fresh dill

2 stems fresh oregano

18 jalapeño chile peppers, sliced to desired thickness

2 large carrots, peeled and sliced to desired thickness

1 clove garlic, smashed

¼ cup extra-virgin olive oil

Pickled Cauliflower and Carrots

ZAHRA MAKBOUSEH

I always thought that my aunt made the best pickled cauliflower until I tasted some at Khazen, a tiny but famous shwarma stand in Haifa. Today, the stand has expanded many times over, but I prefer to remember it as the place we always stopped to eat shwarma sandwiches generously topped with briny golden pickled cauliflower before heading for a swim in the glorious Mediterranean. It didn't get any better than that.

In a 1-quart sterilized jar with a tight-fitting lid, combine the cauliflower, carrots, chile pepper, if using, garlic, dill, coriander, citric acid, turmeric and curry powder, if using. Fill a third of the jar with vinegar and add 2 tablespoons salt. Fill the jar to the top with water in 1-cup portions. For each cup of water added, add 1 tablespoon salt. Cover tightly and set aside at room temperature, not to exceed 75°F, for at least 5 days. Refrigerate after opening.

MAKES 1 QUART

1 head cauliflower, florets and stem cut into small pieces
1 large carrot, peeled, quartered and cut into matchsticks
1 chile pepper, seeded and thinly sliced (optional)
2 cloves garlic, sliced
2 stems fresh dill, chopped
1 tablespoon coriander seeds
1 tablespoon citric acid
1 teaspoon turmeric
½ teaspoon curry powder (optional)
Distilled white vinegar and sea salt for pickling

Pickled Stuffed Bell Peppers

FILFIL MAHSHI MAKBOUS

I don't know of any other Galilean home cook who stuffed bell peppers the way my mother did. When she put these on the table, they would disappear in seconds. Get creative with the stuffing here if you like; I typically use whatever is fresh and crisp at the farm stand or market.

Remove the stem end of each pepper about ¼ inch beyond the stem and reserve. Using a spoon, remove the seeds.

Make the stuffing: In a medium bowl, combine the celery, carrots, tomatoes, cucumbers, cabbage, jalapeños, vinegar and garlic and mix together.

Spoon the stuffing into the peppers, dividing it evenly among them. Replace the stem tops on the peppers and arrange, stem-end up and stacked on top of each other, in a 1-gallon jar with a tight-fitting lid. Fill a third of the jar with vinegar and 2 tablespoons salt. Fill the jar to the top with water in 1-cup portions. For each cup of water added, add 1 tablespoon salt. Add the citric acid, cover tightly and set aside at room temperature, not to exceed 75°F, for at least 5 days. Refrigerate after opening for up to 3 months. To serve, cut each pepper into quarters, lengthwise.

MAKES 6 PICKLED PEPPERS (ENOUGH FOR 24 SERVINGS)

6 bell peppers, any color
Distilled white vinegar and sea salt for pickling
1 tablespoon citric acid

For the Stuffing

2 celery stalks, chopped
2 carrots, peeled and diced
2 green tomatoes, chopped
2 Persian or Kirby cucumbers, diced
2 cups shredded white cabbage
2 jalapeño chile peppers, seeded (optional) and diced
4 tablespoons distilled white vinegar
2 tablespoons garlic, finely chopped

Pickled Eggplant in Olive Oil

BATINJAN MAKBOUS

Magic happens when eggplant stuffed with chile paste and garlic is cured in olive oil. The eggplant softens, the chile paste mellows and the garlic pops. Note that this version of stuffed eggplant is different than the richer, walnut-stuffed *Makdous*, page 50—it's lighter and plays the role of condiment, making a wonderful addition to a falafel sandwich or to serve spooned next to almost any main course. Growing up, many families couldn't afford walnuts in quantity, so this is what was on offer during the week.

Bring a large pot of water to a boil. Slide the eggplant into the water and cook until fork-tender but not mushy, about 10 minutes. Transfer to a colander to drain and cool. Once cool enough to handle, make a 1½-inch incision lengthwise down the middle of each eggplant. Do not cut all the way through.

In a small bowl, combine the salt and citric acid. Rub half of the salt mixture around the outside of the incisions in the eggplants. Set the eggplants aside in a colander or strainer for 2 hours more to drain of moisture. Meanwhile, combine the chile peppers, garlic and chile paste with the remaining salt mixture.

Stuff 1 teaspoon of the chile-pepper mixture into each incision in the drained eggplants, then stack them, one on top of the other, in a 1-gallon sterilized jar with a tight-fitting lid. Pour the oil over them to cover completely, adding more if necessary. The eggplants will keep, refrigerated, up to 3 months.

VARIATION *For vinegar-packed eggplants, follow the steps below after placing the stuffed eggplants in the jar.*

Fill the jar a third full with distilled white vinegar. Fill to the top with water, adding in 1-cup portions. For every cup water added, add 1 tablespoon sea salt. Cover tightly and set aside at room temperature, not to exceed 75°F, for at least 5 days. Refrigerate after opening for up to 3 months.

MAKES 12 PICKLES (ENOUGH FOR 12 SERVINGS)

- 12 baby eggplants, about 4 pounds
- 3 tablespoons sea salt
- 1 teaspoon citric acid
- 2 green chile peppers, such as jalapeños, finely chopped
- 3 tablespoons chopped garlic
- 3 tablespoons seedless Middle Eastern or Turkish chile paste
- 2 cups extra-virgin olive oil, plus more, if necessary, to cover

Basil Pesto

The first time I ever tasted pesto, I was hooked. I remember the first meal I made using it like it was yesterday—linguini tossed with pesto, topped with fried eggplant and served with fresh home-baked bread. When I use pesto this way, as a sauce, I generally make it with pine nuts. If I'm going to incorporate it into a dish, I use almonds, which are less expensive.

Put the garlic in the bowl of a food processor and pulse until coarsely chopped. Toss in the nuts, Parmesan, if using, pepper and salt and chop until the nuts are finely crushed, about 1 minute. Add the basil, oil and lemon juice and pulse for 1 minute more, until smooth. Stir in red pepper flakes, if desired.

To store, transfer the pesto to a sterilized jar with a tight-fitting lid. Pour a thin layer of olive oil on top of the pesto, seal and refrigerate up to 10 days or freeze up to 3 months.

MAKES 2 CUPS

3 to 5 cloves garlic

1 cup pine nuts, slivered almonds or walnut halves

2 tablespoons grated Parmigiano-Reggiano cheese, or to taste (optional)

1 teaspoon freshly ground black pepper

½ teaspoon fine sea salt

4 packed cups chopped fresh basil leaves

½ cup extra-virgin olive oil, plus more for storage

Juice of 2 lemons

Crushed red pepper flakes to taste (optional)

Garlic Sauce

THOUM

This is the sauce that is traditionally used on kebabs or roasted chicken. I know some people who refuse to eat either without it! The key to making a beautiful, smooth sauce is to drizzle the oil into the mixture very slowly in a thin stream, like you would to make mayonnaise. The slower you drizzle, the silkier it will be.

Place the garlic in a blender and chop until the machine won't chop anymore. With the blender running, add the vinegar, egg whites, salt and lemon salt through the opening in the top of the lid. Blend until the garlic mixture is superfine. Drizzle the oil, a few drops at a time, through the opening—this may take 5 to 10 minutes. Continue blending until the sauce is thick and silky; it should have the consistency of thick cream. The sauce will keep, in a tightly covered container, up to 1 week in the refrigerator.

MAKES 2 CUPS

40 garlic cloves
3 tablespoons distilled white vinegar
2 large egg whites
1 teaspoon sea salt
1 teaspoon lemon salt
1½ cups corn oil

Homemade Hot Sauce

HARISSA

There's nothing quite like a homemade batch of hot sauce. Back in Nazareth, we dried our own red chile peppers, then soaked, drained, chopped and froze them in small batches. My sister still sends me the special peppers from Nazareth, since I've had no luck finding them in the States. Here, I prefer Middle Eastern chile pastes to all others; the Turkish seedless brands are fantastic. You can find them at Middle Eastern specialty stores or online. Serve this hot sauce with fish or stirred into any one of my lentil soups.

Heat the oil in a saucepan over medium heat until hot. Add the garlic and cook until golden brown, 2 to 3 minutes. Sprinkle in the chile paste, cumin, caraway and dill seeds, if using, and pepper and cook, stirring, for 2 minutes. Pour in the lemon juice and ⅓ to ⅔ cup water, depending on desired consistency, and bring to a boil for 2 to 3 minutes.

Remove from the heat, let cool and season with salt. Transfer to a jar with a tight-fitting lid. The hot sauce will keep, refrigerated, for up to 1 month.

MAKES 2 ¼ CUPS

6 tablespoons extra-virgin olive oil
6 cloves garlic, finely chopped
2 cups chile paste
1 teaspoon ground cumin
½ teaspoon ground caraway seeds (optional)
½ teaspoon ground dill seeds (optional)
½ teaspoon freshly ground black pepper
⅔ cup fresh lemon juice
Sea salt

Olive Spread

This is wonderful to have on hand for all manner of occasions. It is a delicious spread for almost any kind of sandwich, especially in Arabic bread stuffed with *Shulbato*, page 202; see the variation. I prefer a smooth spread, but the beauty of preparing this yourself is that you can make it whatever texture you like. For a milder spread, replace 1 cup of the pitted Kalamata olives with canned pitted black olives, drained.

In the bowl of a food processor, combine the olives with the garlic, shallot, capers, sun-dried tomatoes and anchovies, if using, lemon juice, oil, cumin and pepper and puree to the desired consistency. Transfer to a jar with a tight-fitting lid. The olive spread will keep, refrigerated, up to 2 months.

MAKES 2 CUPS

2 cups pitted black Kalamata olives
2 cloves garlic, chopped
1 shallot, chopped (2½ tablespoons)
6 capers in brine, rinsed and drained
5 sun-dried tomatoes in extra-virgin olive oil, chopped (optional)
4 anchovies, thoroughly rinsed of salt, chopped (optional)
Juice of 1½ to 2 lemons
¼ cup extra-virgin olive oil
½ teaspoon ground cumin
½ teaspoon freshly ground black pepper

Thick Tahini Sauce

Tahini sauce, a smooth blend of toasted sesame paste, lemon juice, garlic and olive oil, is ubiquitous in Middle Eastern kitchens. It is *the* condiment. There is hardly a dish that isn't enhanced by it—drizzled on Falafel sandwiches, page 56, and over Brussels Sprouts with Panko, page 49; blended with pureed chickpeas for Hummus, page 38, and with charred eggplant for Baba Ghanouj, page 44. My favorite Whole Fried Fish, page 145, is served with this sauce mixed with parsley. At Tanoreen, I mix it into salad dressings and drizzle it into cauliflower casseroles. My daughter? She dips French fries into it! Learn to make this and you will have a simple, delicious, versatile sauce to add to your repertoire.

In the bowl of a food processor, combine the tahini, garlic, lemon juice and salt and process on low speed for 2 minutes or until thoroughly incorporated. Turn the speed to high and blend until the tahini mixture begins to whiten. Gradually add up to ½ cup water until the mixture reaches the desired consistency.

Transfer the sauce to a serving bowl and garnish with the parsley. Leftover tahini sauce can be stored, tightly covered in the refrigerator, for up to 2 weeks.

VARIATIONS

Spicy Tahini Sauce Add ¼ cup pomegranate molasses and 2 tablespoons chile paste to the bowl of the food processor and pulse until thoroughly incorporated.

Sandwich Sauce To make a thinner version for drizzling on falafel, kafta or cauliflower tagine, add water to the mixture and pulse to thin to desired consistency.

Fetti Sauce Combine 1 cup of the tahini sauce with 1 cup of plain yogurt in the bowl of a food processor and pulse until smooth to make a wonderful, simple sauce for Chicken Fetti, page 154.

MAKES 2½ CUPS

1½ cups tahini (sesame paste)
3 to 4 cloves garlic, crushed
About 1 cup lemon juice or to taste
1 teaspoon sea salt
Chopped parsley for garnish

Tomato and Dill Spread

DAGGA

This Gazan specialty is a delicious dip as well as a sauce for virtually any fish. Open a can of sardines and you can make the best sandwich by tucking them into Arabic bread or between two slices of Italian or French bread swabbed with this spread. I always leave the seeds in the chile peppers to impart a properly spicy flavor; leave them out for a milder version.

In a large bowl or mortar, combine the garlic and the salt. Using a pestle, pound the mixture to a paste. Sprinkle with the dill seeds and pound into the paste until incorporated. Toss in the fresh dill and pound until incorporated. Add the chile peppers and pound to release their fragrance. Toss in the tomatoes and pound gently until the mixture is the consistency of a thick sauce. Stir in the lemon juice and oil and season to taste with salt. Store, tightly covered, in the refrigerator for up to 3 days.

MAKES 8 CUPS

8 cloves garlic, finely chopped
1 teaspoon sea salt plus more to taste
1 generous tablespoon dill seeds
½ packed cup chopped fresh dill
2 chile peppers, such as jalapeños, finely chopped
10 plum tomatoes, or 5 beefsteak tomatoes, peeled and roughly chopped
Juice of 1½ lemons
5 tablespoons extra-virgin olive oil

Seasoned Garlic Sauce

TEKLAI

This recipe makes more sauce than you will need for any single recipe, but you can refrigerate it in a container with a tight-fitting lid for up to one month. If you're using the *teklai* straight from the refrigerator, reheat it first: Heat 1 teaspoon of olive oil in a skillet over medium-high heat. Add the *teklai* and saute just until it begins to sizzle.

Heat the oil in a small skillet over medium-high heat. Add the garlic and cook until fragrant and soft, 3 minutes. Stir in the salt, pepper and coriander and cook until the mixture is fragrant and the garlic is golden brown. Remove from the heat and spread in a thin layer on a baking sheet to cool. Transfer to a jar with a tight-fitting lid and keep in the refrigerator for up to 1 week.

MAKES 1 CUP

½ cup extra-virgin olive oil
20 cloves garlic, finely chopped
½ tablespoon sea salt
½ tablespoon freshly ground black pepper
½ cup ground coriander

Seasoned Garlic Sauce with Lemon

TEKLAI FOR MLOOKHIA

I prefer to make only as much of this version of *teklai* as I need; it is best used immediately. That said, it will keep in a container with a tight-fitting lid for up to one week in the refrigerator.

In a small skillet, melt the butter over medium heat. Add the garlic and salt and saute until golden brown, 3 to 5 minutes. Stir in the coriander and saute another minute. Using a large spoon, skim the foam from the surface of the mixture and remove the skillet from the heat. Add the lemon juice, cool the *teklai*, then transfer to a container with a tight-fitting lid and keep in the fridge for up to 1 week.

MAKES ½ CUP

4 tablespoons (½ stick) butter or ghee
3 heaping tablespoons finely chopped garlic
Pinch sea salt
3 heaping tablespoons ground coriander
Juice of 3 lemons

Spicy Seasoned Garlic Sauce

TEKLAI FOR CAULIFLOWER STEW AND OKRA WITH POMEGRANATE

A mix of cilantro and jalapeño give this *teklai* variation quite a kick—it adds a bright layer of flavor to Cauliflower and Lamb Stew, page 108, and Okra Stew with Lamb and Pomegranate Molasses, page 119. This *teklai* will keep, tightly covered, in the refrigerator up to one month.

In a medium skillet, heat the oil over medium-high heat. Toss in the garlic and saute until golden, 3 minutes. Sprinkle in the coriander, black pepper and salt and saute, stirring until fragrant, about 30 seconds. Add the cilantro and jalapeño, if using, and stir to incorporate. Stir in the lemon juice. Cool, then transfer to a container with a tight-fitting lid. Refrigerate up to 1 month, if you like.

MAKES 1 CUP

¼ cup extra-virgin olive oil
8 to 10 garlic cloves, finely chopped
3 tablespoons ground coriander
½ teaspoon freshly ground black pepper
Pinch sea salt
⅓ packed cup chopped fresh cilantro
1 jalapeño chile pepper, partially seeded, finely chopped (optional)
Juice of 1 lemon

Tanoreen Spice

Tanoreen Spice is the secret to many of our dishes. It is a secret signature blend, which we sell in our restaurant, but if you are not able to visit us, here is a recipe that will get you close.

Mix the ingredients together well and store in an airtight container in your pantry.

MAKES 3 TABLESPOONS

2 teaspoon ground allspice
2 teaspoon ground black pepper
2 teaspoon ground coriander
2 teaspoon ground cumin
Good pinch of freshly grated nutmeg

DESSERTS

Satisfying a Sweet Tooth

Weekends in our Nazareth home revolved around food. Friday or Saturday were synonymous with raw kibbeh and fried fish, but Sunday morning invariably meant awakening to the unmistakable aroma of fresh baked Coconut Semolina Cake (*Harisa*; page 232). My mother would rise long before the rest of us, so that by the time we sauntered into the kitchen, she could present us with a piece of the dense, golden treat, soaked in sugar syrup infused with orange blossom and rose water. She baked the cake in a huge sheet pan, in hopes that a large batch would take us through to the following Sunday.

It only barely did, since in the Middle East, it is not unusual to eat dessert for breakfast as well as any other time of the day. Macaroni cookies, page 244, Date Cookies (*Ka'ik*; page 242) and Mamool Walnut Cookies, page 239, for example, are typically served with strong Turkish coffee in the morning. Flower-Scented Custard with Pistachios and Syrup (*Sahlab*; page 230), a soothing, chilled custard, is often eaten after lunch.

The hallmarks of Middle Eastern desserts are few yet distinct. Unlike any other course in a meal, the portions are generally quite small. Because they are made with such rich ingredients, a bite or two is all one needs to satisfy a sweet tooth. In the recipes that follow, you'll notice a handful of ingredients that show up in most Middle Eastern desserts. Fragrant rose and sweet orange blossom water almost always infuse the simple syrup, or *attir*, that tops desserts, such as *Knafeh*, page 245, as well as the dough used for Rolled Date Cookies, page 243, the poaching liquid for Stuffed Fresh Dates, page 241, and the custard in *sahlab*. Nuts, too, are a primary dessert ingredient. In fact, the only other ingredient I use more than nuts at Tanoreen is parsley! If pistachios, walnuts, pine nuts or almonds are not layered, stuffed or folded into a dessert, then we sprinkle some on top for good measure. Various combinations of sweet spices—cinnamon, nutmeg and cloves—are also ubiquitous. These earthy seasonings are mixed into date and nut fillings and stirred into sugar syrup to infuse it with distinctly Middle Eastern flavors.

The combination of fragrant flower waters, nuts and spices is hard to compete with. So, you will find that, more than in any other chapter in this book, I stay fairly true to traditional Middle Eastern recipes, with only a few variations and additions I have experimented with at Tanoreen.

> "My mother would rise long before the rest of us, so that by the time we sauntered into the kitchen, she could present us with a piece of the dense, golden treat, soaked in sugar syrup infused with orange blossom and rose water."

Flower-Scented Custard with Pistachios and Syrup

SAHLAB

My gluten-sensitive customers go wild for this creamy dessert, fragrant with just a hint of rose and orange blossom waters. It can be prepared as either a hot drink—in which case, I add a dash of cinnamon, some raisins and crushed walnuts—or a chilled custard topped with crushed pistachios and fragrant syrup, as I make it here.

Place the mastic and ½ teaspoon of sugar in a small bowl. Using the back of a spoon, crush the mastic to a coarse powder.

Pour the milk into a medium pot and stir in the mastic mixture. Heat over medium heat until the milk comes to a boil. Stir in the diluted cornstarch, rose water and orange blossom water. Using a hand mixer, mix until the liquid begins to thicken slightly and coats the back of a spoon, about 2 minutes. Transfer to a 9-inch round cake pan. Let cool slightly, cover with plastic wrap and refrigerate until firm and thoroughly chilled, at least 3 hours.

Invert a serving platter at least 4 inches wider than the cake pan over the pan. Flip over to release the *sahlab* and the syrup that has formed on the bottom of the pan. Sprinkle the top with the pistachios. Cut into wedges with a pie server and serve cold.

**SERVES 6 TO 8
(ONE 9-INCH-ROUND CUSTARD)**

1 teaspoon ground mastic
1 cup plus ½ teaspoon sugar
8 cups cold milk
1 cup cornstarch, diluted with ½ cup water
2 tablespoons rose water (optional)
2 tablespoons orange blossom water
1 cup chopped pistachios

Ruby Red Fruit Compote

This raspberry and cherry sauce is very versatile—it is not only delicious over *sahlab*, above, but can brighten a scoop of ice cream or a slice of cake, too.

In a medium saucepan, combine the raspberries and cherries with the sugar, Grand Marnier, vanilla and lemon juice. Cook over high heat until the fruit begins to break down, about 5 to 8 minutes. Reduce the heat to low and simmer until the mixture thickens slightly, 20 to 25 minutes. Remove from the heat and let cool before serving. The compote will keep, tightly covered, in the refrigerator for up to 2 weeks.

MAKES ABOUT 3 CUPS

1 pound fresh or frozen raspberries
1 pound fresh or frozen cherries, pitted
½ packed cup brown sugar
2 tablespoons Grand Marnier liqueur
1 tablespoon vanilla extract
5 drops fresh lemon juice

Coconut Semolina Cake

HARISA

Not to be confused with the North African hot sauce pronounced the same way, this toothsome, sweet cake is known as *namoura* or *basboosa* in some regions of the Middle East, but in Galilee, it is *harisa*. This particular version is one of my mother's most treasured recipes, perfected as only she could, by adding her own touch. In this case, it's coconut, an ingredient you wont find in other *harisas* (omit it if you want to make the traditional version). This cake is quite simple to make, but its richness and exotic flavor make it a special dessert—and its size is perfect for a crowd. It freezes well, but the recipe can also be halved and baked in a 6- by 9-inch cake pan to yield a smaller cake.

> **COOKING TIP** You probably won't need all of the simple syrup called for here. But it's nice to have on hand for the next semolina cake, or to stir into iced tea or lemonade. It will keep, covered, in the refrigerator for up to 4 months.

Preheat the oven to 350°F. In a large mixing bowl, stir together the sour cream and baking powder and let stand for 1 minute, or until the sour cream begins to rise. In a small bowl, stir together 4 tablespoons of the sour cream and baking powder mixture with 4 tablespoons melted butter and set aside.

In another large bowl, combine the farina with the remaining melted butter and the coconut, sugar, baking soda, and vanilla extract. Blend with a rubber spatula or your hands until thoroughly incorporated, about 5 minutes. Alternately, combine the ingredients in the bowl of a stand mixer fitted with the paddle attachment and beat on medium speed until thoroughly incorporated. Add the sour cream mixture to the farina batter and mix thoroughly until the ingredients are thoroughly incorporated.

Spread half of the reserved sour cream and butter mixture in the bottom of a 12 by 17-inch baking sheet. Spread the farina batter evenly over it, pushing it out to the corners with a rubber spatula. Spread the remaining sour cream and butter mixture evenly on top. Bake for approximately 30 minutes or until golden brown. While still warm, pour the simple syrup over the cake. Transfer the pan to a wire rack to allow the cake to cool to room temperature.

Cut the cake into 12 squares, garnish each piece with the pistachio nuts and serve. The cake will keep, covered with plastic wrap, at room temperature, up to 3 days or refrigerated up to 2 weeks. Reheat in a low oven before serving.

VARIATION **Walnut Cake** *With the simple addition of 3 cups of chopped walnuts, 1 cup pitted, chopped dates and 3 tablespoons cocoa powder to the farina batter, you can transform the semolina cake into an entirely different dessert.*

**SERVES 12
(ONE 12- BY 17-INCH CAKE)**

4 cups sour cream

2 tablespoons baking powder

¾ pound (3 sticks) unsalted butter, melted and cooled

1 (28-ounce box) white farina such as Cream of Wheat

2 cups shredded unsweetened coconut

1 cup sugar

¼ teaspoon baking soda

3 tablespoons vanilla extract

Simple Syrup (page 245), at room temperature

½ cup chopped pistachio nuts (optional)

> **PUTTING BAKING POWDER TO THE TEST**
>
> Combining the sour cream with baking powder is a good method for testing the power of your baking powder. If the sour cream doesn't rise, your baking powder has exceeded its expiration date.

Chocolate-Raspberry Cake

I am a chocoholic, a condition I'm afraid I've passed on to my daughter who can't resist a bite of the darkest variety every night. So it makes sense that I would occasionally offer a chocolate dessert at Tanoreen. I created this cake for a Valentine's Day menu; it was born out of a challenge I presented to myself to make the chocolatiest chocolate cake possible. After a bit of experimentation, I came up with this. The secret lies in multiple but distinct layers of chocolate flavor—dark cocoa powder, strong chocolate liqueur and dark chocolate. There's also a bit of instant coffee in the mix, an addition that imparts a certain earthiness that intensifies the chocolate flavor even more. This is a wonderful celebration cake; you can find a large single-layer, 12- to 14-inch round cake pan at a baking supply store.

Preheat the oven to 350°F. Dust the bottom and sides of a 12- to 14-inch round baking pan with a thin coating of flour. Tap out the excess. Chill a medium mixing bowl and the beaters of a hand mixer or large hand whisk in the refrigerator.

In a medium bowl, combine the flour, baking powder and baking soda.

In the bowl of a stand mixer, beat the eggs on medium speed until pale yellow, about 4 minutes. Add the sugar, olive oil, cherry juice and vanilla and beat until smooth. With the beater running, gradually add the flour mixture to the bowl and beat until the batter is smooth, about 5 minutes. With a rubber spatula, fold in the coconut, if using, the walnuts and chocolate chips.

Pour the batter into the prepared pan and bake until a toothpick inserted in the center comes out clean, 25 to 30 minutes. Let the cake cool slightly while preparing the syrup and whipped cream.

To make the syrup, bring ½ cup water to a boil in a medium saucepan. Add the Grand Marnier, if using, maple syrup, ground coffee, sugar and cocoa powder and stir, using a wooden spoon, for 1 minute. Remove from the heat and set aside.

To make the whipped cream, pour the cream into the chilled bowl. Fit a hand mixer with the chilled beaters and beat the cream on medium speed until it begins to thicken. Alternatively, use a large hand whisk to beat the cream, making large strokes and changing direction every so often. Add the vanilla and sugar and continue to whisk until peaks begin to form and the desired stiffness is reached.

Run a knife around the rim of the pan to loosen the cake from the edges. Invert a rimmed platter or large plate over the pan and flip the cake out onto it. Allow the cake to cool completely then pour the syrup over it, allowing it to soak through. Chill the cake in the refrigerator for at least 15 minutes before serving. Cut into wedges and serve topped with the whipped cream and the fresh berries, dusted with confectioners' sugar.

MAKES 10 TO 12 SERVINGS

For the Cake
2 cups all-purpose flour, plus more for dusting the pans
4½ teaspoons baking powder
½ teaspoon baking soda
4 large eggs, beaten
1 cup superfine sugar
¾ cup extra-virgin olive oil or melted unsalted butter
1 cup cherry or raspberry juice
2 tablespoons vanilla extract
1 cup shredded coconut (optional)
1 cup chopped walnuts
1 cup semisweet chocolate chips

For the Syrup
5 tablespoons Grand Marnier liqueur (optional)
3 tablespoons organic maple syrup
2 tablespoons ground instant coffee
2 tablespoons sugar
1 tablespoon unsweetened cocoa powder

For the Whipped Cream
2 cups chilled heavy cream
1 tablespoon vanilla extract
1 tablespoon sugar

1 pound fresh raspberries, strawberries or blackberries
Confectioners' sugar for dusting

Flourless Tangerine Apricot Cake

As time goes on, more and more of my customers are requesting gluten-free dishes. It is easy to put together a meal with this in mind, since many of our savory dishes are naturally free of gluten. Of course, cakes and pastries are a challenge, but one I was happy to take on. I experimented with various gluten-free alternatives to flour and found that a combination of ground almonds and pistachios result in a flour with wonderful texture. Grind the nuts in a nut grinder to a consistency similar to farina; take care not to grind too finely or it will affect the cake's texture. Serve with whipped cream, fresh fruit or ice cream.

Place the tangerines in a large pot with enough water to cover and bring to a boil. Continue to boil until the fruit is soft, 25 to 35 minutes, depending on the ripeness of the fruit. Transfer to a colander to drain, then put the tangerines in a blender and puree until smooth. Alternatively, use a hand mixer to puree the tangerines.

Place the apricots in the same pot with enough water to cover and bring to a boil. Continue to boil until the fruit is soft, 15 to 20 minutes, depending on ripeness of fresh apricots or freshness of dried apricots. Transfer to a colander to drain, then put the apricots in a blender and puree until smooth. Alternatively, puree the apricots using a hand mixer.

Preheat the oven to 350°F. Prepare a 16-inch round baking pan with nonstick cooking spray.

Meanwhile, in a medium bowl, combine the sugar, almonds, pistachios, walnuts, coconut, if using, and baking powder. Set aside.

In the bowl of a stand mixer, beat the eggs until pale yellow. Add the pureed apircots, the Frangelico, if using, and vanilla and beat until thoroughly incorporated. With the motor running, gradually sprinkle in the nut mixture to the egg mixture and mix until smooth, 3 to 5 minutes.

Pour the batter into the baking pan and bake until a cake tester inserted in the middle comes out clean, 35 to 40 minutes. Transfer the pan to a wire rack to cool slightly.

To serve, run a knife around the edge of the cake pan to loosen it. Invert a serving platter over the pan and flip it over to release the cake. Serve the cake warm.

MAKES 10 TO 12 SERVINGS (ONE 16-INCH ROUND CAKE)

8 tangerines, peeled, sectioned and seeded

8 apricots, peeled and pitted or 4 ounces dried

1 cup sugar

1 pound peeled raw almonds, ground to the texture of semolina

1 cup pistachios, skinned and ground to the texture of semolina

1 cup crushed walnuts

½ cup shredded coconut (optional)

2 tablespoons baking powder

8 large eggs

4 tablespoons Frangelico liqueur (optional)

2 tablespoons vanilla extract

Easter in Nazareth

When I was a young girl, my uncle, who lived in the U.S., came to visit Nazareth for Easter after a nearly ten-year absence.

Easter tradition back in those days dictated that in the week leading up to the Sunday celebration, neighbors and family baked together during the day, then shared a lively, hearty dinner together each night at a different home. Upon his arrival, my mother greeted my uncle with a huge hug and, to his great surprise, a gaggle of women—at least ten—behind her, mixing, rolling and baking traditional Easter cookies. Some were in charge of the *mamool*, little dome-shaped sweets filled with cinnamon-spiced walnuts or pistachios, perfumed with orange blossom water and sprinkled with sugar. Others were presiding over the wreath-shaped, date-filled *ka'ik*, fragrant of cinnamon, cloves and nutmeg.

Our guest was in awe of our assembly line; we set up three stations, one for making the dough, another for making the stuffing and a third for rolling the stuffing into the dough. Clouds of flour filled the air, and the counters were piled high with semolina, nuts, sugar, shortening, spices and dates. Each woman stuffed, rolled and decorated cookies by the dozen and, once a baking pan was full, called on one of her children to carry it to the village baker, since homes in those days didn't have their own ovens. Not surprisingly, the children were always standing by, eager to help . . . and sneak some nuts, date filling or a cookie, warm from the oven.

Why bake alone when you can bake together? Why make one batch of cookies when you can make hundreds? That is the Palestinian philosophy. Back then, Easter week was synonymous with the smell of brewed coffee and those spiced, earthy cookies. There were platters mounded high everywhere, as if dropped from heaven. And, curiously enough, the cookies were shaped in ways to make a young girl believe they just may have. *Ka'ik*, shaped in circlets for the holiday, symbolized the crown of thorns Jesus wore on the cross and *mamool*'s dome shape was said to resemble Jesus' tomb. Sadly, these rituals and traditions have faded over time, but I'll never forget how they embodied the generosity of my community back then.

"Upon his arrival, my mother greeted my uncle with a huge hug and, to his great surprise, a gaggle of women—at least ten— behind her, mixing, rolling and baking traditional Easter cookies."

Mamool Walnut Cookies

Making *mamool* by hand is in my DNA, so I forego the molds that are now available to make the process go faster. Of course, using them will not impact the taste of the cookie, but they will make a pretty design on top. They are available in Middle Eastern grocery stores and specialty kitchen stores. If you opt to use pistachios, soak them for 30 minutes, then drain them to help maintain their gorgeous green color. If you want to go dairy-free here, you can substitute orange blossom water for the milk.

Make the filling: In a large bowl, combine the nuts with the butter, rose water, orange blossom water, sugar, cinnamon and cloves; stir to thoroughly coat the nuts. Set aside.

Make the dough: In a large bowl, combine the semolina, farina and flour. Sprinkle the mastic and mahlab over the dry ingredients. Make a well in the middle of the dry ingredients and add the yeast and sugar to the well. Add 3 tablespoons warm water to the yeast mixture and let sit until it begins to foam, about 1 minute. Pour in the milk or orange blossom water and, with a fork, gradually mix the wet and dry ingredients together until a dough forms.

Transfer the dough to a clean work surface and knead until it is pillow soft and workable. If the dough becomes too stiff to work with, gradually sprinkle in water to bring it to a workable consistency. Return the dough to the bowl and set aside on the counter for 1 hour, covering the bowl with a clean kitchen towel to prevent the dough from drying out as you shape the cookies.

Preheat the oven to 370°F. Prepare two baking sheets with parchment paper.

Place about 3 tablespoons dough in the palm of one hand and use the other palm to roll it into a ball. Make an indentation in the ball with your finger. Spoon 1½ tablespoons of the nut mixture into the indentation, then bring the edges of the dough up around the filling. Pinch the edges all around to seal in the filling. Flip the cookie over into the other hand, seam-side down, and gently press until the seam side is flattened. Decorate as you wish. Place the cookie on a prepared baking sheet and repeat with the remaining dough.

Bake until the cookies are pale blond, 12 to 15 minutes. Transfer to a wire rack to cool. The cookies can be stored at room temperature for 2 days; they will keep in an airtight container in the refrigerator up to 2 weeks or in the freezer up to 3 months. Before serving, dust liberally with confectioners' sugar.

MAKES 3½ DOZEN COOKIES

For the Filling

3 pounds pistachio or walnuts, shelled and coarsely chopped
3 tablespoons butter, ghee or corn oil
3 tablespoons rose water
3 tablespoons orange blossom water
1 cup superfine sugar
½ teaspoon ground cinnamon
Pinch ground cloves

For the Dough

2 pounds fine semolina flour
1 pound white farina
1 pound all-purpose flour
1 tablespoon mastic
1 tablespoon mahlab
1 teaspoon active dry yeast
1 tablespoon sugar
2 cups milk or orange blossom water
Confectioners' sugar for dusting

Stuffed Fresh Dates

Admittedly, dates fresh off the tree are not easy to find in the States, but I see them with increasing frequency at farmers' markets or from online vendors. Their season is short—just three months beginning in August—but the memory of that first bite will last forever. Fresh dates are as crisp as a Granny Smith apple, as hard and yellow as a Golden Delicious, but taste just like a date. Look for dates in the *khalal* stage of ripeness, when they are golden and a bit crunchy; it comes after the green, or *kimri*, stage and just before the *rutah*, or soft and gooey, stage. Most dates you find in the market are firm and dark, in the fourth and final stage of ripeness called *tamir*.

Stuff each date with an almond and set aside.

In a large saucepan, bring 2 cups water to a simmer over medium heat. Add the sugar, stirring until dissolved. Pour in the orange juice, Frangelico, orange blossom water, rose water, cloves and cinnamon stick. Raise the heat and bring to a boil. Stir in the lemon juice. Reduce the heat and simmer for 10 minutes; the mixture will begin to thicken.

Gently slip the dates into the saucepan, taking care not to let the almonds fall out. Return to a simmer and let simmer for 12 minutes. Turn off the heat and let cool, uncovered, until the dates reach room temperature.

Transfer the dates and syrup to a heatproof container and refrigerate until completely chilled. Divide the dates among four plates and serve with a scoop of the ricotta and a drizzle of the simple syrup.

**SERVES 4
(8 STUFFED DATES PER SERVING)**

32 fresh *khalal* dates, stem end trimmed, pitted
32 raw skinless almonds or walnuts
¾ cup sugar
¼ cup fresh orange juice
2 ounces Frangelico, Amaretto or Grand Marnier liqueur
1 tablespoon orange blossom water
1 tablespoon rose water
5 whole cloves
1 cinnamon stick
2 drops lemon juice
1 cup ricotta cheese
Simple Syrup (page 245) for drizzling

Date Cookies

KA'IK

You might notice that the dates you buy are a bit tough or dry in places. To soften them, place the dates in a skillet over very low heat and mash with a wooden spoon or spatula as they warm. If you like a sweeter cookie, you can add additional sugar to this dough. I prefer to use less since I find the dates to be sweet enough.

Make the dough: Put the flour in a large bowl. Add the melted butter and knead with your hands until the butter is completely absorbed into the flour. Make a well in the center of the bowl and add the yeast, sugar and 2 tablespoons hot water. Let sit for 1 minute. Add the mastic and mahlab to the flour mixture. Pour the orange blossom water into the yeast mixture and knead it all together until it forms a soft dough. Cover with a kitchen towel and let rest for 30 minutes.

Make the filling: In a large bowl, combine the dates with the oil, rose water, cinnamon, cloves and nutmeg. Knead with your hands until the mixture has the consistency of a soft paste.

Preheat the oven to 370°F. Prepare two baking sheets with parchment paper.

Place about 3 tablespoons dough in the palm of one hand and use the other palm to roll it into a ball. Make an indentation in the ball with your finger. Spoon 1½ tablespoons of the date mixture into the indentation, then bring the edges of the dough up around the filling. Pinch the edges all around to seal in the filling. Flip the cookie over into the other hand, seam-side down and gently press until the seam side is flattened. Place the cookie on the prepared baking sheet and repeat with the remaining dough.

Bake until the cookies are golden brown, 15 to 20 minutes. Transfer to a wire rack to cool. The cookies can be stored at room temperature for 2 days; they will keep in an airtight container in the refrigerator up to 2 weeks or in the freezer up to 3 months. Before serving, dust liberally with confectioners' sugar.

MAKES 3½ DOZEN COOKIES

For the Dough
6 cups all-purpose flour
2 pounds (8 sticks) unsalted butter, melted
1 tablespoon active dry yeast
1 tablespoon sugar
1 tablespoon mastic
1 tablespoon mahlab
2 cups orange blossom water or warm milk

For the Filling
3 pounds Medjool dates, pitted
3 tablespoons corn oil, butter or ghee
2 tablespoons rose water (optional)
½ teaspoon ground cinnamon
Pinch ground cloves
Pinch ground nutmeg
Confectioners' sugar for dusting

Rolled Date Cookies

MAOROOTA

I have tried in vain to replicate the date roll my mother used to make. This is pretty close, though I believe she used more butter. These days, since we're all trying to eat more healthfully, I often make it with olive oil instead of ghee, to nice results. If you do, in fact, use olive oil, add 2 tablespoons of anise seeds to the dough. Serve with coffee or tea.

In a large bowl, combine the dates with the oil, cinnamon, cloves and allspice. Work with your hands until the mixture forms a paste. (If the dates are hard, first combine them with the oil in a large pot and cook over low heat to soften. Then add the spices and work into a paste.) Set aside.

In a large bowl, whisk together the flour, yellow and white farinas, mahlab, if using, mastic and all but 1 tablespoon of the sugar. Make a well in the center of the mixture. Pour the ghee into the well and, working with your hands, incorporate the flour into the ghee. Cover and set aside to rest for 30 minutes to 1 hour.

When the dough has finished resting, combine the remaining 1 tablespoon sugar with a drop of warm water and the yeast in a small bowl. Make another well in the center of the dough and pour in the yeast mixture. Add the orange blossom water and work the dough from the interior of the well out for 3 to 5 minutes. Alternatively, put the dough in the bowl of a stand mixer fitted with the dough hook, make the well, add the yeast mixture and orange water and mix on medium until the dough is smooth and soft.

Shape the dough into four balls and place on a clean surface. Cover with a clean kitchen towel and let rest for about 15 minutes. Meanwhile, preheat the oven to 400°F. Grease two baking sheets with olive oil.

Dust a clean work surface with flour and roll out each ball of dough to ½ inch thickness to make a 16-inch round. Divide the date mixture among the rounds, spreading it evenly out to the edges. Evenly top each round with the walnuts. Roll each round of dough up like a jelly roll, arranging them on the prepared baking sheets at least 2 inches apart.

Bake the rolls for 10 minutes, then check to see if the dough is taking on too much color; it should be pale. Reduce the heat to 300°F and bake for 15 to 20 minutes. Set aside to cool.

Slice into 1-inch-thick cookies and serve. The cookies will keep in a covered container in a cool, dry place up to 2 weeks or up to 3 weeks in the refrigerator.

VARIATIONS *To make Rolled Fig Cookies, replace the date mixture with fig preserves and use pistachios in place of the walnuts. Spread the preserves onto the dough as you would on a sandwich. For truly indulgent rolled cookies, sprinkle some grated semi-sweet chocolate onto the filling before rolling.*

MAKES 3 DOZEN COOKIES

4 pounds pitted fresh dates, chopped
2 tablespoons corn oil
½ teaspoon ground cinnamon
Pinch ground cloves
Pinch ground allspice
2 cups all-purpose flour, plus more for dusting
1 cup fine yellow farina
1 cup white farina
1 teaspoon mahlab (optional)
1 teaspoon mastic
½ cup sugar
1½ cups melted ghee or extra-virgin olive oil, plus more for greasing
1 tablespoon active dry yeast
1½ to 2 cups orange blossom water, milk or water
1 pound crushed walnuts

> **COOKING TIP** Sometimes I parbake the roll and freeze it, then thaw and finish off the baking just before serving. To do so, bake the roll for 10 to 12 minutes, cool completely, then wrap tightly and freeze up to 2 months.

Macaroni Cookies

Around the time that the olives from our trees were first pressed, my mother invariably made these subtle, anise-flavored cookies. She never made less than two months' worth of them—about 25 pounds of cookies!—because they store well and are wonderful to have on hand to serve with coffee or tea when unexpected guests stop by. The cookies are so named for their hollow interior, like the pasta. I enjoy them dipped in cold Simple Syrup (see opposite page), or in melted chocolate. Lately, I've begun stuffing them with dates.

Sift the flour into a large bowl. Stir in the sugar, sesame seeds and the ground and whole anise seeds. Add the oil and work it into the flour with your hands until the flour has taken on as much as it can, 3 to 5 minutes (there will be excess oil after kneading that you can discard). Gradually add up to 1 cup of cold water and mix with your hands after each addition until a dough forms. If the dough does not come together, add more water, a few teaspoons at a time, until it does.

Preheat the oven to 375°F. Prepare two baking sheets with parchment paper.

To shape the cookies, pull a piece of dough the size of a ping pong ball from the batch. Place it on a flat sieve or an overturned strainer. Press it into a 2 by 3-inch rectangle. Using four fingers, roll the dough from the top toward you so that it is folded onto itself. Place the cookie on a baking sheet, seam side down. Repeat with the remaining dough, spacing the cookies ½ inch apart.

Bake the cookies until very lightly browned, 12 to 15 minutes. Let cool. The cookies will keep, tightly wrapped. Or wrap them in two layers of plastic wrap, place in a resealable plastic bag and freeze up to 2 months.

VARIATION **Lenten Macaroni Cookies** *My mother made a spiced, date-stuffed version of this simple cookie during Lent by working ¼ teaspoon ground cinnamon and a pinch each of ground cloves and allspice into 2 pounds of fresh pitted dates. She added 1 teaspoon of nigella seeds to the dough. To fill, flatten a walnut-sized piece of dough into a 2 by 1-inch rectangle. Roll 2 teaspoons of the date stuffing between your palms to the same length as the dough, set it in the center of the dough and wrap the dough up around it, pinching the seam together. Bring the ends of the dough around to meet each other to form a wreath. Bake as described above.*

MAKES 5 DOZEN COOKIES

6 cups all-purpose flour

1½ cups sugar

1½ cups unhulled sesame seeds (shells on)

½ cup ground anise seeds

½ cup whole anise seeds

3 cups extra-virgin olive oil, or 2 cups extra-virgin olive oil plus 1 cup corn oil

Knafeh

Katayfeh is the name given to the shredded filo pastry used to make these traditional cheese- or walnut-filled desserts, which are found all over the Middle East. I use ghee when I make this pastry at the restaurant, but butter works well, too. Either way, use the best-quality ghee or butter you can afford. If you don't feel confident flipping the pan over to release the *knafeh*, leave it in the pan, drizzle with the syrup and serve the pastry straight from the pan.

> **COOKING TIP** *Knafeh* freezes beautifully and is very good reheated in an oven (never in a microwave); in fact, it will taste as if you just made it. The unbaked pastry can be frozen, tightly wrapped, for up to 3 months. After it's baked, it will keep in the refrigerator for 1 week.

Preheat the oven to 450°F. Set out an 18-inch round or 12 by 17-inch baking pan. Break the dough apart and put it into the bowl of a food processor. Pulse until you have ⅛-inch pieces.

Put the shredded dough in a large bowl and pour the melted butter over it. Using your hands, work the dough until it soaks up all the butter or ghee. The mixture should feel soft with no dry patches. Divide the dough into two equal portions. Add a few drops of food coloring to one portion, if you wish, mixing until evenly colored. At this stage, the dough can be tightly wrapped and frozen up to 1 month.

Pack one portion of dough into the pan, evenly spreading it with your hands (use the colored dough if you plan to turn the *knafeh* out to serve it). Spread the cheese or walnut filling to completely cover the dough. Sprinkle the remaining portion of dough over the filling, and using the palms of your hands, firmly pat down and spread the dough to entirely cover the filling. Take care not to leave any filling exposed (or it will burn) and make sure the dough doesn't touch the edges of the pan (or the *knafeh* won't release).

Bake until the cheese is entirely melted and the top is golden brown (for the cheese *knafeh*) or the nut filling is hot and the dough is golden brown and crisp (for the walnut *knafeh*), about 20 minutes. While still hot, invert a larger baking sheet or serving platter over the pastry and flip it over to release it. Pour the simple syrup all over the hot pastry. If making the cheese *knafeh*, sprinkle the pistachios all over the top. Cut into 2-inch squares or diamonds with a pizza cutter and serve.

Recipe pictured overleaf.

MAKES ONE 18-INCH ROUND OR 12 BY 17-INCH KNAFEH (ABOUT 3 DOZEN SQUARES)

1½ pounds *katayfeh* (shredded filo), thawed
1 pound (4 sticks) unsalted butter or ghee, melted
Orange food coloring (optional)
Cheese or Walnut Filling (page 247)
Simple Syrup (see below), at room temperature
½ pound pistachios, chopped, for garnish (for Cheese *Knafeh*)

> **MAKING SIMPLE SYRUP**
>
> In a saucepan, stir 5 cups sugar into 8 cups water over medium heat until it boils. Add ½ teaspoon lemon juice, 2 tablespoons orange water and 2 tablespoons rose water. Lower the heat slightly, but continue to boil for 30 minutes. For thicker syrup, allow to simmer longer until you've reached the desired consistency. Remove from the heat and let cool. The syrup can be used hot or cold; when using hot syrup make sure the dessert is cold and vice versa. This can be refrigerated in a tightly sealed container for up to one month.
>
> **Variation**: To add additional pops of flavor consider adding a piece of ginger, orange peel or cloves.

Cheese *Knafeh* Filling

I typically make my own cheese for this when I am preparing it at the restaurant, but it's not necessary if you have access to top-quality cheese curds, ricotta and mozzarella. Cheese curds are often offered at farmers' markets or can be found in specialty cheese shops, some gourmet food shops and online. You can substitute additional mozzarella for the ricotta if you wish.

MAKES ENOUGH FOR ONE 18-INCH ROUND OR 12 BY 17-INCH *KNAFEH*

2 pounds sweet cheese curds
½ pound ricotta cheese
1 pound fresh mozzarella cheese, grated

In a large bowl, combine the cheese curds, ricotta and mozzarella and thoroughly mix together. Refrigerate until ready to use.

Walnut *Knafeh* Filling

This is traditionally made with just walnuts, but I prefer to add almonds and pistachios to the mix. Whatever the combination, use three pounds total.

MAKES ENOUGH FOR ONE 18-INCH ROUND OR 12 BY 17-INCH KNAFEH

2 pounds walnuts, chopped
1 pound almonds whole or slivered almonds or pistachios, skinned and chopped
½ pound raisins, preferably golden
½ pound unsweetened coconut flakes
¼ cup orange blossom water
3 tablespoons rose water (optional)
3 tablespoons corn oil
1 teaspoon ground cinnamon
Pinch ground nutmeg
Pinch ground cloves

In a large bowl, combine the walnuts and almonds with the raisins, coconut flakes, orange blossom water, rose water, if using, oil, cinnamon, nutmeg and cloves. Mix together with your hands until the ingredients are evenly distributed. Set aside until ready to use.

Index

allspice 10
almond 204, 215, 236
apricot
  jam 14
  tangerine cake, flourless 236–7
Armenian tabbouleh 82
artichoke
  cleaning 165
  lamb & vegetable soup 102–3
  salmon in pesto 143
  stuffed with meat & pine nuts 164–5
arugula 86–7

baba ghanouj 44, 128–9, 209
baking powder 232
basil pesto 209, 215
  beet salad 76–7
  eggplant Napoleon 128–9
  salmon in 143
basmati rice 10
bass
  fisherman's dish 139
  tagine 140–1
  Tanoreen baked 135
beef
  baked spaghetti 189
  hossi for kibbeh 34
  kafta 174–9
  meat filling 67
  meat stuffing 166
  & potato stew 117
  seasoned, & stock 90, 112
  with spinach stew 112–3
  stuffed artichoke 164–5
  & white bean stew 116
beet
  salad 76–7

  & turnip, pickled 210–1
bell pepper
  green 74, 84–5, 125, 135, 140
  pickled stuffed 213
  red 74–5, 85, 125, 135
  red, & onion flatbread 65
  red, & walnut spread 46
black pepper 10
bread *see* flatbread
Brussels sprout & panko 49, 209
bulgur 10
  Armenian tabbouleh 82
  kibbeh 37
  lentil pilaf 198
  tabouleh 80–1
  in tomato sauce 202–3
  vegetarian stuffed cabbage 130
  vegetarian stuffed vegetables 126
butternut squash & red lentil stew 114–5

cabbage
  boiled 172
  stuffed 172
  vegetarian stuffed 130
cakes
  chocolate-raspberry 234–5
  coconut semolina 228, 232–3
  flourless tangerine apricot 236–7
  walnut 232
calamari, seafood soup 104–5
cardamom 10
carrot
  & cauliflower, pickled 213

  carrots & jalapeño, pickled 210
chicken tagine 161
lamb & vegetable soup 102–3
sweet salad 83
warm salad 83
cauliflower
  & carrot, pickled 213
  & lamb stew 90, 108
  salad 72, 84–5, 209
cheese
  knafeh filling 247
  pie filling 60
  see also specific cheeses
cherry, fruit compote 230–1
chicken
  chickpea & pearl onion, with Palestinian couscous 156–7
  fetti 154–5
  kebabs 162
  pizza 158–9
  with potatoes 160
  seasoned with stock 90, 100
  simple soup 100
  tagine 122, 161
  whole stuffed 152–3
chickpea
  bulgur in tomato sauce 202
  falafel 56–7
  & fava bean breakfast 24
  harira 97
  hummus 38–9
  my mother's hummus 40
  pearl onion & chicken, with Palestinian couscous 156–7
  yogurt tahini with 26
chile
  homemade hot sauce 220
  paste (*hossi*) 34–5
  red, paste 11

chocolate-raspberry cake 234–5
cinnamon 10
citric acid 10
coconut semolina cake 228, 232–3
compote, ruby red fruit 230–1
cookies
  date 228, 242
  macaroni 228, 244
  mamool walnut 228, 239
  rolled date 243
coriander 10
couscous, Palestinian 156–7
  chicken, chickpea & pearl onion 157
cream, whipped 234–5
cucumber
  fattoush salad 78
  Turkish salad 49
cumin 10
custard, flower-scented, with pistachios & syrup 228, 230–1

dandelion greens, sauteed, with caramelized onions 195
date(s)
  cookies 228, 242
  rolled, cookies 243
  stuffed fresh 228, 241

Easter 238
egg
  kaak sandwich 20
  & meat 15, 18–19
  & potatoes 15, 17
  in purgatory 122, 125

scrambled, with halloumi 19
simple omelet 20
with za'atar 15, 16
eggplant 125, 162–3
  baba ghanouj 44, 128–9, 209
  baked 124
  baked, with lamb 188
  eggs in purgatory 125
  mutabal 45
  Napoleon 122, 128–9
  pate 43
  pickled, in olive oil 214
  pickled, stuffed 50–1
  salad 74–5
  stuffed 116–17
  stuffed with lamb, in lemon sauce 167
  stuffed, in tomato sauce 166
  tomato & squash soup 93
  upside-down lamb & vegetables 180–1

falafel 32, 56–7
fattoush salad 72, 78
fava bean 15
  breakfast 21
  & chickpea breakfast 24
  Tanoreen's specialty 24–5
feta
  cheese pie filling 60
  salad 79
fetti sauce 221
  & chicken 154–5
fettuccini
  lentil noodle soup with greens 94–5
fish
  fisherman's dish 139
  Friday fish-fries 142
  roasted 150–1
  spicy baked 136
  tagine 122, 140–1
  Tanoreen baked 122, 135
  whole fried 144–5

see also specific fish
flatbread
  Arabic 61
  kaak 20
  red pepper & onion 65
  za'atar 15, 62
foul 15, 21, 24–5, 208
freekeh 10
  with lamb 186–7
  soup 90, 101
  spicy vegan Swiss chard rolls 131

garlic sauce 217
  seasoned 222
  seasoned, with lemon 223
  seasoned, spicy 223
  shrimp in 122, 146
ghee 10
goat, kibbeh 36–5
grape leaves 10
  grilled red snapper in 148
  kafta-stuffed 179
  stuffed 169
  stuffed, and squash 170
  vegetarian 53

halloumi with scrambled eggs 19
harira 97
harissa 11
hashwi stuffing 172
herbs, dried 78
hossi
  kibbeh in the tray 176–7
  for kibbeh 34–5, 36
hot sauce, homemade 209, 220
hummus 32, 38–9, 221
  with meat 29
  my mother's 40

ingredients, pantry 10–11

jalapeño & carrot, pickled 210

kaak 20
kafta 174–9
  stuffed grape leaves 179
  & sweet pea stew 114–5
  with tahini or tomato sauce 175
  Tanoreen roll 177
kale 192
  lentil noodle soup with greens 94–5
  shallot & olive oil 196
katayfeh 245
kebabs, chicken 49, 162
kibbeh 54–5
  for *hossi* 34–5
  in the tray 176–7
knafeh 228, 245–7

labneh 14
lamb
  with baked eggplant 188
  & cauliflower stew 90, 108
  eggplant stuffed with, in lemon sauce 167
  harira 97
  hashwi stuffing 172
  hummus with meat 29
  kafta 174–9
  kibbeh 36–7
  meat & eggs 15, 18–19
  meat filling for pies 59, 67
  meat pies 58–9
  meat stuffing 166
  pine nuts & rice with 122, 173
  & pomegranate molasses with okra stew 118–9
  seasoned, with stock 90, 112
  with freekeh 186–7
  spiced shank 72, 184–5
  with spinach stew 112–3
  stuffed artichoke with meat & pine nuts 164–5

stuffed cabbage 172
stuffed grape leaves 168–9
stuffed grape leaves & squash 170–1
& vegetables layered rice with 182–3
& vegetable soup 102–3
& vegetables, upside-down 180–1
layered rice with lamb and vegetables, 182–3
leek & potato soup 92
lemon sauce 167
lentil 10
  harira 97
  noodle soup with greens 94–5
  pilaf 192, 198
  pureed soup 96
  red, & butternut squash stew 114–5
lettuce
  fattoush salad 78
  Tanoreen green salad 86–7

macaroni cookies 228, 244
maftool 11, 156–7
mahlab 11
mamool cookies 228, 238–9
  walnut 239
mastic 11, 59
mlookhia stew 90, 109
mujadara 72, 198–9
mutabal 45

noodle lentil soup with greens 94–5
nutmeg 11

okra
  stew, with lamb & pomegranate molasses 118–9
  with tomatoes 202–3
olive oil 11
olive(s) 208
  eggplant salad 74–5
  spread 209, 220
  omelet, simple 20
onion
  caramelized, & dandelion greens 195
  & red pepper flatbread 64
  see also pearl onion
orange blossom water 11, 204

panko
  with Brussels sprouts 48–9, 209
  eggplant Napoleon 128–9
parsley
  Armenian tabbouleh 83
  sauce, with tahini 41
  tabouleh 80–1
pate, eggplant 43
pea(s)
  basmati vegetable rice 205
  sweet, & kafta stew 114–5
  pearl onion 117, 156
  beef & tomato stew 117
  chicken & chickpeas, with Palestinian couscous 156–7
  chicken tagine 161
  maftool 156–7
pesto see basil pesto
pickles 208
  cauliflower & carrot 213
  eggplant in olive oil 214
  jalapeños & carrots 210
  stuffed bell pepper 213
  turnips & beets 210
pies
  cheese filling 60
  meat 58–9
  meat filling 61

savory 58–60
  spinach filling 60
  vegetable filling 61
pilaf, rice & vermicelli 116, 204
pine nuts
  rice with lamb 173
  jasmine rice & raisins 204
  stuffed artichokes with meat 164–5
pistachio
  flour-scented custard with, & syrup 228, 230
  flourless tangerine apricot cake 236
  knafeh 245
  mamool walnut cookies 239
pizza, chicken 158–9
pomegranate molasses 11
  & lamb with okra stew 118–9
potato
  baked eggplant 124
  baked eggplant with lamb 188
  & beef stew 117
  with chicken 122, 160
  and eggs 15, 17
  kafta with tahini or tomato sauce 175
  & leek soup 92
  in soups 90, 102–5
  spiced lamb shank 184–5
  spicy mashed 200–1
  stuffed cabbage 130
  Tanoreen baked fish 135
  Tanoreen salad 74–5
  vegetable pie fillings 67

quail, grilled 163

raspberry
  chocolate cake 234–5
  ruby red fruit compote 230–1
red pepper paste (harissa) 11

red snapper
  grilled, in grape leaves 148–9
  seafood soup 104–5
  spicy baked 136
  tagine 140–1
  Tanoreen Baked Fish 135
rice
  basmati vegetable 205
  chicken *fetti* 154
  lamb & pine nuts 173
  fisherman's dish 139
  hashwi stuffing 172
  jasmine, with pine nut & raisin 192, 204
  layered rice with lamb and vegetables 182–3
  simple chicken soup 100
  spicy 205
  upside-down lamb & vegetable 180–1
  vegetarian stuffed vegetables 126–7
  vegetarian grape leaves 52–3
  & vermicelli pilaf 116, 204
rose water 11

salad dressings 78, 86–7
salads
  beet 76–7
  cauliflower 72, 84–5, 209
  eggplant 74–5
  fattoush 72, 78
  feta 78
  sweet carrot 83
  Tanoreen green 86–7
  Tanoreen potato 85
  tomato 72, 76–7
  Turkish 49, 72
  warm carrot 83
salmon in pesto 143
sandwich sauce 221
sandwiches, egg *kaak* 20
seafood soup 104–5
semolina coconut cake 228, 232–3
sesame seeds 11

shrimp
  in garlic sauce 122, 146
  seafood soup 104–5
soup
  freekeh 90, 101
  harira 97
  lamb & vegetable 102–3
  lentil noodle, with greens 94–5
  pureed lentil 96
  pureed split pea 98–9
  seafood 104–5
  simple chicken 100
  Tanoreen leek & potato 92
  tomato & squash 93
spaghetti, beef-baked 189
spatchcocking 163
spice, Tanoreen 225
spicy mashed potatoes 200–1
spinach
  pie filling 60
  stew, with beef/lamb 112–3
  Tanoreen green salad 86–7
split pea
  pureed soup 98–9
  spinach stew with beef or lamb 112–3
squash
  baked eggplant 124
  & red lentil stew 114–5
  stuffed 126–17
  stuffed, in tomato sauce 166
  & tomato soup 93
  & grape leaves, stuffed 170
stew
  beef & potato 117
  cauliflower & lamb 90, 108
  chopped *mlookhia* 90, 109
  string bean & tomato 111
  okra, with lamb & pomegranate molasses 118–9
  red lentil & squash 114–5
  spinach, with beef/lamb 112–3
  sweet pea & *kafta* 114–5
  white bean & beef 116

stock
   & seasoned chicken 100
   & seasoned lamb/beef 90, 112
string bean
   sauteed 194
   & tomato stew 111
stuffing
   hashwi 172
   meat 166
   for pickled bell peppers 213
sumac 11
Swiss chard
   spicy vegan Swiss chard rolls 131
syrup 230

tabouleh 32, 72, 80–1
tagine
   chicken 122, 161
   fish 122, 140–1
tahini 11
   baba ghanouj 44
   hummus 38
   with parsley sauce 37
   sauce, kafta with 175
   spicy sauce 221
   thick sauce 32, 41, 44, 49, 59, 84–5, 140, 154, 175, 221
   yogurt, with chickpeas 26
   yogurt sauce 154
tangerine apricot cake, flourless 236–7

Tanoreen 6–8, 32, 36, 90, 122, 192, 208, 228
   baked fish 135
   green salad 86, 151, 160
   kafta roll 177
   leek & potato soup 92
   potato salad 85
   specialty fava beans 24
   spice 131, 179, 225
tomato
   Armenian tabbouleh 83
   & string bean stew 111
   beef-baked spaghetti 189
   cheese pie filling 60
   & dill spread 209, 222
   eggplant pate 43
   eggplant salad 74–5
   eggs in purgatory 125
   fattoush salad 78
   feta salad 79
   fisherman's dish 139
   fried 196–7
   mutabal 45
   with okra 202–3
   red pepper & onion flatbread 65
   salad 72, 76–7
   salmon in pesto 143
   sauce 174
   sauce, bulgur in 202
   sauce, *kafta* with 175
   sauce, stuffed eggplant/squash in 166
   sauteed string bean 194
   spiced lamb shank 184–5
   spicy rice 205

   & squash soup 93
   & string bean stew 111
   stuffed 126–17
   sweet pea & *kafta* stew 114–5
tabouleh 80–1
Tanoreen baked fish 135
Tanoreen green salad 86–7
vegetarian grape leaves 52–3
white bean & beef stew 116
Turkish salad 49, 72
turnip & beet, pickled 210

vegetable(s)
   basmati rice 205
   filling for pies 60
   & lamb, upside-down 180–1
   & lamb soup 102–3
   & lamb, layered rice 182–3
   vegetarian stuffed 126–17
   see also specific vegetables
vegetarian
   grape leaves 52–3
   stuffed cabbage 130
   stuffed vegetables 126–17
vermicelli
   chicken *fetti* 154
   harira 97
   & rice pilaf 204
   simple chicken soup 100

walnut
   beet salad 77
   cake 232
   knafeh filling 247

mamool cookies 228, 239
pickled stuffed eggplant 50–1
   & red pepper spread 46–7
rolled date cookies 243
spicy baked fish 136
stuffed fresh dates 241
weddings 54–5
white bean & beef stew 116

yogurt
   Brussels sprouts with panko 48–9
   fetti sauce 221
   meat pie filling 59
   sauce 154
   tahini, with chickpeas 26

za'atar 11, 14–15, 63
   bread 62
   cheese pie filling 60
   feta salad 79
   with egg 16
zucchini
   lamb & vegetable soup 102–3
   tomato & squash soup 93
   see also squash

Acknowledgments

To my daughter and business partner, Jumana, my joy, who stands by me every day at Tanoreen: Your motivation and belief in our family and this book is infinite and I am most grateful.

To my son, Tarek, my light and pride: Your dedication to bringing this book to life was immeasurable, invaluable and appreciated beyond words.

To my husband, Wafa, my partner in life for the last forty years, who has stood by me every step we took on the remarkable road we have shared thus far: I love you.

To Rawda, Azmi, Marwan and Samia, my siblings, whose stories we shared growing up were the basis for this book, and with whom I still cook, eat and stand, together: You bring me great joy.

To my best friends, Yolanda, Soumaya, Suhair and George: We like to eat, and you encouraged me to turn my flourishing passion for cooking into what Tanoreen is today.

To my staff at Tanoreen, who have been loyal for all these years and who helped test endless recipe ideas: Thank you.

To my amazing customers, who supported me from a small ten-table storefront into what Tanoreen has become, and beyond: Many thanks.

Thanks to my team on this book:

Including my writer, Kathleen, for tirelessly reviewing recipe after recipe, working hard and staying motivated this last year.

My agent, Judith, for seeing the light at the end of the tunnel every time.

To our photographer, Pete Cassidy, and to Vicki Murrell, and the family and friends who hosted us abroad at the photo shoot, for bringing every recipe to life and travelling through my childhood with me: Many thanks.